FEMINISM AND THE
ABYSS OF FREEDOM

FEMINISM AND THE ABYSS OF FREEDOM

LINDA M. G.
ZERILLI

The University of Chicago Press | Chicago and London

LINDA ZERILLI is professor of political science at Northwestern University. She is the author of *Signifying Woman: Culture and Chaos in Rousseau, Burke, and Mill.*

The University of Chicago Press, Chicago 60637
The University of Chicago Press, Ltd., London
© 2005 by The University of Chicago
All rights reserved. Published 2005
Printed in the United States of America
14 13 12 11 10 09 08 07 06 05   1 2 3 4 5

ISBN: 0-226-98133-9 (cloth)
ISBN: 0-226-98134-7 (paper)

Library of Congress Cataloging-in-Publication Data

Zerilli, Linda M. G. (Linda Marie-Gelsomina), 1956–
    Feminism and the abyss of freedom / Linda M. G. Zerilli.
        p.   cm.
    Includes bibliographical references and index.
    ISBN 0-226-98133-9 (hardcover : alk. paper) —
    ISBN 0-226-98134-7 (pbk. : alk. paper)
    1. Feminism.   2. Feminist theory.   I. Title.
    HQ1154.Z435 2005
    305.42'01—dc22

                                    2004028618

⊚ The paper used in this publication meets the minimum require-
ments of the American National Standard for Information Sciences—
Permanence of Paper for Printed Library Materials,
ANSI Z39.48-1992.

FOR GREGOR

We start something. We weave our strand into
a network of relations. What comes of it we
never know. We've all been taught to say: Lord
forgive them, for they know not what they do.
That is true of all action. Quite simply and
concretely true, because one *cannot* know.
That is what is meant by a venture.

—HANNAH ARENDT

CONTENTS

FOR A LONG time I thought about this book as an attempt to find my way back to what once brought me to feminism: the radical demand for women's political freedom, the right to be a participant in public affairs. Although feminism is composed of a wide range of practices—aesthetic, social, economic, and cultural—the feminist challenge to the androcentrism of the public sphere and the constitution of alternative spaces of freedom is what captured and held my interest. Increasingly, however, I found myself both fascinated by but also ambivalent about developments in second- and third-wave feminism, especially the centrality accorded by both waves to questions of identity and subjectivity. However important these questions seemed—and still seem—to me, I worried about the framework in which they were posed. I could not find in this framework the feminist demand for political freedom that so inspired me. Instead of insistently claiming political freedom, it seemed, feminism was now devoted to overcoming the cultural constraints of normative masculinity and femininity. As important as such a struggle is, I had trouble seeing how it could possibly occur in the absence of the demand for freedom as I understood it.

Concerned as I was about this reframing of freedom as freedom from the constraints of subjectification, I also resisted the nostalgic longing for early second-wave feminism that began to take hold in the 1990s in the wake of the debates around identity politics. I strongly agreed with third-wave critics who questioned the coherence of the category of women as the subject of feminism, though I remained uneasy about the consequences of such questioning for politics. Not least, I worried about a certain tendency toward a renewed dogmatism on the part of feminists for whom critiques of the category of women turned into a politically destructive skepticism. At a certain point, it seemed that feminists were talking past one another, quarreling about something that was in any case an accomplished fact and hardly the result of anyone's deliberate choice. The view that the collapse of women as a unified category was the fault of "poststructuralist" feminist theorists and to a lesser extent "women of color" struck me as an attempt to kill the message by killing the messenger. It also seemed like a troubling displacement of feminist politics itself.

If we no longer speak unthinkingly of women as a group with common interests based on a common identity, surely that is not attributable solely nor even primarily to the considerable critical energies of third-wave thinkers like Judith Butler, Chantal Mouffe, or Joan Scott. The economic and social developments of late capitalism (for example, the breakup of the labor movement, globalization, and the homework economy) have resulted in exceedingly complex stratifications among women nationally and internationally which cannot be grasped solely in terms of gender relations. More to the point, the breakup of women as a coherent group is attributable to feminism itself: feminism is a political movement that has striven to unite women in a struggle for freedom largely by refuting the naturalized femininity on which the illusion of a given, common identity of women is based. Rather than willfully destroy the category of women, then, thinkers like Butler, Mouffe, and Scott tried to clarify—in deeply critical and non-nostalgic terms—the political consequences of its historical loss for the future of feminism.

Trying to understand the pathos of the category of women debates, I began to think it might be symptomatic of the epistemological framework within which most second- and even third-wave feminisms were articulated. As strange as it seemed to blame poststructuralists for the loss of something that—insofar as we can speak of a loss—was more the product of history and politics than of nihilistic scholarship, it seemed even stranger to think that the future of feminism, as a political movement, could possibly hang on the status of an analytic category of feminist theory. Apart from the fact that few feminist activists understand theory as a guide for praxis—save in some very loose sense—it seemed important to move out of the details of "the subject of feminism" debates and question their underlying assumption: What could be made of the idea that any claim to speak in the name of women must function like a rule under which to subsume particulars, lest it have no political significance at all? Was there not perhaps some guidance to be had for feminism in this moment from nonfeminists who had thought about the relation of politics and freedom to rules and their application?

These thoughts and questions led me back to the thought of Hannah Arendt, who had nothing to say about feminism, but a lot to say about the loss of traditional categories of thought for making sense of political reality—the very sort of loss, it seemed to me, represented by the crisis of the category of women, a loss bemoaned by second-wave feminists and often scripted as a theft for which third wavers were made responsible. In Arendt's view, the break in tradition, already begun with the scientific revolution in the seventeenth century, culminated with the political catastrophes of the twentieth. It is not only pointless but dangerous to try to recover categories of thought that no longer resonate within our current political and historical context, Arendt held. Unfortunately, as she also recognized, just because a tradition has come to an end, traditional concepts have not lost their power over us. On the contrary, they can become even more tyrannical, for a confused moral and political orientation can seem more appealing than no orientation at all.

As I reflected on the loss of women as a category of traditional political theory and feminist political thought, Arendt's remarks on the break in tradition took on special significance. Writing this preface in 2004, I am struck by the strange compromise we feminists have reached on matters that once called forth a fairly militant articulation of oppositional political stakes. The pathos is no longer there, but neither is any clear sense of how to theorize or act politically without the inherited categories of feminist thought. We nod to the importance of acknowledging difference among women, yet we persistently return to the idea that feminism demands a unified subject. Alternatively, we vigorously refuse such a subject, but are at a loss about how to say or claim anything beyond the particular case.

This book cannot resolve all the puzzles it describes. But perhaps it can help us think them through by clarifying how we got where we are and how we might think differently about political freedom, political claims, and the political role of feminist theory. "Our inheritance was left to us by no testament," says Arendt, citing René Char. What if we took that opaque aphorism as a challenge to welcome, rather than bemoan, the irreversible break in tradition that characterizes politics in late modernity, including feminism? In that spirit of possibility, I present my reflections.

ACKNOWLEDGMENTS

MANY PEOPLE HAVE contributed their time and energy to this project. Thanks first to Benjamin Barber, Susan Carroll, Cynthia Daniels, Samantha Frost, and Marcia Ian, friends and former colleagues at Rutgers University, who inspired me to begin work on the project. At Northwestern I have found an intellectual community that has likewise been highly supportive of my work. Sara Monoson, Miguel Vatter, Peter Fenves, and Robert Gooding-Williams have provided me with very helpful comments. Special thanks to my friends in the Gender Studies Program, in particular former directors Tessie Liu and Alex Owen, for affording me the opportunity to lead a faculty seminar on issues related to this book. I thank as well Ann Orloff, who provided insightful criticisms on earlier versions of the chapters and reminded me of what really matters; Michael Hanchard, who saw the blind spots in the work and, with his strong friendship, helped me endure; Richard Flathman, who commented on various chapters and whose work on Wittgenstein is an inspiration to me; Christine Froula, who gave very thoughtful criticisms of chapter 4; Kirstie McClure, who inspired my reading of the Milan Women's Bookstore Collective; and Peter Meyers, whose creative scholarship on the rhetorical tradition and deep appreciation of Arendt's political thought stimulated my own thinking. Mary Dietz and Ernesto Laclau read the manuscript for the University of Chicago Press and gave me enormously useful comments. For his generosity and critical reading of the entire manuscript I thank George Shulman, who remains my model of intellectual curiosity and generosity. I have benefited from conversations with Chantal Mouffe, Sonia Kruks, William Connolly, and Patchen Markell. Zillah Eisenstein, teacher and friend, provided insight and encouragement in the earliest stages of the project. Thanks to the students in my graduate seminars at

Northwestern, who challenged me, among other things, to think clearly about why Hannah Arendt might be relevant for feminists.

I have been very fortunate to have had superb research assistants, both at Rutgers and Northwestern. Crina Archer, Lida Maxwell, Ella Myers, Laurie Naranch, and Torrey Shanks have all been involved at various stages of this project, tracking down articles, checking citations, and keeping me focused in the midst of the many piles of paper. Thanks especially to Lida Maxwell and Crina Archer for their help with the preparation of the final manuscript. My colleague and dear friend, Bonnie Honig, has read more versions of this manuscript than either of us care to remember. Her creative energy, intellectual focus, and good judgment have been invaluable to me. It is not possible to put into words how much I owe her. I wish also to acknowledge my incalculable debt to my teacher, Michael Rogin, whose example of intellectual vitality and personal integrity will survive his untimely death.

I am once again grateful to my family—Marie A. Zerilli, Armand F. Zerilli, Amanda Zerilli, and Jeffrey Zerilli—for their love and support. Finally, I want to thank my companion, Gregor Gnädig, for his affirming spirit and unerring belief in me. To him I dedicate this work.

This project was supported by generous research leaves from both Rutgers and Northwestern University. Thanks also to the Institute for Advanced Study and especially Joan Scott for providing a hospitable environment at the earliest stage of this project. Chapter 2 was published in *On Monique Wittig: Theoretical, Political and Literary Essays* (Champaign: University of Illinois Press, 2005). Chapter 3 was published in *differences: A Journal of Feminist Cultural Criticism* 15, no. 2 (Summer 2004): 54–90. Portions of chapter 4 were published in *Political Theory* 20, no. 10 (April 2005): 158–88.

Why *Feminism* and *Freedom*
Both Begin with the Letter *F*

The *raison d'être* of politics is freedom,
and its field of experience is action.

—HANNAH ARENDT

JUDGING FROM THE spate of publications declaring the "end of feminism," it would seem that feminism, as a social and political movement, has more or less reached its limit.[1] For some critics, this end is given in the supposedly incontrovertible fact that the discrimination feminism set out to challenge is more or less a thing of the past. In their view, gender equality is a legal fact awaiting its full social realization, which, in accordance with the logic of historical progress, is imminent. For other critics, this is clearly not the case. Changes in law do not automatically result in social changes but require the vigilance of an ongoing political movement. If these same critics declare the end of feminism, then, it is more with a sense of loss than triumph. And perhaps they are right: it is increasingly hard to identify the "movement" in the feminist movement; for feminism, when it is not safely ensconced in the formal institutions of the liberal democratic state, can indeed look like a dispersed collection of diverse grassroots struggles that have lost the orientation once provided by its collective subject: "women."

Critics who long for the clear sense of direction that they identify as the sine qua non of feminist politics like to charge third-wave feminism, especially its poststructuralist variant, with the destruction of the collective subject "women," but their accusation flies in the face of political history. Anyone even slightly acquainted with the history of first- and second-wave American feminism will immediately recognize that the orientation provided by this putatively collective subject was illusory at best. Feminism has always been shot through with deep internal conflicts about the subject in whose name its equally conflict-ridden social and political aspirations were to be achieved.[2] The breathless pace with which members of the earliest second-wave feminist groups split off to found other groups, only to find members of the new group splitting off to found yet other groups, indicates what we might call a retroactive fantasy about the wholeness of political origins, a fantasy that is by no means unique to feminism.[3] Far from united at origin, feminism, like all modern democratic political movements (including the American and French revolutions), was divided from the start, wracked by differences over the causes or form of oppression, disputes over the meaning of liberation, and competing understandings of what democratic ideals like freedom and equality and the public realm in which they were to find expression should look like.[4]

Such differences and even deep divisions, visible at particular moments in history, appear self-defeating only if we assume that the raison d'être of a democratic political movement like feminism is foremost the social advancement of the group, that such advancement can only be attained if it is in someone's name, and that this name must be known in advance of the political struggle itself. The most trenchant critics of identity politics, such as Judith Butler, Ernesto Laclau, and Chantal Mouffe, have strongly argued that politics (including not only a post-Marxist notion of radical democracy but the more traditional forms of social democratic politics) is indeed possible without such a unified and pre-given subject. Although these criticisms are well taken—especially insofar as they disclose the troubling exclusions that a collective subject like "women" or "workers" given in advance of politics carries with it—what they do not squarely address is the fraught question of whether the raison d'être of politics, feminist or any form of democratic politics, is indeed the social advancement of the group in whose name members of a political movement claim to speak.

Freedom as a Social Question

If it is difficult to imagine the raison d'être of politics as anything other than the social advancement of a group and its members, that may be because we tend to think of politics in terms of what Hannah Arendt calls "the social question." The social question arises wherever it is assumed that classic social welfare problems such as hunger, inequality of wealth, housing, a living wage, and so on are problems that can be solved by political means.[5] For Arendt, the social question—already fatefully (in her view) posed in the French Revolution—comes to be definitive of what politics is with the rise of "the social" in the nineteenth century. Although Arendt is not clear in her definition, the social is a kind of enlarged "housekeeping," whereby the public/private distinction is dissolved and citizens are situated in a relatively passive relation to the bureaucratic apparatus of the welfare state, which becomes the sole addressee of political claims and responsible for the distribution of goods and the maintenance of life. The assimilation of the political to the social restricts political action to an instrumental, means-ends activity that entails the micro- and macro-management of social relations. Since "society always demands of its members that they act as if they were members of one enormous family which has only one opinion and one interest," writes Arendt, the rise of the social is identical with the rise of conformism and "behavior," and with the consequent reduction of the possibility of spontaneous action (*HC*, 39).[6]

His crit.
of J.D.

family =
society

Arendt's account of social conformity and the rise of the social resonates with critiques of modern disciplinary society (such as Michel Foucault's), which have strongly influenced the shape of recent feminist theory.[7] But Arendt's tendency to define all issues related to the body as dangerous forms of necessity that are best kept private if not hidden and her antipathy toward the "administrative housekeeping" of the modern welfare state have made her a controversial figure both on the progressive Left and in contemporary feminism. Notwithstanding a recent shift in feminist attitudes toward Arendt, which reflect a willingness to consider the potential value of her work for a postidentity politics, what stubbornly remains at the end of the day is her apparent refusal to include social issues among the concerns of politics.[8] An ungenerous but not entirely inaccurate reading of Arendt on the social question (found in the secondary literature) accuses her of eliminating from politics anything that we could possibly recognize as political.[9] If issues of housing, poverty, fair wages, and child care are by definition social, not political, what on earth would people talk about when they come together politically? Why would they come together politically at all?

A more generous reading of Arendt would respond to these legitimate questions by suggesting that she does not in fact exclude social concerns from politics but warns against the introduction of the instrumentalist attitude that such concerns often carry with them. Insofar as expediency is held to be the highest criterion, the instrumentalist attitude treats democratic politics as a means to an end, which almost inevitably leads citizens to allow the actions and judgments of experts to substitute for their own. But if Arendt's point is that expediency is an attitude we tend to take toward social issues, it is also one we could not take. Thus one could well speak politically about something such as fair wages while guarding against what Bonnie Honig, deepening a point originally made by

Compare
JD's Dem.
As "good in
itself"

Here JD's Ambivalency
About "ends" is at issue
— since Dem. is incompatible it is
always an "end in view," it has a means.

Hanna Pitkin, calls "the laboring sensibility," that is, "a sensibility that is taken to be characteristic of laboring as an activity [for example, a process- and necessity-driven attitude] but which may or may not be characteristic of the thinking of any particular laborer."[10] There is neither a determinate group of persons nor a determinate class of objects that is by definition social, not political. Instead, there is a tendency to develop an antipolitical sensibility, which arises whenever we seek political solutions to social problems, against which we need to be on our guard.

Although this more generous reading of Arendt is a valuable correc- tive to dismissive critiques of her work, it is not meant to be a definitive riposte to what many readers find to be the most difficult aspect of her political thought. Arendt's unqualified claim that the social question has displaced and, indeed, led to the virtual ruin of democratic politics stands there—if only we will let it—as a bold challenge to "think what we are doing," as she once unceremoniously put the task of political theorizing (*HC*, 5). A difficult but valuable partner in feminist dialogue, the non- feminist Arendt presses us to ask, how does the frame of the social ques- tion blind us to whatever does not fit inside the frame? How is feminism, in particular, limited in its vision by its perceived identification with the social question? Are there other political visions and practices with which feminism might instead be partnered?

Of the many topics through which we might engage these questions, none is more urgent than freedom. It is a commonplace to state that fem- inism has been the struggle for women's freedom. For the most part, however, Western feminists on both sides of the Atlantic have tended to justify the claim to freedom in terms of the social question, social jus- tice, or social utility. When Mary Wollstonecraft famously argued for the rights of women, for example, she demanded freedom as the unqual- ified right to participate in government based on the criterion of all republican citizenship, which, in her view (as in that of other radical republicans, such as Thomas Paine), was the faculty of reason. But she also felt the need to qualify that radical demand: "Contending for the rights of women, my main argument is built on this simple principle, that if she [woman] be not prepared by education to become the com- panion of man, she will stop the progress of knowledge and virtue."[11] And besides, women were the virtuous sex that had so much to con- tribute to the moral advancement of society. Writing over a half a cen- tury later, John Stuart Mill strongly argued for women's unqualified claim to political freedom, warning that, should women not be given their rights, British civilization was doomed.[12] And besides, society was wasting half its brainpower and talent, in particular women's facility in all social matters that required moral virtue and delicate sensibility. Likewise, in the early nineteenth-century United States, the suffragist Carrie Chapman Catt asserted, in the irrefutable logic of the syllogism, democracy is rule by the people, women are people, ergo women have the right to participate in government. And besides, women would bring to public life the special virtues of femininity, especially "in areas where mothers' skills were needed, such as schooling, caring for criminals, or dealing with unemployment."[13]

According to Nancy Cott, the demand for women's freedom in the writings of most late eighteenth- and nineteenth-century feminists exhibits an uneasy but ultimately successful combination of equal-rights arguments and expediency arguments, sameness arguments and difference arguments. Whereas the first set of arguments turns mostly on the idea of social justice, the second set turns on what Arendt called the social question. Cott captures this combination in the struggle for the vote.

> [I]t was an equal rights goal that enabled women to make special contributions; it sought to give women the same capacity as men so they could express their differences; it was a just end in itself, but it was also an expedient means to other ends. "Sameness" and "difference" arguments, "equal rights" and "special contributions" arguments, "justice" and "expediency" arguments existed side by side.[14]

Cott's broader intellectual agenda here, like that of Joan Scott in her work on the struggle for rights in French feminism, is to break the deadlock of the sameness-difference debate that has plagued American feminist historiography and theory.[15] Both Cott and Scott try to reframe modern feminism as constituted by paradox, by the need both to accept and refuse sexual difference. The question, however, is whether the tenacity of the impossible choice framework of equality or difference that they would expose can be properly understood, let alone overcome, without attending to the larger frame in which feminist struggles for political rights have been posed: the frame of the social question and its means-ends conception of politics.

Attending to the social question and how it has framed what can be heard as a political claim, I am more troubled than Cott by the ways in which feminists have tried to justify the demand for women's freedom. The two arguments she describes, though logically distinct, came, in the course of their articulation in concrete political contexts, to be deeply entangled in each other—entangled such that a claim to freedom could not be articulated or heard *unless* it was uttered as a claim to social justice, which in turn could only be heard in the idiom of the social question. Women's claim to freedom, in other words, was a claim to social justice, which would allow for a more just solution to the social question. In this way, issues of social justice and the social question became almost synonymous, and the feminist claim to freedom more often than not took the form of a rather complex set of justifications. These justifications, which almost always referred to something unique in femininity (be it a certain sensibility or simply a practical skill associated with the social role of women), turned, in the last instance, not on freedom as the very practice of democratic politics or as the reason we engage in such politics. Instead, freedom became a means to some other end: an attenuation of the problems associated with the social question. The "besides" that often qualified feminist claims to social justice—usually in the form of a long list of all the special contributions women would make if only they were participators in government—came to look like the very reason for women's freedom itself: the betterment of society. Thus, we might well wonder whether the claim to political freedom is perhaps being not enabled, but rather displaced, by the social question.

In her brief but perspicuous tracking of changes in the meaning of "women" from the eighteenth to the twentieth century, Denise Riley observes that the social "was constructed so as to dislocate the political."[16] Although this dislocation, which Arendt bemoaned, was in no way restricted to women's political demands, the emerging sphere of the social in the nineteenth century was deeply feminized.[17] By the early- to mid-twentieth century, Riley writes, "the very word 'women' was imbued in all political languages with domesticity in a broad sense, with a limiting notion of sociality."[18] Tracking this development, she argues that the inherited idea of a naturalized femininity in the early- to mid-nineteenth century was redeployed, by advocates and opponents of women's rights alike, in relation to the emerging idea of the social. This redeployment, Riley observes, resulted in a "bland redistribution and dilution of the sexual onto the familial," as well as a dispersal of the "irresistibly sexualized elements of 'women' onto new categories of immiseration and delinquency—which then became sociological problems [that women, in their sociologically defined capacity as citizens, were called upon to solve]."[19] Doubly positioned as "both agents and objects of reform in unprecedented ways with the ascent of the social," women came to be seen more as a sociological group with a particular social agenda than as an emerging political collectivity with unqualified democratic demands.[20] Claims to the political status of citizen increasingly had to be made as claims to a certain sociological status; the claim to political freedom was heard as the claim to participate in the public "social housekeeping" that Arendt so disdained.

The entanglement of women and the social, then, has deeply influenced what can be heard as a political demand for freedom. Whatever its problems, the term *social feminism*—coined by the historian William O'Neill to describe the women who were municipal civic reformers, club members, settlement house residents, and labor activists—captures the new idiom in which the struggle for American women's political rights after 1900 came to be fought.[21] Social feminism, I hasten to qualify the accepted narrative, developed as more than a claim to sexual difference, the difference women would make if only they were granted political rights. What feminists faced was not just conventional conceptions of femininity that had to be strategically redeployed for political purposes, but a significant displacement of the political by the social. Within the increasingly all-encompassing framework of the social question, the earlier claims to women's full political membership as a good in itself, made by feminists like Susan B. Anthony and Elizabeth Cady Stanton, were seen as selfish and narrow. Indeed, these feminists and their unqualified demand for the right to be participators in public affairs came to be seen as "hard-core." For social feminists and, indeed, for anyone who made the case for women's rights on the basis of social utility, be it in terms of difference or equality, the ballot was not an end in itself but a means to an end: the betterment of society.[22]

In some sense, the displacement of the political by the social is intrinsic to the history of democratic politics more generally. Far from unique to feminism, the articulation of political demands in the language of the social is a rhetorical strategy that has been, and continues to be, taken up by many disenfranchised groups (for example, the struggle for the gradual extension of "manhood suffrage" in nineteenth-century England, for the rights of African Americans in the United States, for workers' rights in capitalist economies, and for women's human rights in a global context), whose advocates, eager to convince those in power of the rightness of their cause, framed it in the language of social utility. Although rhetorical strategy—whether conscious or not to those involved in making political claims—is surely a crucial component in any struggle for political freedom, rhetoric is often treated by historians and political theorists, to say nothing of philosophers, as if it were the mere form in which an independent argument is made. In that case, one could, as it were, package an argument for freedom in the rhetoric of expediency or the social question and then, after freedom has been "attained," shed the packaging like a snake sheds its skin. But things are not so simple.

Apart from Riley's account of modern feminism, which suggests that rhetoric does not merely reproduce but also constitutes the conditions of political visibility, it is also the case that rhetorical strategies have unintended meanings and effects. Indeed, in feminism, arguments for freedom were not always advanced but rather crippled by their entanglement in social justice arguments and expediency arguments. The point here is not to issue some sort of political complaint or directive (asserting, say, that feminists ought to have made, or ought now to make, arguments for freedom free of social justice claims or expediency claims, or that they should make social justice arguments for freedom free of any trace of utility). The rise of the social, as described by Arendt, and the entanglement of women in it, as portrayed by Riley, is an established fact; it is the politically problematic inheritance of contemporary feminism. If the task is to try to understand more fully the consequences of that inheritance for feminist democratic politics today, then we need to think carefully and critically about how the social question (and the economy of utility in which it dwells) has framed both our conception of what freedom is (for example, a means to an end: the betterment of society) and what an argument for freedom must look like if it is to be heard as such (for example, point to something beyond the practice of freedom). Most important, it is to become critically aware of the costs of the social question to freedom itself.

The history of first- and second-wave feminism shows that to enter into the language game of justifications, be it in the name of social justice or the social question, was more often than not to find oneself in the losing position, and this is true even if specific goals such as women's suffrage were won. To speak with Arendt on Women's Liberation, "The real question to ask is, what will we lose if we win?"[23] With every attempt to answer their critics in terms of social justice, which was really an argument about expediency, feminists found themselves only falling deeper into the logic of social utility or function that has historically governed every iteration of the "woman question": what is a woman *for*?[24] Feminists have challenged truncated conceptions of what woman is for, usually by questioning the naturalized femininity that supposedly determines her social function. What has been harder to challenge is the logic of social utility itself. This logic keeps women's radical demand for freedom, for unqualified participation in common affairs, bound to an economy of use that deeply restricts their emergence as a political collectivity (unless, of course, we define politics itself in terms of that same economy).

Feminist efforts to substitute the idea of women as a social group (gender) for women as a natural group (sex) may question the substantive social tasks assigned on the basis of sex differences, but without in any way disrupting the logic that tightly binds political life to social utility. The problem with this binding is not only the entanglement of women's citizenship with the social functions of femininity but also the tendency for the value of expediency to trump claims to freedom. If we value women's freedom because it is useful in solving certain social problems, we may not value freedom when it interferes with social utility or when more expedient ways of reaching the same social results can be shown. Freedom disturbs the use of politics as a means to an end; it is always "out of order."

There is a way to counter the demand that freedom be a means to an end, but it requires that we pose the question of freedom anew and try to find examples of the demand for political freedom that are not easily folded into the social question (or any economy of utility and means-ends thinking whatsoever). Before we can do that, however, we need to consider another problematic framing of freedom, namely, in terms of the subject question.

Freedom as a Subject Question

"Since the whole problem of freedom arises for us in the horizon of Christian tradition on one hand, and of an originally anti-political philosophic tradition on the other," writes Arendt, "we find it difficult to realize that there may exist a freedom which is not an attribute of the will but an accessory of doing and acting."[25] At once commonsensical and deeply strange, Arendt's account of freedom as political action is highly critical of the notion of freedom as a phenomenon of the will, which we, feminist and democratic thinkers alike, have inherited from the Western philosophical and political tradition.[26] Based on Man in the singular, freedom of the will—clearly crucial to but hardly exhausted by the liberal concept of freedom that is dominant in most Western democracies— is entangled in a dangerous fantasy of sovereignty, writes Arendt, according to which "perfect liberty is incompatible with the existence of society."[27] Further, genuine freedom is defined as the freedom not only from the interference of others, or what we call "negative liberty," but also from politics itself.[28]

Like the displacement of the political by the social, the identification of freedom with the free will of a sovereign subject is the problematic inheritance of democratic and feminist politics.[29] Although second- (and to a lesser extent first-) wave feminism criticized the masculinist fantasy of sovereignty that—argued Beauvoir long ago—turns on women's submission, it nonetheless inclined toward a conception of freedom that either sets the individual woman against "all her sex" (that is, the exceptional woman who escapes or denies the social condition of her gender) or requires a woman's full identification with "her sex" (that is, an antipolitical kinship relation in the form of an all-powerful sisterhood that obliterates particularity and with it plurality).[30] In both cases, freedom is articulated as sovereignty, be it an "I" against all the others or an "I" multiplied and extended into an omnipotent "we."

The entanglement of feminism in the ideal of sovereignty is symptomatic of a tendency to think about freedom in terms of what I will call the "subject question." This question centers primarily on the subject's very formation and on the external and internal forces that hinder its freedom. The subject question is the larger frame within which a fantasy of sovereignty has been presupposed, but such a fantasy is in no way exhaustive of the frame. What defines the frame is not a certain *theory* of the subject (autonomous, dependent, or interdependent) but the fact that *the* subject (be it as a philosophical, linguistic, or psychoanalytic category) is the nodal point around which every political question of freedom gets posed. The subject question is not meant to stand as the other to the social question in the way that, say, the "demand for recognition [of identity]" is meant to stand opposed to the "demand for redistribution [of social goods]" in Nancy Fraser's well-known essay.[31] By contrast with "the redistribution-recognition dilemma," the subject question and the social question are part of the same frame, namely, an instrumental and adjudicative conception of politics that minimizes the possibility of freedom as action.

In its second-wave iteration, freedom as a subject question was famously posed in *The Second Sex*.[32] Raised to remain within the social confines of proper femininity, argues Beauvoir, woman is subject to strong external constraints on her freedom, but she also hinders herself: rather than take the risk of freedom, woman is complicit in her own subjection. On the one hand, Beauvoir's account of a socially constituted femininity—"one is not born, but becomes, rather, a woman"—is a bold attempt to rethink "the woman question" in terms of the inner and outer constraints on the subject as they have been described in the Western philosophical tradition and, more specifically, in the existentialist ethics of Sartre. On the other hand, Beauvoir departs from philosophy and gestures toward the specificity of politics when—as if refusing to substitute "Woman in the singular" for the tradition's "Man"—she suggests that freedom can never be strictly a subject question, for freedom is only possible in political community. Contra Sartre, for whom freedom is a subjective inner state that persists even under the most oppressive social conditions (for example, torture), Beauvoir holds that to be free is to be able to do. The woman in a harem is not free, maintains Beauvoir against Sartre, for freedom requires not only an "I-will" but an "I-can," to borrow Arendt's concise formulation.[33] "I-can" points to the worldly conditions that enable one to do what one wills. Thus the problem of freedom for women—initially formulated as a subject question and in terms of the free will of Woman in the singular—turns out to be a problem of transforming the conditions of the common world, hence as a problem of political action: women must learn to act in concert, to say "we," concludes Beauvoir.[34]

The problem of freedom that inspired Beauvoir's account of femininity was both reiterated and occluded in later interpretations of her work, which mostly focused on the identity thematic (that is, gender is made, not given) and tended to lose sight of freedom as a political problem of the I-can. More precisely, freedom comes to be formulated, in the so-called category of women debates of the late 1980s and the 1990s, strictly as a subject question, while subject formation comes increasingly to be interpreted in terms of radical subjection to agencies outside the self that Beauvoir did not see. In this spirit, Judith Butler famously takes up Beauvoir's insight, "one 'becomes' a woman, but always under a cultural compulsion to become one," to argue that the subject is deeply constrained to reiterate the very social norms that constitute it as subject/ed.[35] Absent such reiteration, holds Butler, the subject would suffer the fate of the most radical skeptic: it would have no sense of its own realness, no sense of social existence at all. Following Michel Foucault's account of *assujetissement* (subjectivation), Butler disputes the very idea of "an agent, a cogito," taken for granted in Beauvoir's account of gender construction, that underwrites the "conventional philosophical polarity between free will and determinism."[36] In Butler's third-wave view, the question for feminism becomes, "Is there a way to affirm complicity as the basis of political agency, yet insist that political agency may do more than reiterate the conditions of subordination?"[37]

I discuss Butler's answer to this question at length in chapter 1. For now it is important only to note the centrality and persistence of the problem of agency in the very mode of feminist critique (that is, poststructuralist) that is typically associated with the demise of the "subject." Could it be that this critique marks a move not out of the subject-centered frame (which governed identity politics) but into its negative space? When Butler and others suggest that the subject can express its freedom by reiteration of the very norms and categories that constitute it as subject/ed, have we not so much left the space of the subject as entered into one of its deepest dramas? The negative space in which this drama unfolds is visible in Butler's troubled recognition that the subject is something feminists cannot, but must, do without, something that is both the condition and the limit of feminist politics.[38] But then it seems as if the paradox of subject formation is installed as a vicious circle of agency at the heart of politics. In that case it would be hard to see how politics could ever be a truly transformative practice that might create something new, forms of life that would be more freedom enabling.[39]

Like the social question, questions of identity and, more recently, subjectification frame our thinking about politics in ways that limit our vision and contain our aspirations more to the problem of the I-will than the I-can. True, thinkers like Butler aspire to a grander politics of freedom than the focus on subjectification and its discontents suggests. Ambivalently beholden to the terms of the subject question, however, they remain tied to a conception of politics that makes agency the condition of any political existence whatsoever. Accordingly, the political formation of the "we" in a feminist practice of freedom seems wholly contingent upon *the* subject's capacity for agency, thus forever returning the subject to the vicious circle in which it plays out the drama of its subjection.[40] Rather than rush to solve the problem of agency, however, let us pause and ask why we think that agency is the paramount problem for feminism after identity politics. Perhaps what we need is a clearer sense of how agency is a requirement of that subject-centered frame, even when the frame itself constitutes a negative space.

What if instead we, together with Arendt, were to shift the problem of freedom outside its current subject-centered frame? Such a shift might prove to be a valuable alternative to our current entanglement in the paradoxes of subject formation and the vicious circle of agency.[41] Once we understand what is at stake in thinking about politics as a mode of human action in our Arendtian way, we will see why agency, as it has been thought within the subject-centered frame, is not only *not* the premier problem of democratic and feminist politics but also a deeply misleading problem that inclines us to misunderstand what we do when we act politically. The requirement of agency is entangled in an identification of freedom with sovereignty and an instrumental conception of politics which deny the very condition of democratic and feminist politics, namely, plurality.

Plurality as the condition of politics—the fact that "men, not Man, live on earth and inhabit the world"—means that one acts into an "already existing web of human relationships, with its innumerable, conflicting wills and intentions, [and consequently that] action almost never achieves its purpose [that is, realizes a goal, an end]," writes Arendt (*HC*, 7, 184). Plurality means that the actor no more controls the effects of her action than she does its meaning, that is, what action reveals about "who" she is. *Who* someone is, by contrast with *what* she is (for example, a white middle-class American woman, qualities she necessarily shares with others like her) is the unique disclosure of human action in Arendt's view (*HC*, 184). This "who" is no substance that can be cognized or in any way known; it can only show itself through "manifest signs" (*HC*, 182). Although any attempt to capture the "who" in language always risks reducing it to a "what," the "who" lives on from the stories, narratives, and other human artifacts which speak of it and without which it would vanish without a trace (*HC*, 184).[42] Most important, says Arendt, the impossibility of saying definitively "who" someone is "excludes in principle our ever being able to handle these [human] affairs as we handle things whose nature is at our disposal because we can name them"—it excludes, in other words, the kind of mastery over action that is assumed in the means-ends thinking that defines most theories of politics, including feminist ones (*HC*, 181–82).

Insofar as Arendt's account of the "who" concerns human action broadly speaking, it is not restricted to the realm of politics. But to talk about the realm of politics is, in her view, always to talk about action and thus the "who."[43] However it might appear as if talk of the "who" is just another way of raising the problem of agency, the Arendtian notion of the "who" is fundamentally different from the subject that haunted the category of women debates. Whereas feminists have focused on the question of whether political agency is possible in the absence of the "what" (for example, an identity such as "women"), Arendt insists that politics is not about the "what" and agency, but always about the "who" and nonsovereignty. By contrast with the feminist sense of crisis that emerged in relation to the critique of the subject, Arendt holds that politics, the realm of action, is possible *only* on the condition that there is *no* agent who can begin a process and more or less control its outcome, use a means toward an end. Refuting claims to mastery, Arendt argues not (as Butler following Nietzsche did) that "there is no doer behind the deed" but that the deed, once done, has effects beyond the doer's control.[44] "Whoever begins to act must know that he has started something whose end he can never foretell, if only because his own deed has already changed everything and made it even more unpredictable," asserts Arendt.[45]

Foregrounded in Arendt's account of action is something less about the *subject* (for example, its stability/instability or its capacity/noncapacity for agency) than about the *world* (for example, its contingency) into which the subject is arbitrarily thrown and into which it acts.[46] As I hope to show in the following chapters, this is not a small but crucially important difference: it turns our attention from the question of *the* subject—which, notwithstanding critical iterations of its social constitution and intrinsically paradoxical formation, almost inevitably restates the solipsism if not will-driven character of the subject-centered frame—to the question of the world. What Arendt calls the "world" is not nature or the earth as such but "is related, rather, to the human artifact, the fabrication of human hands, as well as to affairs which go on among those who inhabit the man-made world together" (*HC*, 52). The world is the concrete objective and subjective "space in which things *become* public," the space in which, when we act politically, we encounter others who, too, act and take up the effects of our action in ways that we can never predict or control with certainty.[47]

If it is hard to shift our focus from the question of the subject to that of the world, the space in which things become public, that is because feminist politics has been centered on the "what" (for example, "women" as a coherent identity) and its transformation. This "what" has so captivated our attention that it seems hard to imagine why politics—just as it obviously concerns agency within the subject-centered frame—would not obviously concern the transformation of socially ascribed forms of subjectivity such as gender difference. The obviousness of this political task was as clear for second-wave feminists such as Ti-Grace Atkinson (who claimed, "those individuals who are today defined as women must eradicate their own definition," in effect "commit suicide" in order to give birth to themselves as "individuals") as it is for third-wave feminists such as Wendy Brown (who albeit far more cautiously and with an entirely different notion of subjectivity call for the transformation of "women" from "wounded subjects" into subjects of freedom).[48]

In light of such calls for subject transformation as the very work of political freedom, Arendt's claim that "at the center of politics stands not concern/care for people, but concern/care for the world" rings as at once

commonsensical (the world clearly matters) and strange (psychic attachments to unfreedom matter too).[49] In Arendt's view, the exclusive concern with the self is an expression of the "world-alienation" that
characterizes modernity.[50] A politics that questions that alienation, she
argues, is not—not in the first place—centered on the subject or the
transformation of subjectivity; it is centered on the world and engaged
in worldliness, that is, the creation of the space in which things become
public. Like her rejection of the social question, Arendt's refusal to count
the subject question among the concerns of politics seems perplexing.
Leaving aside the social engineering she criticizes and with which hardly
a feminist would disagree, how could a politics concerned with freedom
not presuppose the transformation of subjectivity?

Let's turn the question around: what is presupposed by a politics of
freedom that centers on the self and its transformation? Consider in this
regard Foucault's well-known claim that a practice of freedom is "an
exercise of the self on the self by which one attempts to develop and
transform oneself, and to attain to a certain mode of being."[51] But this
idea of freedom as a practice centered on the relation of the self to itself
(what Foucault calls *rapport à soi*), lest it remain an I-will in the absence
of an I-can, surely has its worldly conditions.[52] If it is hard to see how
such conditions could obtain in Foucault's account of freedom, that is
because Foucault—like any theorist working from within the frame of
the subject question, albeit in its negative space—takes for granted the
idea that freedom would begin with changes in subjectivity that then
bring about changes in the world, while begging the question of how one
changes subjectivity, save in the guise of a highly individualized conception of work on the self.[53]

The point here is neither to exclude creative work on the self as potentially relevant for political freedom—as Arendt herself might—nor to
decide what comes first: changes in the structure of subjectivity or
changes in the social structures that constitute subjectivity. It is to think
about how the subject question and the (ethical) idea of freedom as the
self's relation to itself (even in the deeply critical iteration given it by
Foucault) might extend, rather than contest, the Western tradition's
philosophical conception of freedom and thus the displacement of political freedom as a relation to the world and to others.[54] Although
Foucault, like Arendt, clearly refutes the idea of free will and sees that
freedom is a practice, not a property of the subject, he does not distinguish adequately between the philosophical kind of freedom that might
be relevant to solitary individuals and the political kind that is certainly
relevant to people who live in communities. Consequently, his otherwise

valuable assertion that freedom is a practice, something "that must be exercised," risks remaining at the individual level without ever founding the new institutions and forms of life that clearly and deeply concerned him.[55] Political freedom in this sense of world-building cannot simply be *rapport à soi* (or its extension) but must involve, from the start, relations with a plurality of other people in a public space created by action, that is, by the very practice and experience of freedom itself.

Freedom as a World Question

"Men *are* free—as distinguished from their possessing the gift for freedom—as long as they act, neither before nor after; for to *be* free and to act are the same," declares Arendt.[56] Like Foucault, Arendt understands freedom to be an activity or practice, but one that takes place in the sphere of human plurality and that therefore has a distinctive, if mostly forgotten, political genealogy. "We first become aware of freedom or its opposite in our intercourse with others, not in the intercourse with ourselves," she writes. In a genealogical attempt to recover a political conception of freedom from the occidental tradition, Arendt, like Foucault, returns to the ancients. For her, however, this return does not recover the Greek idea of care of the self (*epimeleia heautou*) or the notion of freedom as self-rule, as it does for Foucault, but shows that an idea of freedom that begins with the self (*rapport à soi*) occludes its origins in freedom "as a worldly tangible reality."[57] This worldly freedom is political: it requires not only an I-will but an I-can; it requires community. Arendt asserts, "Only where the I-will and the I-can coincide does freedom come to pass."[58] And further: "If men wish to be free, it is precisely sovereignty they must renounce."[59]

Rethinking freedom in terms of nonsovereignty is called for once we take account of plurality. Equating freedom with sovereignty, the Western tradition since Plato, argues Arendt, has held plurality to be a "weakness," at best an indication of our unfortunate dependence on others, which we should strive to overcome. Consequently, "If we look upon freedom with the eyes of the tradition, identifying freedom with sovereignty, the simultaneous presence of freedom and non-sovereignty, of being able to begin something new and of not being able to control or even foretell its consequences, seems almost to force us to the conclusion that human existence is absurd" (*HC*, 235). Bemoaning the idea that "no man can be sovereign" (*HC*, 234), the tradition, beholden to the impossible fantasy of sovereignty, has tended "to turn away with despair from the realm of human affairs and to hold in contempt the human capacity for freedom," Arendt observes (*HC*, 233). In fact, when freedom is equated with sovereignty, it seems as if the only way to preserve both is by not acting or entering the public realm at all, for to enter is to be subject to forces beyond one's control.

"If it were true that sovereignty and freedom are the same, then indeed no man could be free, because sovereignty, the ideal of uncompromising self-sufficiency and mastership, is contradictory to the very condition of plurality," Arendt remarks (*HC*, 234). The question of whether freedom and nonsovereignty are indeed mutually exclusive, as the tradition has held, is important for feminists who are concerned to take account of plurality. Although feminist theorists of the third wave have been deeply critical of the fantasy of sovereignty (be it in the form of Woman in the singular or women as a unified group), they could not really think plurality without occasioning a crisis of agency. I said earlier that agency is a false problem that leads us to misunderstand what we do when we act politically. But the problem is false because it is posed within a subject-centered frame. That frame occludes a way of responding to the crisis of agency that would not require a denial of plurality. This is where third-wave feminism arrives at an impasse: how to take account of plurality (differences among women) without relinquishing the capacity to act politically. For surely action in concert, a feminist might object, must involve *some* sense of agency. If we had no sense of agency when we act politically, why would we so act?

Recognizing the dilemma posed by the tradition, Arendt's answer is neither to resurrect its idea of agency as sovereignty nor to discount what she calls "the disabilities of non-sovereignty" (that is, that we cannot control or foretell with certainty the consequences of action). It is to ask whether action does not harbor within itself capacities that might attenuate these disabilities. Arendt remarks,

> The possible redemption from the predicament of irreversibility—of being able to undo what one has done though one did not, and could not, have known what he was doing—is the faculty of forgiving. The remedy for unpredictability, for the chaotic uncertainty of the future, is contained in the faculty to make and keep promises. . . . Without being forgiven, released from the consequences of what we have done, our capacity to act would, as it were, be confined to one single deed from which we could never recover. . . . Without being bound to the fulfillment of promises, we would never be able to keep our identities [*who* we are]. . . . [Keeping them is possible only in] the public realm

through the presence of others, who confirm the identity between the one who promises and the one who fulfills. . . . Both faculties, therefore, depend on plurality, on the presence and acting of others, for no one can forgive himself and no one can feel bound by a promise made only to himself. (*HC*, 237)

Although the importance of forgiveness in human affairs arose in a religious context, says Arendt, it is by no means irrelevant to secular communities (*HC*, 238–39). Forgiveness sounds strange as a political concept in part because we think about action in terms of sovereign individuals who use a means to an end, know what they do, and are to be held accountable for their actions. Arendt does not question accountability (though her understanding of it is complex), but she refutes the assumption of sovereignty. Her concern is that human beings will, in the spirit of the tradition, turn away from the public realm for fear that, in this realm, "they know not what they do," they cannot possibly control the effects of their actions (*HC*, 239). Likewise, promising sounds strange as a political concept (though it is surely the basis of any idea of the social contract), for we think about the agreements that constitute political community as guaranteed by law. Arendt does not question the role of law in sustaining community, but she refutes the idea that community originates in law or can be so guaranteed. What holds a community together is, among other things in her view, the capacity to make and keep promises, which is an exercise of freedom. This capacity erects, as she puts it, "isolated islands of certainty in an ocean of uncertainty," namely, the unpredictability that belongs to human action (*HC*, 244). Those who are mutually bound by promises gain what Arendt calls a "limited sovereignty," not the spurious sovereignty claimed by an individual setting himself apart from all others, but a certain release from the incalculable future that accompanies human action.

Finding resources in action to counteract the defining features of action, Arendt does not claim to have discovered perfect safeguards that will protect us from action's boundlessness and unpredictability. Being themselves forms of action, promising and forgiving could hardly play such a role. Her point, rather, is to emphasize that we might live human plurality in ways (for example, through promising and forgiving) that attenuate the problems associated with plurality as the condition of action. That we act into a context characterized by multiple wills and intentions; that others take up our actions in ways we can neither predict nor control, Arendt suggests, is the irreducible condition of human action *tout court*. Rather than seek solace in an impossible fantasy of sovereignty, declare a crisis of agency, or turn away from the public realm to preserve sovereignty or avoid crisis, we might take leave of the tradition and affirm freedom as nonsovereignty.

Nonsovereignty is the condition of democratic politics, the condition of the transformation of an I-will into an I-can and thus freedom. This is a simple point, but also one we are forever in danger of forgetting (which is why Arendt never tired of repeating it). Political freedom requires others and is spatially limited by their presence. No subjective relation of the self to itself, freedom requires a certain kind of relation to others in the space defined by plurality that Arendt calls the "common world."

The common world is another way of talking about the nature of democratic—and, I argue, feminist—political space. "It is the space between them that unites them, rather than some quality inside each of them," to cite Margaret Canovan's succinct phrasing of the Arendtian difference between a community based on "what" someone is (that is, on identity) and one based on "who" someone is (that is, on world-building).[60] If identities come to have political significance for us, it is because the "what" has been rearticulated as the "who" in the in-between space of the common world. In this space, plurality is not merely a numerical matter of the many identities of people who inhabit the earth or a particular geographical territory, nor is it an empirical question of the wide variety of groups to which they belong (that is, *what* people are). A political rather than ontological relation based on the ongoing constitution of the world as a public space, plurality marks the way in which subjects as members of political communities, as citizens, stand to one another.[61] What is crucially important for democratic and feminist politics, but mostly occluded by the subject question, is that citizens be situated in a relation of distance and proximity, relation and separation. "To live together in the world means essentially that a world of things is between those who have it in common, as a table is located between those who sit around it; the world, like every in-between, relates and separates men at the same time," writes Arendt (*HC*, 52). Relates *and* separates: the common world "gathers us together and yet prevents our falling over each other, so to speak" (ibid.). Politics requires and takes place in this in-between space.

In mass societies such as our own, comments Arendt, the world has lost its power to relate and separate us. It is as if the table had suddenly disappeared from our midst, she writes, such that "two persons sitting opposite each other were no longer separated but also would be entirely unrelated to each other by anything tangible" (*HC*, 53). Couldn't that also be interpreted as the state of contemporary feminism, in which the price for attending to differences, what separates us, appears to be the absence of anything that relates us? The point is not to assert, in the nostalgic tone attributed—falsely in my view—to Arendt, the loss of something we (feminists) supposedly once had. It is, rather, to see what it would mean to affirm, in a democratic political sense, freedom as a world-building practice based on plurality and nonsovereignty. To assume, as many first- and second-wave feminists did, that a shared gender identity is what relates women politically is flawed not only because, as third-wave feminists claimed, differences among women matter and the very category of identity itself is suspect. It is flawed because it does not answer to the question of what possible relevance identity can have for feminist politics absent a space in which to articulate it as a *political* relation. Third-wave critiques, too, are mostly silent on how to constitute the political space in which the transformation of social relations, including gendered forms of subjectivity, is to occur.

The common world as the space of freedom is not exhausted by existing institutions or the citizen as the subject of law, but "comes into being whenever men are together in the manner of speech and action," that is, whenever they come together politically. Such a "space of appearance," says Arendt, "predates and precedes all formal constitution of the public realm and the various forms of government" (*HC*, 199). Not restricted to a set of institutions or to a specific location, this space is highly fragile and must be continually renewed by action. In Arendt's view, the space of appearance "can find its proper location almost any time and anywhere" (*HC*, 198). If we think about the coffeehouses, living rooms, kitchens, and street corners that served as the meeting places for early second-wave feminism, for example, we can begin to appreciate the value of an action-centered conception of politics. We can see how any physical space can be transformed into a political one and, indeed, how it is that things become public. The peculiarity of such a space of appearance is that it exists only so long as people are engaged in speech and action. The formal public realm itself (that is, that which is protected by law) is "a potential space of appearance," but only a potential one. There is nothing in its institutionalized character that guarantees it as a site of political action or practice of freedom.

What keeps the public realm, the potential space of appearance, in existence is power. Power, not as a relation of rule operating from above and forcing the submission of otherwise autonomous subjects (which is how the Western political tradition and most first-, second-, and some third-wave feminists have tended to see it); power, not as a relation of rule understood as a productive force that circulates throughout the entire social body, constituting subjects as subject/ed and generating relations of resistance (which is how Foucault and many third-wave feminists have understood it); but power as that which "springs up between men when they act together and vanishes when they disperse," as Arendt puts it (*HC*, 200). Although the relations of domination we call power clearly exist in Arendt's view, her idiosyncratic use of the term is an invitation to think about politics as involving something other than relations of rule. "The commonplace notion . . . that every political community consists of those who rule and those who are ruled" (including the idea of democracy as rule of the many), she argues, is once again an "escape from the frailty of human affairs into the solidity of quiet and order" (*HC*, 222).[62] It is an escape from the unpredictability and boundlessness of action and the disturbances of plurality and nonsovereignty.

Understood as a relation of no-rule that depends on the presence of others, politics involves power, only power as that which is "generated when people gather together and 'act in concert,' [and] which disappears the moment they depart" (*HC*, 244). The political space created by action, says Arendt, is both an objective and subjective "in-between," which at once gathers individuals together and separates them. Far from denying that objective worldly interests (for example, the interests at stake in iterations of the social question) are what bring people together politically in the first place—as her critics accuse and as her own critique of the social could be taken to imply—Arendt redefines the very meaning of interests by shifting the frame in which they appear. She writes,

[Reducible to neither the social nor the subject question, such] interests constitute, in the word's most literal significance, something which *inter-est,* which lies between people and therefore can relate and bind them together. Most action and speech is concerned with this in-between, which varies with each group of people, so that most words and deeds are *about* some worldly objective reality in addition to being a disclosure of the acting and speaking agent ["who" she is]. Since this disclosure of the subject is an integral part of all, even the most "objective" intercourse, the physical, worldly in-between along with its interests is overlaid and, as it were, overgrown with an altogether different in-between which consists of deeds and words and owes its origin exclusively to men's acting and speaking directly *to* one another. This second, subjective in-between is not tangible, since there are no tangible objects into which it could solidify; the process of acting and speaking can leave behind no such results and end products. But for all its intangibility, this in-between is no less real than the world of things we visibly have in common. We call this reality the "web" of human relationships. (*HC*, 182–83)

Foregrounded in Arendt's account is politics neither as a subject question nor as a social question but as a world question or, more precisely, as a world-building activity, for which the pursuit of interests may be enabling or corrupting but is, either way, certainly secondary to the practice of freedom. In contrast with the idea, central to liberalism and to most forms of feminism, that the function of politics is to pursue individual and group interests (that is, people come to the table with certain interests already in hand, which then need to be articulated as claims and adjudicated in terms of their validity), we have the idea that interests serve as the occasion, a catalyst of sorts, to engage in politics. The instrumentalist or adjudicative approach to politics sees the pursuit of interests not only as the motor but also the raison d'être of politics itself, for which speech and action are a means (preferably minimizable if not fully eliminable in the interests of expediency). Arendt, by contrast, holds that speech and action can themselves be political, regardless of the interests we may pursue or the ends we may realize when we come together politically. In a very specific sense, then, politics may involve the articulation of interests but is not driven by questions of expediency; it is not a means toward an end. Political are not the interests as such but the world-building practice of publicly articulating matters of common concern.

Feminists familiar with the "endless meeting" will immediately understand why this alternative conception of politics is at once crucially important and exceedingly difficult to affirm. The moment we think about politics in terms of interests and as a means to an end, it is hard to see why we should not hand certain matters over to "those who know" and go home early for a change. Were we to hand over speaking and acting to those who know, however, we would no longer be engaged in the world-building that is surely crucial for feminist and democratic politics, nor experiencing freedom as the right to be a participator in common affairs, but merely registering our claim to a certain distribution of goods and services. Surely we can imagine far less democratic and even antidemocratic organizations and societies that would be far more efficient.

Arendt's idea of politics as a world-building practice of freedom is unintelligible if we think about politics as something that is everywhere or that has always existed and will always exist. The feminist claim "the personal is political," when it identifies power with politics, risks effacing the very special character of democratic politics and also underestimating the possibility that it could be driven out of the world. At issue here is not only the logical problem that, if everything is political, nothing is, but also the difficulty of seeing that nothing is political in itself; for political relations, I argue in the following chapters, are external to their terms: they are not given in objects themselves, but are a creation. Politics, as Jacques Rancière puts it, "consists in building a relationship between things that have none."[63] There is nothing intrinsically political about, say, housework, any more than there is something intrinsically political about the factory or for that matter the government: the word *political* signifies a relation between things, not a substance in any thing.[64] Housework *becomes* political when two things that are not logically related, say, the principle of equality and the sexual division of labor, are brought into a relationship as the object of a dispute, that is, as the occasion for the speech and action with which people create the common world, the space in which things become public, and create it anew.

The same could be said about the practices associated with subject-constitution that are discussed in both Butler's and Foucault's work. Once again, the point is not to exclude as politically irrelevant those issues that have been framed by the subject question, but to understand what it would mean to frame them anew. Arendt herself did not really consider the possibility of such reframing. She can be read as rejecting not only the *frames* of both the subject and the social questions, but also the *concerns* that are associated with each of those frames. She seems not only to reject the possibility that such questions could be relevant to politics but also to see them as destructive of democratic politics, regardless of how they are articulated. Rather than exclude these concerns, feminists need to redescribe them in ways that are less likely to lead to the displacement of political freedom by the very frames of the social and the subject in which freedom has been thought.

If we adopt a world- and action-centered frame, we will open a space for thinking about feminism as a practice of freedom that is creative or inaugural. Although the capacity to start something new has been central to feminism as a political movement, feminist theory, caught within the frames of the social question and the subject question, has tended to lose sight of it. We have lost sight of the possibility that counterpractices of political association need not reproduce subjected identities as the condition of having anything political to say, but might create public spaces in which something is said that changes what can be heard as a political claim and also alters the context in which identities themselves are presently constituted as subject/ed. This possibility is related to the inaugural power of speech and action. Our ability to project a word such as *women* into new and unforeseen contexts is connected to the power of political association to create new (more freedom-affirming) attachments to the world and to others. How else could we understand or care about feminism if we did not keep our eyes on the prize: the world-transforming power of political association and speech?

In the chapters that follow I try to think about political freedom and association in terms of the power of beginning: "the freedom to call something into being, which did not exist before, which was not given, not even as an object of cognition or imagination, and which therefore, strictly speaking, could not be known," as Arendt puts it.[65] This includes the formation of the "we" of feminism. Thinking about women as a political collectivity, rather than a sociological group or social subject, means thinking the "we" of feminism anew: as the fragile achievement of practices of freedom. The achievement is fragile because action's "tremendous capacity for establishing relationships," Arendt reminds us, is inseparable from its "inherent unpredictability" and "boundlessness" (*HC*, 191). The "we" may be pursued as willful purpose, but is rarely if ever achieved as such. Its formation remains irreducibly contingent. When we reflect on the history of feminism, however, we tend to lose sight of this contingency. Telling a story according to which freedom is identical with the struggle for liberation from oppression, feminists are inclined to narrate the formation of the "we" as if it were somehow the necessary outcome of a historical process, the necessary response of women to their centuries-long subjection. And not only necessary but justified too. For it appears once again that freedom must point beyond the demand or practice of freedom itself, be it to social justice or social utility. We find ourselves entangled in justifications that—like the social and subject questions—miss what is most important: the creation of something new, something that could not have been foretold, that was no result of some logical or historical development but rather an "infinite improbability," to borrow Arendt's poetic phrasing.[66]

What would it mean to think about feminism as an "infinite improbability"? What would come of rethinking the "we" of feminism as something utterly contingent, that is, something that could just as well have been left undone, something highly fragile that could be driven out of the world? *Contingency* is a familiar word in contemporary feminist theory, but it has been hard to see it as the *condition* of the world-creating and world-building power of feminism as a practice of freedom. Rather, in contingency we often see the threat that deprives feminism of the all-important political ability to speak authoritatively in someone's name. Yet Arendt tells us that the "frightening arbitrariness" of action (that is, our sheer capacity to start something that is neither the effect of a past cause nor the predictable cause of a future effect) is "the price of freedom."[67] It is a price that feminists—like the "men of action" that figure in Arendt's account of revolutionary movements—are reluctant to pay. When understood as the power of beginning, freedom has an abyssal or aporetic character that we tend to deny or cover over. What authorizes beginning? What legitimates, say, *this* form of political association, *this* constitution of community, *this* practice of freedom, *this* "we"?

I discuss the various ways in which feminists have answered these questions in the chapters that follow. For now it is useful to note that attempts to authorize feminist politics by seeking grounds for inaugural forms of political action have entangled feminists in epistemology, in claims to truth or normative rightness. If we want to understand the epistemological turn in feminism (for example, standpoint theory), which animated the divisive and all-consuming feminist "foundations debate" of the 1990s, we might consider it one problematic response to what Arendt calls "the abyss of freedom."[68] Once again, it is as if women's claim to freedom demands justification, in this case the supposedly truer account of the world that belongs to them as an oppressed group. Although an attempt to authorize the claims of feminism in this way is an understandable, and far from unique, response to the boundlessness and unpredictability of action, Arendt invites us to ask, what are the political costs of this particular recoil from the abyss?

Feminism's "Lost Treasure"

One risk associated with the tendency to recoil from the abyss of freedom is visible in the stories we tell—or fail to tell—ourselves about the revolutionary origins of feminism. Although modern feminism did not originate in a world-historical event like the American Revolution, it partook of the revolutionary spirit that animates such events, namely what Arendt calls "the exhilarating awareness of the human capacity of beginning."[69] Akin to the failure of postrevolutionary thought to remember the simple fact that, writes Arendt, "a revolution gave birth to the United

States and that the republic was brought about by no historical necessity and no organic development," contemporary feminism, too, seems to have lost sight of its own origins in the revolutionary spirit and the contingency of action. The first two waves of feminism denied the abyssal character of political freedom by framing freedom as a social question or a subject question or by scripting the claim to freedom as a necessary historical development that flowed directly out of women's liberation from oppression. Feminism of the third wave, for its part, seems to be so thoroughly caught in the problems associated with these two frames as to have lost sight of what Arendt poignantly called the "lost treasure" of the American Revolution—political freedom itself.

Recent attempts to reclaim feminism as a practice of freedom include narrative accounts of early second-wave feminism that recreate the exhilarating sense of beginning anew that animated the individuals and groups involved. But these accounts, generally written by the feminist political actors themselves, are often characterized by a tone of incredulity and defensiveness, as if third-generation feminists were, when not downright ungrateful, dangerously ignorant of their own political past. Guided by the familiar motto of didactic political historiography—that is, "those who forget the past are destined to repeat it"—many of these accounts treat the past as if it dictates—or ought to dictate—what the future can be.[70] A freedom-centered feminism needs not more rallying cries to carry on the cause of past generations—well, it can use this too—but *disturbing* examples of feminist practices of political freedom: disturbing—if we will only pause and let them disturb us—because they resist being incorporated into the social- and subject-centered frames that shape most stories of feminism, frames in which freedom as action has mostly disappeared.

In the following chapters I offer examples of such disturbance in the form of recuperative readings of familiar and unfamiliar, celebrated and castigated, feminist texts that both foreground freedom as a practice and imagine the various practices that freedom can take: freedom as a non-rule-governed theoretical practice (chapter 1); freedom as an inaugural practice of action (chapter 2); freedom as a world-building practice of promising (chapter 3); and freedom as a critical practice of judging (chapter 4). Although I consider classic claims to political freedom (for example, "Seneca Falls"), the chapters focus on less likely examples: a founding third-wave feminist theory text that is entangled in the ideal of critical reflection it also powerfully contests (Butler's *Gender Trouble*); a work of literature that relates the world-historical event of a global feminist revolution organized around the political principle of freedom (Monique Wittig's *Les guérillères*); a collectively authored account of the founding of freedom in an Italian feminist community (the Milan Women's Bookstore Collective's *Sexual Difference*); and an unfinished project to develop the faculty of judgment on which any capacity to affirm human freedom depends (Arendt's *Lectures on Kant's Political Philosophy*).

My choice of Wittig and the Milan Collective as disturbing examples of a feminist practice of freedom may strike some readers as curious. Have their flaws not already been identified (for example, Wittig is a "humanist," the Milan women are "essentialists")? What significance can they have in the larger scheme of feminist political thought now? It is part of my intention, however, to show how our received frames of the social and subject questions have distorted feminist readings of these authors, blinding us to their concern with freedom and its creation of alternative forms of political association. I reread Wittig and the Milan Collective not only to uncover their rich imagination of political freedom in its various forms, but also to show, in so doing, how it is that we fail to apprehend freedom even when it is instantiated right before our eyes. In the more familiar case of Butler, I examine the critical reception of her early writings on gender, in particular the charge of voluntarism. Although I read (early) Butler as being entangled in a (skeptical) critical enterprise that supports this charge, I also see something else in her project: a contribution to an imaginative, non-rule-governed conception of feminist theory and a nonsovereign practice of freedom.

My attempt to read against the grain of feminist interpretation should be understood as an exercise in the (reflective) judgment that (in chapters 3 and 4) I argue is crucial to recognizing and affirming freedom and thus to feminism. My choice of authors and texts is guided by a concern to develop the multifaceted idea of political freedom, for each thinker offers a different angle from which to see it. Although it is important to emphasize the inaugural character of such freedom, the power to begin anew, we cannot stop there, for freedom so conceived simply turns in on itself—or at least it risks doing so. An account of *political* freedom involves more than spontaneity; it must keep sight of freedom as practices of world-building (such as founding, promising, and judging). The power of beginning a new series would have no meaning for us in the absence of our capacity to create and sustain a worldly space in which to act and judge objects and events in their freedom. For that reason, I take issue with thinkers who cast freedom strictly in terms of constituent power, setting it at odds with the (non-freedom-centered alternative of) constituted power of law, institutions, and the state. As I show in relation to the question of constitutionally guaranteed rights for women in chapter 3, that is a false choice: the point is not to reject but to reclaim legal artifacts such as rights as part of a practice of freedom in its multiple dimensions.

The tendency to construe false choices in feminism (for example, constituent versus constituted power; equality versus difference; recognition versus redistribution) is largely, in my view, an effect of the frames of the social and subject questions that have guided the development of feminist theory. In chapter 1, I show how the epistemological debates of the 1990s, which centered on the problem of justification, inflected these choices with a sense of crisis, namely, the collapse of "women" as the subject of feminism. The crisis, I argue, was precipitated by a means-ends conception of politics, according to which the ability to make a political claim relies on the application of categories as rules to particulars, and by an understanding of feminist theory as the activity of constituting universal rules. Thus the loss of women as a coherent category in theory was the loss of a rule that could be so applied. As theory gives the rule to praxis on this view, in the absence of such a category, we have only "differences," no political movement in the name of "women." Or so the story goes.

At the heart of these debates was Butler's performative theory of gender. What concerns me in chapter 1 is why *Gender Trouble* was interpreted in the epistemic terms of a (politically) devastating form of skeptical doubt (for example, "There are no women"), whereas Butler's whole point was to question these same terms. Reading Butler's antirealist account of gender with Wittgenstein's notion of following a rule, I interrogate her paradoxical entanglement in the skeptical problematic she rejects in favor of a genealogical approach. Butler's alternative to the epistemic concern with concept application, I argue, emerges with her mostly maligned account of drag. Contesting received interpretations, I see in Butler's discussion of drag a "figure of the newly thinkable," to borrow Cornelius Castoriadis's phrase. Such figures, given by radical imagination, are the very condition of critical thought. Whatever doubts we may raise about an "established truth" such as gender always begin with a productive moment of figuration, not (as skepticism would have it) by revealing the ungrounded nature of belief. If we arrive at the insight that a particular belief is ungrounded (as Butler does about a realist idea of gender), that is because we have created a new way of seeing that enables us to recognize the contingency of a particular social arrangement. Feminist critique, I conclude, must always have this productive moment of figuration as its condition. It does not rely—and need not rely—on a form of doubt that is impossible because it is radical and totalizing.

Having indicated the potential role of imagination for negotiating the impasses associated with the epistemological turn in feminism, I go on in chapter 2 to develop a nonepistemic, action-centered conception of politics and the idea of freedom as the power of beginning. Vividly exhibited in the revolutionary poetics of Monique Wittig, feminism is an inaugural practice: the capacity to bring into existence that which could have been neither predicted nor caused, partly because it exceeds the category of sex. Like Butler's project, Wittig's work is often taken to be skeptical, as if the category of sex were something we could doubt in its entirety. By contrast with that view, I argue that Wittig fully recognizes the limits of doubt for contesting sex as central to our form of life. Her critical approach is not skeptical but productive and creative. Wittig, too, offers a figure of the newly thinkable: *les guérillères*, the beginners who break the series of normative heterosexuality and fight for the sole principle of freedom.

But Wittig is less successful in showing the need for and creation of a worldly in-between, that is, the relations that both unite and separate people engaged in a political practice of freedom. For that, I turn to the Milan Women's Bookstore Collective, which conceives freedom as action, but is also concerned with world-building. By contrast with Wittig, the Italians insist that feminist world-building requires the social inscription of sexual difference, not as a form of subjectivity but as a resolutely political practice of "free relations among women." These relations involve the articulation of a new social contract organized around not female identity (be it natural or social) but the willingness to make judgments and promises with other women in a public space. Wholly based on such practices, female freedom requires no other justification (for example, the betterment of society). Its only raison d'être is itself.

Demonstrating the importance of a worldly in-between, the Milan Collective foregrounds the importance of judgment for feminism, but stops short of giving any theoretical account of such a practice. And so, taking up the collective's insight that feminist community ought to be founded not on identity but on a critical practice of making shared judgments, I turn, in chapter 4, to Arendt's idiosyncratic reading of Kant's third *Critique*. In its reflective mode, judgment is the faculty that allows us to apprehend and affirm objects and events *in their freedom*, to take pleasure in the otherwise frightening arbitrariness of action, and to create feminism as critical community. Emphasizing imagination, rather than understanding and reason, as crucial to such judgment and as the political faculty par excellence, Arendt helps us understand why the collapse of the category of women need by no means spell the end of feminism, for a freedom-centered feminism never relied on concept application in the first place. Political claims rely on the ability to exercise imagination, to think from the standpoint of others, and in this way to posit universality and thus community. The universality of such claims depends on their being not epistemologically justified, as most feminists have tended to assume, but taken up by others, in ways that we can neither predict nor control, in a public space. This space called the world is an ever-changing one in which, positing the agreement that may or may not materialize, feminists discover—daily—the nature and limits of community.

In the conclusion I argue that the project of a freedom-centered feminism cannot be developed apart from an understanding of some of the well-known paradoxes and tensions much studied by democratic theorists. By bringing feminism into a critical dialogue with democratic theory, I try to develop further a resolutely political way of working through the problems associated with the subject question and the social question. This dialogue, already initiated in the preceding chapters through an engagement with Arendt, can open a space for thinking anew some of the most tenacious problems in feminist theory. The difficulties associated with constituting a political community that remains open to critical questioning are hardly unique to feminism. The same might be said of the problem of founding a free people where the institutions and spirit of freedom are minimal or do not yet exist. These are dilemmas that belong to the theory and praxis of democracy. Feminists have rightly criticized canonical political theory for its inscription of gender hierarchy into the very grammar of politics. Perhaps it is now possible to return to some of the classic thinkers and see what they have to offer us as we negotiate our way through the impasses that have arisen in recent years and that have led to a sense of exhaustion or crisis.

Working within the tradition of democratic theory, Arendt will aid us in restarting the critical dialogue between it and feminism. Although she never had a (good) word to say about feminism, her fierce commitment to a fully conventional, artificial or non-natural understanding of the political realm as the space of a nonsovereign freedom, I hope to show in this book, offers feminists a valuable alternative to the impasses associated with both the subject question and the social question. Admittedly, other dilemmas, paradoxes, and tensions will arise once we turn our attention to democratic thinkers like Arendt, but perhaps we will be better able to see and accept them as belonging to the difficult and unruly work of feminist and democratic politics, rather than despair at our failure to solve them once and for all. As Joan Scott and others have pointed out, feminism is full of paradoxes. Thus it should be unsurprising that together with the feminist authors discussed in the following chapters, the nonfeminist Arendt will help us refuse the "end of feminism" and take up the project of affirming feminism anew.

CHAPTER ONE

Feminists Know Not What They Do:
Judith Butler's *Gender Trouble* and
the Limits of Epistemology

Theory in itself is a doing, the always uncertain
attempt to realize the project of clarifying the world.

—CORNELIUS CASTORIADIS

A CELEBRITY FEMINIST theorist of the postmodern variety goes to a
conference on identity in New York City. After presenting a paper chart-
ing the demise of women as a unified category, she is confronted by a hostile member of the audience who accuses her of betraying feminism.
Feminism, the practice, needs a subject called women, declares the irate
spectator; a subject that feminism, the theory, has dissolved in its skeptical flight from the ordinary. In a voice pitched well above the ordinary,
this spectator emphatically asserts her confidence in the existence of "real
women" (like herself) and concludes by asking the speaker, "How would
you know that there are women right here in this room?" To this agitated
rhetorical query the weary postmodern feminist replies rather matter-of-
factly, "Probably the same way you do."[1]

With debates concerning the so-called category of women mercifully
behind us, such scenes would appear to have little continuing significance,
save as illustrations of the peculiar pathos of that particular episode in the
development of American feminist theory.[2] To say that these debates are
over, however, is by no means to declare them settled. True, the dramatic
escalation of the stakes of theorizing in the 1990s has yielded to a bland
consensus about "the differences among women." But what does that
consensus really mean? What kinds of shared assumptions and deep divisions does it conceal?

Although the call to attend to difference helped unmask a false homo-
geneity in the fundamental categories of feminism, it has in turn masked the
discontents of feminist theorizing itself. It is as if the concept of difference
were a magical substance that could not only eviscerate the legacy of exclusion in feminism but also settle fundamental questions about what theory
is and how it relates to praxis. Both second- and third-wave feminists have

been deeply concerned with the relation between the theoretical and the practical—agreeing implicitly or explicitly with the Marxist dictum that the point is to change the world, not merely interpret it—but they have not really clarified the relationship between interpretation and change. Proclaiming that theory ought to relate to praxis, feminists have for the most part either left the exact nature of the relation obscure or, worse, tended to define it (albeit often unwittingly) as unidirectional, with theory comprising the universal concepts that are applied in rule-like fashion to the particulars of politics. Should that one-sided relation be deemed untenable, as many feminists of the third wave hold, it seems as if our only recourse is to abandon theory and settle on mere description. But then it appears as if the price for refusing the universalizing impulse of theory is the inability to say something beyond the particular case.

If feminist critique entails "the transfiguration of the commonplace," to borrow Arthur Danto's phrase, then mere description—leaving aside the whole question of whether any description is not always theory-laden—does nothing to bring particulars into an unexpected, critical relation with each other such that we can see any particular object, not to mention our own activity, anew.[3] Likewise, if feminist critique entails taking account of the inaugural character of what Arendt calls action, then a theoretical enterprise centered on formulating hypotheses, concepts, or models that can explain and predict the regularities of sex/gender relations fails to comprehend its own subject matter and leads us to misunderstand what is at stake in our own political praxis. We need a freedom-centered mode of feminist critique that would resist the temptation to reach beyond the common to transfigure the commonplace, that is, a place outside our practices from which to form universal concepts under which to subsume particulars in the name of predicting and achieving social change. If that be the task of this chapter, it should be understood in therapeutic rather than prescriptive terms. Rather than offer yet another feminist theory of sex/gender that could function as a rule to be applied to the contingencies of politics, we want to understand at once the nature of the demand for, and rejection of, such a theory.

Theory—The Craving for Generality?

Let us begin by clarifying the two distinct but related views of theory mentioned above: (1) theory is the critical practice of forming universal concepts that can be applied in rule-like fashion to the particulars of lived experience; (2) universal theory as such is fully bankrupt and must be replaced with the art of description which refuses to say anything beyond the particular case at hand. The tendencies are related because, as we shall see below, they both assume that the critical theoretical enterprise itself consists in a universalizing function that illuminates particulars by subsuming them under concepts to produce a total critique. One of the reasons for the use and abuse of postcolonial feminist writings, for instance, may well be that feminists look to those writings to attenuate what appears to be the necessary consequences of this kind of enterprise, what Wittgenstein calls the "craving for generality" and with it "the contemptuous attitude towards the particular case."[4] This craving is a product of centuries of philosophical and political thinking; it is a disposition to generalize against which feminists, working with and against that inheritance, are by no means invulnerable. What drove some feminists to produce unified categories that did not attend to the particular case was in part this craving for generality, a craving that animated the hegemonic strand of the feminist theoretical enterprise through the 1980s and into the 1990s and that continues to haunt it even today, if only in the form of its nemesis, the refusal of theory, be that skepticism or radical particularism.

Barely concealed in the category of women debates is the unspoken wish that feminist theory can, and ought to, give an exhaustive account of gender relations and provide a kind of "super-idealized guidance" on how to change them.[5] We might think of this wish as a desire for solace, a desire that would be satisfied by, and thus incessantly searches out, the perfect theory. The phenomenal influence of Judith Butler's *Gender Trouble* in American feminist circles of the third wave speaks not only to the author's polemical brilliance but also to our desire for such a theory (even when, as in Butler's case, the theorist herself calls into question our desire for solace).[6] Is this desire unreasonable? Hasn't second-wave American feminist theory itself incited our desire for solace by generating a long chain of causal explanations of women's oppression which, if rightly understood, could be rightly remedied? Few American feminist theorists writing today would speak of the origin or cause of (all) women's suffering. But has the desire for solace, that is, for a total theory and a maxim that would tell us how to act politically, disappeared? In light of what we have learned from the category of women debates, surely it is not a matter of creating once and for all a theory that would be so encompassing of the diversity of lived experience, so accurate in its account of cause and effect, so final in its articulation of normative commitments, that it could in fact tell us how so to act.

Driving the tenacious but impossible idea of such a theory is a conception of politics as an instrumental, means-ends activity centered on the pursuit of group interests. This pursuit requires a coherent group (for example, women) with shared concerns. It requires as well the production of knowledge in the form of concepts that function as rules under which to make sense of and order the particulars of women's lives, knowledge that can be used to articulate political claims and authorize them in the coinage of modern scientific rationality and its practices of justification. In light of many feminists' more or less uncritical acceptance of this conception of politics, it is not surprising that the critique of a total theory, as it was expressed in the call to attend to differences, precipitated a sense of total political crisis. The source of that crisis, in other words, lies not in the loss of women as the subject of feminism, but in a means-ends view of politics that requires such a coherent, pregiven subject. The possibility of a total theory that this understanding of politics implies treats people themselves as means to an end, as the "*passive* objects of its theoretical truth," writes Cornelius Castoriadis, and the world itself as a static object: the last thing it can account for is their political activity, whatever cannot be assimilated to a closed system, namely the new.[7]

Following Castoriadis's critical account of the crisis of orthodox Marxism, we might say that the exposure of this total theory as a feminist pipe dream led, in the course of the category of women debates, to two different but related responses, which we might now think of as contemporary (and therefore attenuated) versions of the old philosophical battle between dogmatism and skepticism: (1) the critique of the alleged certainties of second-wave feminist theory might well be right, but we have to shut our eyes and blindly affirm them nonetheless in the interests of radical politics (for example, "strategic essentialism"), for such politics cannot get off the ground without foundational knowledge claims and the theory that articulates them; (2) since a total (feminist) theory cannot exist, we are led to abandon the theoretical enterprise if not the feminist project itself, for the latter, to speak with Castoriadis, is now "posited as . . . the blind will to transform at any price something one does not know into something one knows even less" (*IIS*, 71–72). The responses are related because, though the second is the position rejected by the first, both share the view that without a total theory there can be no conscious action whatsoever, no sense of a common project whose ideals we at once debate and fight for in someone's name. Absent the rational knowledge that allows us to think present and future social organizations as totalities and gives us at the same time a criterion permitting us to judge them, there is no feminist politics save a decisionistic one (that is, a politics devoid of any particular ideals or normative commitments). In that case, we might as well declare "the end of feminism," for there is little to differentiate a feminist project from other political projects, including nonfeminist and even antifeminist ones.

To demand that a revolutionary project (such as feminism) "be founded on a complete theory," writes Castoriadis, "is . . . to assimilate politics to a technique, and to posit its sphere of action—history—as the possible object of a finished and exhaustive knowledge. To invert this reasoning and conclude on the basis of the impossibility of this sort of knowledge that all lucid [that is, theoretically, critically informed], revolutionary politics is impossible amounts, finally, to a wholesale rejection of all human activity and history as unsatisfactory according to a fictitious standard" (*IIS*, 75). Beholden to an instrumentalist conception of politics, feminists, though most see that such knowledge is neither possible nor desirable, have a harder time seeing how feminism could possibly continue without it or, more precisely, something that approximates it in the sense of providing objective criteria according to which political claims could be defined, articulated, and justified. Feminists therefore find themselves tempted by dogmatism and skepticism, either affirming what they may well know is not the case (for example, "women" is a coherent group) or denying that one can affirm anything political that one does not know (for example, speak in the name of women). And this same logic, carried to its absurd conclusion, hinges the future of feminism on our ability to make a cognitive judgment along the lines of "There are women in the room."

Castoriadis's critique of the tendency to assimilate politics to a technique recalls Hannah Arendt's account of the tendency to think about politics as a form of fabrication or making. To think about politics in this way, Arendt argues, is to imagine "[t]he construction of the public space in the image of a fabricated object," that is, as an object that exists first as a model in thought, as a set of rules that guide the realization of the model in praxis.[8] Countering this instrumentalist conception of politics with an action-centered view, Arendt claims that political actors "know not what they do."[9] She does not accept here the (Platonic) separation of doing and knowing and the hierarchical distinction between those who know (the philosophers or rulers) and those who do (the demos or ruled).[10] Rather, she questions the very idea that politics as action is a rule-governed activity, prefigured by theory in the form of a model, which has outcomes that can be known in advance of the actual activity itself. Political actors know not what they do, then, not because there are others (the theorists or the philosophers) who do so know, but because, when we act, we cannot know (predict or foresee) what the consequences of our action will be.

This inability to predict the outcome of political action (Arendt) or praxis (Castoriadis) is a problem only according to the requirements of a means-end conception of politics and its fictitious standard of knowledge. Both Castoriadis and Arendt question the idea that politics, as a register of human doing, requires its participants to supply, or be able to supply, a complete theory of their activity. Neither thinker associates this lack of total knowledge with the failure to think critically, with nonreflexive activities, or with the mindless compulsion of habit. Like Wittgenstein, they affirm that our rule-governed practices are underdetermined, that is, that they are neither justified all the way down nor in need of such justification to count as part of a creative and critical relation to the world. More specifically, both Arendt and Castoriadis reject the idea that politics is a means-ends activity based on practices of knowing, that is, of adducing evidence, establishing truth or falsity, providing justification or nonjustification. If politics were "a 'purely rational' activity," writes Castoriadis, "based on an exhaustive, or practically exhaustive, knowledge of its domain," then "any question relevant for practice and arising out of this domain would be decidable"—decidable, that is, in theory and quite apart from actual praxis—and "confined to positing in reality the means to reach the ends it aims at, and establishing the causes that would lead to the intended results" (*IIS*, 72).

A Wittigensteinian Reading of the Feminist Foundations Debate

That hardly a feminist would claim politics to be a purely rational activity in no way alters the tendency to cast politics as if it ought to approximate a technique with adequate epistemic tools for establishing the truth or falsity of feminist claims. Some feminists are knowledge producers, working to transform, in the broadest sense, what we know and how we come to know it, as well as the relationship between knower and known. That work is valuable, but the work of feminism as a political movement is not first and foremost epistemic.[11] The idea that political claims must be redeemed as claims to knowledge and truth leads feminism away from politics as a practice of freedom (that is, as a contingent, world-building activity, rooted in action and situated in the realm of the probable) and in the direction of either strong or weak versions of both dogmatism and skepticism. As we shall see more clearly in chapter 4, the notion that political claims are either grounded (and therefore not contestable) or ungrounded (and therefore not persuasive) occludes a third possibility: rather than knowledge claims that must be redeemed as true or false by means of a logical or cognitive (determinant) judgment, political claims are based on contingently formed public opinions that call for our (reflective) judgment without the mediation of a concept.

In the feminist debates of the 1990s, epistemic commitments included the obsessive focus on foundations, to the virtual exclusion of everything else: defending them or critiquing them on the basis of what they authorize and what they foreclose.[12] Whatever position one may have taken in this acrimonious debate, both sides shared (even when they asserted otherwise) the assumption that political claims are at bottom knowledge claims; hence, what must be either protected (in the view of some feminists) or questioned (in the view of others) is a foundation, a piece of (noninferential) knowledge. On the one hand, this debate over foundations in feminism was immensely productive inasmuch as it brought to light a series of exclusions (for example, racism, heterosexism, and Eurocentrism) that were associated with a feminism whose organizing principle was "women and their interests." On the other hand, this same debate was influenced by problematic assumptions concerning the nature of critical reflection. As James Tully has shown in an article on Wittgenstein and political philosophy, these assumptions include both the notion that there is a sharp distinction between our everyday practices and the practice of critical thought, as well as the idea that our words and acts are rational only insofar as we can give grounds for them.[13] Following Wittgenstein, he holds that critical thinking will always take for granted things that we neither do nor must justify in order to act rationally.[14] Critique could not get off the ground if it were not reasonable to take certain things for granted.

From the reception of *The Second Sex* to that of *Gender Trouble*, this conception of critical reflection (that is, not taking anything for granted) has strongly influenced our understanding of the tasks of feminist theory. Second-wave feminism claimed that theory ought to be rooted in praxis and women's everyday lives. But it also assumed that theory is the activity of forming critical concepts that will free us from our otherwise blind adherence to social convention. Although feminist theory of the third wave has, for the most part, questioned the idea of a total theory that would so free us, it too tends to conceive of the critical enterprise as that which cuts through the always-already-there quality of our two-sex system, revealing the ungrounded character of our agreement in judgments. The problem with this notion of theory as a critique of our customary ways of acting and thinking arises when the practice of critical reflection is seen as being somehow of an entirely different order than that of all other (nonreflective) practices. As David Hume powerfully argued, such a view of critique sees its agent in the form of autonomous reason, which thoroughly emancipates itself from custom and prejudice. Although few feminist theorists imagine they can occupy—and many feminists are critical of attempting to occupy—the Archimedean standpoint that was the target of Hume's critique of philosophical reflection, there persists a tendency to view feminist critical reflection as an interpretive enterprise that is noncontinuous with customs and habits. This in turn has contributed to two mistaken assumptions: (1) that the two-sex system is fundamentally a problem of epistemic claims, which can be unsettled by classically skeptical questions about the possibility of knowledge or truth; (2) that such skeptical questioning defines the task of feminist theory, which unsettles our prereflective habits and customs and sets the agenda for feminist political practice.

Curious in the debate over foundations is that feminist critics of foundationalism were often deeply at odds with the elevation of theory as an autonomous critical practice; moreover, they were hardly blind to the noncognitive dimensions of the two-sex system. The performative theory of gender developed by Butler, for example, includes genealogical features that are irreducible to knowledge claims. Even the more empirically based work of the feminist biologist Anne Fausto-Sterling acknowledges the extent to which the broader symbolic framework that limits embodiment to two sexes also limits the political effect of the scientific claim that there are at least five.[15] Both Butler and Fausto-Sterling see that we may well *know* something (for example, that there are bodies that do not conform to our concepts of sexual dimorphism) and continue to *act* as if we did *not know* it (for example, treat intersexed bodies as anomalies or exceptions that in no way disturb those concepts). But they sometimes seem to assume that it ought to be possible to throw our system of reference into question, all at once, by means of classically skeptical questions about the certainty of our knowledge of sex difference.[16]

Feminists like Butler and Fausto-Sterling rightly raise questions about our two-sex system by exposing the contingency of our criteria. Criteria are supposed to be the means by which the existence of something is objectively established; they are the means by which we judge. We say that empirical propositions can be tested, and that our criteria constitute the objective measure according to which we test. If you say, "This is a female and this is a male," and I pose the skeptic's question "How do you know?" you might invoke standard criteria of sex difference such as chromosomes, hormones, and genitalia. But what if those principles of judgments themselves are judgments? What is to be tested by what if the yardstick itself is a judgment? At what point have we got an objective means of testing our empirical proposition?[17]

As Wittgenstein shows, at a certain point our criteria disappoint us—therein consists the impulse to radical doubt, to skepticism. Consider the International Olympic Committee's move, in 1968, from the genitalia test for femaleness to the chromosome test, only to return, in 1992, to the genitalia test. (From parading nude in front of judges, female athletes were then asked to submit their DNA, only to parade nude once again.) In each instance there were individuals who did not meet the criteria, but could not be discounted as female. There were those who "looked" like females and saw themselves as women, but had male sex chromosomes; those who had female sex chromosomes, but due to defects in hormone production had men's muscles and male genitals; those who had two X chromosomes, but an extra Y one as well. And so on.

The Olympic Committee's quest for a definitive test for femaleness exhibits what many feminists argue: there are no definitive criteria for sex difference. But that doesn't mean that there are no criteria or that in our everyday encounters with other people we will not make a judgment about such difference, usually without thinking, certainly without thinking about chromosomes or, for that matter, even genitalia. We do make these judgments, mostly in a flash, without thinking, on the basis of unreflective responses that constitute what Wittgenstein calls a prior "agreement in judgments." "This is not agreement in opinions [matters of fact] but in form of life," he writes.[18] It is an agreement in language that makes it possible to establish criteria in the first place.[19] Needless to say, this is not an agreement any of us signed: it is neither conventional in that sense nor based on rational consent. But neither is it natural, if by *natural* we mean somehow determined and determining of our criteria. It is more like our mutual attunement in language; we normally do know what another person means when he or she uses a word.[20]

It is important for feminists to point out exceptions to the two-sex system, but if these exceptions do not unsettle the deeply imbricated hinge propositions "there are males and there are females; there are men and there are women," it may be because we never learned those propositions as empirical ones. What stands fast for us does so not because it is obvious or convincing, but because "it is . . . held fast by what lies around it," writes Wittgenstein (OC §144). Accordingly, every form of representation provides a means for accommodating that which is "deviant" (for example, the "females" with "male" sex chromosomes) without having to surrender the form of representation. Paraphrasing §79 of *Philosophical Investigations*, I would put these points like this: Should one of my definitions be called into question—say, a female human being has two X chromosomes—is it not the case that I have, so to speak, a whole series of props in readiness, and am ready to lean on one if another should be taken from me and vice versa? How much of what I think a female human being is must be proved false for me to give up my definitions as false? The point is that there is no fixed point at which I'd have to abandon my definitions, though I may well abandon them at some point. I use the concept "female" (like any other concept) without fixed meaning. That may be why cases that do not meet the criteria of the two-sex system tend to remain exceptions to the rule, mere anomalies that may give us pause about the accuracy of our criteria but in no way destroy the very concept for which those criteria are to serve as the test. A three-legged table may wobble a bit, but that doesn't mean we won't call it a table. The Olympic Committee changed the test (twice in fact), but it never doubted that what it was testing for (sex difference) existed.

The Olympic Committee's deliberations indicate that we can include members in a class who do not meet the prototypical descriptions we associate with membership in that class. As Hilary Putnam, working off Wittgenstein, argues, all so-called natural kinds ("lemon," "water," "tiger," or "gold") are not definable; that is, it is impossible to provide a set of descriptions that constitute the necessary and sufficient conditions for identifying the members of the class they designate. All natural kinds have "abnormal members," and yet few people would question whether they belong to those groups. "A green lemon is still a lemon—even if, owing to some abnormality, it *never* turns yellow. A three-legged tiger is still a tiger. Gold in the gaseous state is still gold."[21] And so on. In short, the extension of a term is not fixed by a concept. For our purposes here, this means that any particular set of criteria for sex difference can be elastic—even to the point of instability, as the Olympic Committee shows—and subject to doubt without fatally undermining our basic sense that there is something called sex difference.[22] And yet this sense is based, not on some objective properties of human bodies, but on an agreement in judgments, that is, in our uses of terms. There is no appeal beyond what *we say.*

The skeptic's doubt is meant to press on, and make visible, the limits of justification for what we say. (Why is the new test any better than the old test? Aren't both just stabs in the dark?) But the skeptical impulse, in its classic form, never questions the ideal of absolute knowledge that governs the dogmatic assertions the skeptic would contest; rather, it dramatizes our disappointment with the impossibility or failure of such knowledge. Wittgenstein's approach to skepticism is to treat it not as a threat that must or can be definitively countered (as common sense philosophers like G. E. Moore would have it) but as a temptation that is irreducibly human. In some important sense the skeptic is right: absolute knowledge is impossible and our criteria inevitably disappoint. Skepticism is not merely the negative thesis that we can never know anything with absolute certainty, however, but the rather different though related idea, as Stanley Cavell clarifies, that our relation to others and to the world is one of knowing.[23] This epistemic characterization of human relations tempts us to read off the specific failure of our criteria in any given empirical instance a total failure of the basis of human community, our mutual attunement in language, an abyss of meaninglessness. This in turn incites the dogmatic temptation to ground meaning outside human practices, to make it into something that has truth conditions quite apart from what we say, to seek an objectively correct way of applying a rule.

Wittgenstein's own account of rule-following and language use, however, far from definitively countering these temptations, could be seen as amplifying the vertigo induced by the skeptical challenge to metaphysical realism. As Cavell vividly puts Wittgenstein's teaching,

> We learn and teach words in certain contexts, and then we are expected, and expect others, to be able to project them into further contexts. Nothing insures that this projection will take place (in particular, not the grasping of universals nor the grasping of books of rules), just as nothing insures that we will make, and understand, the same projections. That on the whole we do is a matter of our sharing routes of interest and feeling, modes of response, senses of humour and of significance and of fulfillment, of what is outrageous, of what is similar to what else, what a rebuke, what forgiveness, of when an utterance is an assertion, when an appeal, when an explanation—all the whirl of organism Wittgenstein calls "forms of life." Human speech and activity, sanity and community, rest upon nothing more, but nothing less, than this. It is a vision as simple as it is difficult, and as difficult as it is (and because it is) terrifying.[24]

The thought that there is no objectively correct way of applying a rule, that all we have is a mélange of subjective responses, seems to remove the ground from under our feet. How could we ever speak of shared language or of any standard of correctness in our rule-following practices whatsoever? Contingency would indeed appear to be what it has always been for the philosophers, the ultimate in meaninglessness.

The realist would halt this vertigo, contending that our understanding the meaning of, say, the rule "add two" commits us in advance to a determinate answer to any new calculation, functioning as a set of directions that instructs us how to add any new combination of numbers. Such an account might see rules as constituting "a series," writes Wittgenstein, figured as "rails invisibly laid to infinity. . . . And infinitely long rails correspond to the unlimited application of a rule" (*PI* §218). In the grip of the sense of vertigo described above, we are inclined to think that there must be something outside our own practices of rule-following that guarantees their success. As Wittgenstein puts it,

> "All the steps are really already taken" means: I no longer have any choice. The rule, once stamped with a particular meaning, traces the lines along which it is to be followed through the whole of space.—But if something of this sort were really the case, how would it help? (*PI* §219)

Wittgenstein questions the idea that something in our minds could in this way determine the correct application of the rule for all future contingencies and, in §201 of *Philosophical Investigations*, famously states the skeptical objection: "This was our paradox: no course of action could be determined by a rule, because every course of action can be made out to accord with the rule." According to Saul Kripke, Wittgenstein shows that we can refuse at once the idea that the world comprises independently existing truth conditions for our rule-following practices and the skeptical conclusion that there can be no shared meaning.[25] Although there is no objective fact that we all mean by, say, the rule "add two" that explains our agreement in particular cases, argues Kripke, what allows us to speak of shared meaning is "the brute fact that we generally agree" about those cases.[26] Wittgenstein shifts the question of meaning from the realist requirement that it meet objective truth conditions, so argues Kripke, to the antirealist requirement that it meet the justification conditions given by a particular community. I follow the rule correctly if I apply it in such a way that other users of the rule with similar training do not object to my application. It is community agreement about matters of fact that staves off the sense of vertigo described by Cavell.

At first glance, the appeal to such an agreement as a solution to the skeptical paradox of rule-following is appealing. Wittgenstein's account of rule-following is, after all, centrally concerned with showing it to be a set of social practices, not isolated acts carried out by solitary individuals speaking private languages: "A game, a language, a rule is an institution," he writes.[27] Agreement is necessary for there to be rules, but that agreement will depend on our specific practices, not on their conformity to the objective nature of concepts. "For if agreement about results or 'particular cases' were all that constrains meaning," observes Donald Barry, "then the contingency of meaning would appear to be too high to sustain any credible continuity in usage at all, and communication would collapse."[28] Barry sees this as reintroducing the problem of idealism, which Kripke thinks he has solved with the appeal to "the brute fact of agreement." It is agreement in form of life, not in matters of fact, that constitutes Wittgenstein's definitive response to this problem, in Barry's view.[29] But neither Kripke nor Barry asks why we think that we need some theory of agreement (albeit an antirealist one) at all. Isn't the attempt to specify justification conditions just an indication of our tendency to be captivated by, and then try to quell, the sense of vertigo described by Cavell?

Whereas Kripke assumes that we agree in matters of opinion or fact and so in form of life, Barry reads Wittgenstein as saying that we agree in form of life and so in matters of fact. Although it is important to consider the difference between these two notions of agreement—and why Wittgenstein suggests that there is one—we risk losing sight of the possibility that what Wittgenstein offers is less an alternative theory of justification to metaphysical realism than a dramatization of the vertigo we feel in the absence of such a theory and a court of appeal beyond what we say.[30] Relocating this court of appeal from (the realist notion of) independently existing truth conditions either to the (antirealist notion of the) brute fact of agreement in matters of opinion (as Kripke does) or to the more diffuse (antirealist) agreement in form of life (as Barry would) attributes to Wittgenstein a theory of meaning, whereas his whole point may well have been to question our desire for such a theory. Seen in this way, then, what Wittgenstein offers is not an alternative theory of meaning (for example, meaning as use) based on an antirealist conception of justification (for example, agreement in matters of opinion or in form of life), but heuristic devices intended to animate critical reflection on our own temptations, especially skepticism and dogmatism in all their varieties.

Wittgenstein's genuine insight, then, is not simply to shift the terms of justification from a realist criterion to an antirealist one, but to call into question the whole problematic of justification in which philosophical accounts of following a rule have been thought. What the dogmatist and the skeptic share is the idea that our practices must be so justified to be meaningful; they merely disagree about the possibility of such justification. In *Philosophical Investigations*, Wittgenstein states the problem of justification as follows:

"How am I able to obey a rule?"—if this is not a question about causes, then it is about the justification for my following the rule in the way I do.

If I have exhausted the justifications I have reached bedrock, and my

spade is turned. Then I am inclined to say: "This is simply what I do."
(*PI* §217)

For the skeptic, such an admission is tantamount to declaring the meaninglessness of rule-following practices: they really are just stabs in the
dark. For other critics of realism reluctant to draw the same skeptical conclusion, Wittgenstein's remarks refute not the possibility of meaning but
of justifying our practices in universal and rational terms. As Richard
Rorty reads it, the place where "my spade is turned" indicates the
absolute limit to attempts at justifying our practices to people who do not
already share them.[31] But does Wittgenstein in fact say what Rorty would
have him say?

Pointing to the place where justification runs dry, Wittgenstein takes
up the demand, issued by his imaginary interlocutor, that they be so justified. He presses us to ask, why do we think that our practices require justification on the order of a total theory of meaning? At issue is not whether
we can or cannot give reasons for our actions in the very specific contexts
in which the demand for such grounds may arise. To put the demand for
justification in terms of what we can or cannot do is already to misunderstand it. The real issue at stake here is why we think that we need a theory
of justification, not to declare in dogmatic fashion that our practices are at
bottom unjustified, which is what Rorty would have us do.

"Giving grounds . . . come[s] to an end sometime. But the end is not
an ungrounded presupposition [as the skeptic accuses]; it is an ungrounded way of acting" (*OC* §110).[32] If Wittgenstein reminds us here
that our reasons run out, it is not to declare the absolute limit of justification, as Rorty would have it, but to reveal the temptation to construe
our action in epistemic terms.[33] He allows us to see that we are making a
certain kind of demand that may lead us to misunderstand our own practice, including that of justification itself. Any practice of justification relies
on unexamined but not unreasonable assumptions, things we simply do
not doubt, need not doubt, and—in specific cases—could not doubt to act
rationally.

Keeping Wittgenstein in mind, we can now see that the Olympic
Committee's "justification" in 1992 for the new test (which was the old
test) amounts to saying "this is what we do." But that need not lead to
the drastic consequences the skeptic would have us draw (for example,
we can no longer speak of the existence of sex differences, for every
knowledge claim must be grounded, justified). Feminists could interrogate "what we do" by trying to expose, in Butler's words, "the foundational premise [of the criteria for sex difference] as a contingent and

contestable presumption."[34] But wouldn't that take for granted the idea that "what we do" must be so grounded and entangle us in the very epistemological problematic of justification Wittgenstein questions? And what if it turns out that this practice is not based on a foundation that can be so exposed?

Doing Gender, Following a Rule

Butler's critical project to unmask foundationalist premises in feminism is often received as an attempt to eradicate foundations or to advance antifoundationalism as a coherent epistemological and political position. "Both of those positions," she rightly observes, "belong together as different versions of foundationalism and the skeptical problematic it engenders."[35] Distancing herself (with Foucault and Derrida) from the epistemological tradition of Western philosophy, Butler's central concern is not with the problem of grounding knowledge claims but with relations of power and their naturalization in forms of identity. She criticizes the tradition for its failure to take into account "the rules and practices" that constitute the subject, constitute it in such a way that (gender) identity appears to be an original and abiding substance.[36] By contrast with this realist account, Butler writes, "genders can be neither true nor false, but are only produced as the truth effects of a discourse of primary and stable identity."[37] If the idea of gender as a property of a subject is not an empirical proposition (true or false) but an effect of a discourse of truth and power, then critique must proceed rather differently from the way it would according to the justification problematic described above. The point can't be to prove that gender is not justified in the sense of grounded, but to show how the illusion of a ground on which we decide the true and the false of gender itself is produced and with what consequences for feminist politics.[38]

How can it be, then, that Butler's *Gender Trouble* was taken by many feminists as a declaration about the "false" or "illusory" character of gender, as if the point of her text were to declare, in skeptical fashion, that feminists have no grounds for making political claims in the name of women since we cannot say with epistemic certainty that there *are* women? That Butler's work was accused of denying the existence of "real women"—much as the irate New York spectator held—reflects anxieties about the possibility of feminism in the face of the changing social, economic, and political realities of the late twentieth century, which deepened existing cleavages among women or created new ones. I have already suggested that these changes unsettled the rule-governed theorizing of second-wave feminism. Third-wave thinkers like Butler did not cause but diagnosed—in deeply critical and non-nostalgic terms—the loss of women as a coherent, foundational category of feminist praxis. What I now want to consider is the possibility that dogmatic feminist responses to *Gender Trouble*—albeit symptomatic of the mistaken understanding of the relationship between feminist theory and praxis discussed earlier— might indicate Butler's own paradoxical entanglement in the skeptical problematic she sets out to challenge.

Rejecting the ideal of total knowledge and the notion of subject-centered reason and signification that classical skepticism assumes, Butler's critical intervention consists in an effort to expose the constitutive effects of gender as a signifying practice and the logic of exclusion that it supports.[39] In a passage that puts into question the idea of an original and abiding gender identity, Butler situates critique in relation to the encounter with the extra-ordinary, the strange:

> The point here is not to seek recourse to the exceptions, the bizarre, in order merely to relativize the claims made in behalf of normal sexual life. As Freud suggests in *Three Essays on the Theory of Sexuality*, however, it is the exception, the strange, that gives us the clue to how the mundane and taken-for-granted world of sexual meanings is constituted. *Only from a self-consciously denaturalized position* can we see how the appearance of naturalness is itself constituted. The presuppositions that we make about sexed bodies, about them being one or the other, about the meanings that are said to inhere in them or to follow from being sexed in such a way *are suddenly and significantly upset* by those examples that fail to comply with the categories that naturalize and stabilize that field of bodies for us within the terms of cultural conventions. Hence, the strange, the incoherent, that which falls "outside," gives us a way of understanding the taken-for-granted world of sexual categorization as a constructed one, indeed, as one that might well be constructed differently.[40]

One could hardly overstate this turn toward the "strange," the extra-ordinary, in Butler's work and in the major texts of feminist theory of the 1990s. An attempt to unsettle normative conceptions of gender, perhaps to imagine other forms of life, feminist invocations of the strange such as Butler's are compelling. But is it possible that this turn to the strange ultimately re-entangles us in problematic assumptions about the nature of critical reflection discussed earlier? In the passage just cited, such reflection is understood as a "self-consciously denaturalized position." What would such a position actually look like?

If doubt presupposes certitude, as Wittgenstein argues, how could we possibly stand outside our form of life and judge it to be arbitrary (or, for that matter, nonarbitrary)? The point here is not to dispute the possibility of feminist critique, but to ask whether it should take the shape Butler seems to suggest. Although it may well be the case that, in certain circumstances, the strange *can* help us to see "the taken-for-granted world of sexual categorization" as—if not exactly "constructed"—mutable, it is also more often the case that the strange is simply accommodated as an anomaly to our everyday practices. If the strange is to transfigure the commonplace, we need an account that, without seeking a place outside the common (that is, the external standpoint), addresses the context in which such a transfiguration might occur. Surely it is not something in the strange as an *object* that enables this critical relation to the taken-for-granted, but rather its place in a network of relations with other objects that we engage as part of a practice, and this practice will involve following rules. Rather than assume that our two-sex system is "suddenly and significantly upset" whenever we are faced with the strange, then, we should ask: what are the conditions under which (1) something or someone appears strange to us, and (2) the strange occasions critical thought?

In *Gender Trouble*, drag serves as the paradigmatic instance of the "strange," which calls forth the act of interpretation that puts into question the naturalness of our two-sex system: "*In imitating gender, drag implicitly reveals the imitative structure of gender itself—as well as its contingency.*"[41] Drag not only reveals to the spectator the illusion of gender as an original and abiding identity, it also serves—crucially in fact— as the paradigm for understanding gender as a performance rather than an essence, a "*stylized repetition of acts.*"[42] In *Bodies That Matter*, Butler, responding to the charge of voluntarism, complicates this account of performativity by distinguishing between gender as "performative" ("the forcible citation of a norm") and drag as a "performance" ("the parodic citation of a norm").[43] What remains, however, is the idea that drag occasions an interpretive act that allows us to see what we normally take to be an object, with inherent and abiding properties, as a contingent and mutable practice. Gender is compulsory in a way that drag is not, but both are imitative performances without an original. Thus drag, as an artistic performance, is not the faithful reproduction of a content that inheres in the original object drag supposedly imitates, but the exposure of this very idea of content as illusory. Another way of putting this point is to say that, when we do gender, we follow a rule, but this rule-following remains invisible to us; when we see drag, we become aware of the rule we are following when we do gender, hence aware of the fact that gender is a performance, not a substance. Revealed thereby, says Butler, is "a radical contingency in the relation between sex and gender in the face of cultural configurations of causal unities that are regularly assumed to be natural and necessary."[44]

In a sense, then, drag occasions critical thought on Butler's account because it calls for an interpretation that exposes the rule-following practice that constitutes gender: "the various acts of gender create the idea of gender, and without those acts, there would be no gender at all."[45] And in some very important way, of course, this way of thinking about gender is right. Gender is a practice, just as Butler shows, and this practice is governed by rules. The question is, what does it mean to participate in such a practice, to follow a rule? And what would it mean to have these rules made visible in such a way that we could obtain a critical stance on gender as a rule-following practice? These questions must be answered before we can decide whether drag, as an instance of the strange, has the critical force Butler ascribes to it.

It is easy to see the convergence between Butler's performative account of gender and Wittgenstein's notion of following a rule. Both thinkers refute the realist notion that rules or norms have meaning apart from their application. For Butler like Wittgenstein, meaning must be understood as a social practice, not as something determined by individual choice. In *Bodies That Matter*, Butler (responding to the charge of voluntarism) takes up the challenge of how "to understand the constitutive and compelling status of gender norms without falling into the trap of cultural determinism."[46] But why would the threat of determinism arise once we think about gender not as "an artifice to be taken on or taken off at will [as drag is] and, hence, not an effect of choice," as a certain reading of *Gender Trouble* might suggest, but rather as a reiterative and citational practice or, in Wittgenstein's terms, as following a rule?[47]

It is not immediately clear how we should understand the idea of the rule as something that is constitutive and compelling (for example, "femininity as the forcible citation of the norm") but not determining. Butler suggests wherein the difference might lie when she claims that rule-following may fail or in some way be incomplete. As she explains in relation to the construction of "sex,"

[C]onstruction is neither a single act nor a causal process initiated by a subject and culminating in a set of fixed effects. Construction not only takes place *in* time, but is itself a temporal process which operates through the reiteration of norms; sex is both produced and destabilized in the course of this reiteration. As a sedimented effect of a reiterative or ritual practice, sex acquires its naturalized effect, and, yet, it is also by virtue of this reiteration that gaps and fissures are opened up as the constitutive instabilities in such constructions, as that which escapes or exceeds the norm, as that which cannot be wholly defined or fixed by the repetitive labor of that norm. This instability is the *de*constituting possibility in the very process of repetition, the power that undoes the very effects by which "sex" is stabilized, the possibility to put the consolidation of norms of "sex" into a potentially productive crisis.[48]

The undeniable appeal of this notion of failure as an inherent possibility in any reiterative or citational practice is deeply linked to an account of norms or rules as things that, were we to apply them successfully, would have precisely the deterministic consequences described above. What saves us from these consequences is the possibility of failure that inheres in the very practice of rule-following itself: the fact, as Butler explains above and will repeat below, that every citation of a norm opens the possibility for that which "escapes or exceeds the norm."

Thinking about a norm (or a rule) and what it means to cite (or follow) it in this way presses Butler in the direction of positing what Derrida, in his response to John Austin's theory of the performative, calls "the essential possibility of cases interpreted as marginal, deviant, parasitical, etc."[49] Derrida's idea that the risk of failure is inherent to the speech act transforms Austin's notion of the possibility of accidents into a condition of language itself. Anomalies are not anomalous at all, but are the internal condition of all the so-called ideal cases involving no accidents. As Butler approvingly summarizes Derrida's account,

Derrida claims that the failure of the performative is the condition of its possibility, "the very law and force of its emergence." That performative utterances can go wrong, be misapplied or misinvoked, is essential to their "proper" functioning; such instances exemplify a more general citationality that can always go awry, and which is exploited by the "imposture" performed by the mimetic arts. Indeed, all performativity rests on the credible production of "authority" and is, thus, not only a repetition of its own prior instance and, hence, a loss of the originary instance, but its citationality assumes a mimesis without end. The imposture of the performative is thus central to its "legitimate" working; every credible production must be produced according to norms of legitimacy and, hence, fail to be identical with those norms and remain at a distance from the norm itself. The performance of legitimacy is the credible production of the legitimate, the one that apparently closes the gap which makes it possible.[50]

What can it mean to think about a norm (or rule) as something that exists apart from any citation of it? We could say that no such gap exists in the so-called ideal cases, that is, those in which performatives do not fail. But if failure is built into the practice of citation as the very condition of its possibility—and in such a way that we can no longer distinguish anomalies from ideal cases (as Austin did)—then it would appear as if the norm (or rule) is being construed here as something that can in fact exist apart from any citation of it. As Butler herself put it above, "every credible production must be produced according to norms of legitimacy and, hence, fail to be identical with those norms and remain at a distance from the norm itself." This is the same point she made earlier about the reiterative practice that constructs "sex." It seems as if, to put this in Wittgenstein's terms, the rule is somehow independent of its application. But then we are right back to the idea of rules and rule-following that was to be questioned in the first place.[51]

The idea of a rule as somehow determining is clearly at odds with Butler's attempt to think "performativity in relation to transformation."[52] Like Derrida, she wants to think at once the rule and the event, not the consolidation of the notion that certain meanings are guaranteed by the rule itself. The essential possibility of failure and the endlessly mimetic character of citationality are crucial for Butler because they reveal the "imposture" that belongs to the performative as the condition of its own "'legitimate' working" (hence the transformative potential of drag).[53] What is this imposture if not the collapse of the space of authenticity that allows us to see that what we take to be a case of plain meaning is really the hegemony of a particular interpretation? The norm is not a rule in the sense that the realist contends (that is, determining from above every instance of its application), then, but a sedimented interpretation or application that is hegemonic and that we tend to repeat without recognizing that it is we who interpret the rule in this way—but could interpret otherwise.[54] Thanks to "the essential possibility of deviant cases," any performative harbors other possible interpretations; it can "break with its prior contexts," break, that is, "with any and all prior usage."[55] Endorsing Derrida's concern to release the performative from the social convention in which Austin would contain it, Butler writes, "Such breaks with prior context or, indeed, with ordinary usage, are crucial to the political operation of the performative. Language takes on a non-ordinary meaning in order precisely to contest what has become sedimented in and as the ordinary."[56]

In some sense, this account of the performative is consistent with what Cavell described as the ability to project a word. Such projection, we recall, had no objective guarantee of success based on prior usage or social convention either. But that lack of guarantee was not construed by Cavell as an essential possibility of deviancy intrinsic to the functioning of language itself. If intrinsic to anything, the failure of meaning was seen as a possibility given in the simple fact that signs only have meaning in contexts, and contexts change. Nothing can guarantee that a sign that had meaning in one context will have any, let alone the same, meaning in another. That, however, is less a statement about what is *nonordinary* in our lives with language than what is deeply *ordinary*. As we saw with Hilary Putnam's argument about natural kinds, abnormal cases are always possible, but they do not indicate an essential possibility of the failure of meaning as the very condition of meaning. Following Wittgenstein, we do not need to posit failure as an internal condition of language to stave off meaning determinism because the successful application of concepts does not carry with it the threat of the closure of meaning that Butler, following Derrida, seems to assume. Language is not a cage from which only the essential possibility of failure in language can save us.

The temptation to think about social transformation as requiring a break with the ordinary, where the latter stands for prior usage or social convention, is linked to the tendency to imagine that the only alternative to a hegemonic application of a rule is to see it as something that is open to transformation insofar as it can be endlessly interpreted. Wittgenstein gives voice to this tendency when he writes,

> A rule stands there like a sign-post.—Does the sign-post leave no doubt open about the way I have to go? Does it shew which direction I am to take when I have passed it; whether along the road or footpath or crosscountry? But where is it said which way I am to follow it; whether in the direction of its finger or (e.g.) in the opposite one?—And if there were, not a single sign-post, but a chain of adjacent ones or of chalk marks on the ground—is there only *one* way of interpreting them?—So I can say, the sign-post does after all leave no room for doubt. Or rather: it sometimes leaves room for doubt and sometimes not. (*PI* §85)

It seems that our only choices are to affirm that every doubt must be eliminated or else all is in doubt: any interpretation of the rule will count as understanding it. To think about rules in this way is to say, either they compel in the sense of deciding in advance of the contingencies of any actual practice how we shall act, or they leave every course of action open.

Is interpretation the best way to think about rule-following? And is it the only way of imagining social transformation and critique, a nonhegemonic application of the rule? Let us approach these questions by considering the difference Wittgenstein draws between interpreting a sign and understanding it. Interpretation (*Deutung*) is "the substitution of one expression of the rule for another" (*PI* §201). The paradox of rule-following described above (in relation to Kripke) follows from a failure to make this distinction. If understanding a rule were the same as interpreting it, we would need yet another interpretation of the rule to understand the rule, and so on in an infinite regress.[57] This leads Wittgenstein to say that "there is a way of following a rule that is not an interpretation." This way is an immediate grasping or understanding, which shows in how we act. It is not that we never interpret a rule, but interpretation is called for only when our normal procedures break down, where there is a sense of doubt and we do not know our way about. When we apply interpretation to ordinary cases of rule-following (as Butler and Derrida do), we misunderstand what it means to follow a rule. To know how to do something (read a signpost, play chess, calculate, or sing a tune) involves an immediate understanding or grasping exhibited through action, not an interpretation.[58] Wouldn't the same point hold for "doing" or "performing" gender?

In part II of the *Investigations*, Wittgenstein clarifies these points in the context of a discussion of "two uses of the word 'see,'" which may give us a better sense of the problems with Butler's claims about the revelatory character of a drag performance. The notion of seeing he has in mind here is not confined to perception in the usual sense but applies as well to our ability to perceive meaning in language. Invoking the famous gestalt image of the duck-rabbit, which can be seen as either a rabbit's head or a duck's, Wittgenstein draws a distinction between what he calls "the 'continuous seeing' of an aspect and the 'dawning' of an aspect."[59] To continuously see an object under an aspect, which characterizes ordinary acts of perception, is to recognize it immediately as a certain kind of object, say, a picture-rabbit. To experience the dawning of an aspect, which certainly occurs but is not characteristic of ordinary acts of perception, is to see the same object, suddenly as it were, as a different kind of object, say, a picture-duck. The object has not changed, but our way of seeing it has. How is this possible?

Wittgenstein rejects arguments about the nature of perception that locate the origin or cause of a certain perception in the object itself. As he proceeds, it becomes clear that the criticism is directed at the empiricist understanding of ordinary acts of perception (which are expressed by statements such as "I see a picture-rabbit") as entailing interpretation (which is expressed by statements such as "I am seeing the picture-rabbit as a picture-rabbit"). Indeed, what appeared to be an inquiry into the strange experience of aspect-dawning turns out to be a critical investigation of ordinary seeing. Wittgenstein suggests that we directly perceive or have an unmediated grasp of objects; their status as a particular type of object is simply taken for granted in our actions and speech. We do not encounter things as material objects of the generic kind, things that are, initially, given to the senses and that, subsequently, must be interpreted or organized in accordance with our concepts. We do not encounter objects about which "we form hypotheses, which may prove false," as we do when we interpret.[60] Continuous aspect perception is a form of certainty. When I see a knife and a fork on the table, says Wittgenstein, it makes no sense to say, "Now I am seeing this as a knife and fork." Quite simply, "One doesn't 'take' what one recognizes as the cutlery at a meal *for* cutlery; any more than one ordinarily tries to move one's mouth as one eats, or aims at moving it."[61]

But isn't that precisely the problem?—a feminist like Butler might ask. Isn't it a problem that we do not take the woman we see *for* a woman, any more than we take the fork *for* a fork? Isn't the whole point of feminist critique to transfigure the commonplace by putting into question the very experience of ordinary seeing? But what would it mean to think about our potentially critical relation to particular signs as requiring a fundamentally interpretive relation to all signs? Whereas Butler seems to say that interpretation is the basis of our relation to signs—only some interpretations get "sedimented" and must be replaced by other nonordinary interpretations—Wittgenstein suggests that we normally understand without interpreting, and that is not a defect of some kind or failing on our part but the nonreflective basis of anything we might call critique. As Tully explains,

[I]t is important not to infer from this that there must be a stock of conventional uses that are permanently beyond interpretive dispute. First, the circumstances of any particular activity of interpreting a problematic sign involves the unmediated grasp of other signs, which, *eo ipso*, places them provisionally beyond interpretation. Second, it is always possible to "step back": to call into question the regular use of these other signs and take it up as an object of interpretation.[62]

In some sense, the experience of aspect-dawning (for example, seeing the duck now as a rabbit), though reasonably rare, is important in the way Tully suggests. Through the dawning of an aspect, we become aware that we are already seeing something as something, we are engaging in continuous aspect-seeing, or we have a way of seeing at all. Wittgenstein clarifies,

> Then it is like *this*: "I have always read the sign 'Σ' as a sigma; now someone tells me it could also be an M turned round, and now I see it like that too: *so* I have always *seen it as* a sigma before"? That would mean that I have not merely seen the figure Σ and read it like *this*, but I have also *seen* it as *this*![63]

The change of aspect shows you that you have previously seen the sign as a sigma, making you aware that you were seeing it *as* something at all. The important thing, however, is not to confuse this ability to see that one sees something as something with the experience of ordinary seeing, as if the interpretive moment of aspect-dawning (for example, my seeing a sigma as an M turned round) were characteristic of our ordinary life with signs (for example, is it a sigma or an M?) or corrosive of our sense of certainty when we use them (for example, it seems like a sigma, but it could be an M). The important thing is not to forget that any dawning of an aspect is always parasitic on ordinary ways of seeing rather than the overcoming of some sort of illusion (for example, seeing that the woman one sees is really performing what one thinks one sees).

The dawning of an aspect allows one to see that what one sees is not ascribable to anything in the object, but is rather based on the use of another concept. Writes Wittgenstein, "[W]hat I perceive in the dawning of an aspect is not a property of the object, but an internal relation between it and other objects."[64] When I see a sign under an aspect—be it continuous aspect-seeing or a dawning—I see it as internally related to other things. These relations are based on concepts. The seeing is immediate (grasped), not mediated (interpreted). The perspective of which I am unaware until something interrupts how I see is not itself an interpretation, nor, for that matter, is what I see now. Likewise, what I see under a change of aspect does not arise because I have placed what I saw before in doubt. If I see the sigma or the duck, I see the sigma or the duck. When I see the M or the rabbit, I see the M or the rabbit. These are not interpretations, not choices about how to see something (as if it were up for grabs), and not subject to doubt (as if I needed grounds for what I see). One might say, upon seeing the rabbit after one has been seeing the duck, "I am seeing this rabbit as a rabbit," or "Now that I see a rabbit I wonder if it was really a duck." But that has to do with the language game in which seeing something as something is in play, that is, with the context in which one sees the object, not something in the object itself.[65]

If seeing drag occasions critical thinking about gender, it is not because, being the "hyperbolic" instantiation of gender norms, to cite Butler, drag "brings into relief what is, after all, determined only in relation to the hyperbolic: the understated, taken-for-granted quality of heterosexual performativity."[66] For one thing, my ability to call into question any particular gender norm is parasitic on others that are provisionally beyond question. For another, there is nothing in a drag performance itself that guarantees I will see drag and gender as the same kind of object—see, that is, the drag performance as the display of what gender really is (that is, performative). It is just as likely that I will see drag when I see drag and see gender when I see gender—just as I might see the picture-rabbit, then the picture-duck, but never any necessary connection between those two objects. To see drag, after all, is to *know* that gender is being performed—otherwise, we would simply see gender. Even if one agreed that drag incites the act of interpretation (under what conditions?), which in turn gives rise (in whom?) to critical reflection about gender norms, it does not follow that gender is *like* drag or that the latter *exposes* the fact that "the gendered body . . . has no ontological status apart from the various acts which constitute its reality."[67]

The conditions of doubt cannot be formulated as a universalizable proposition.[68] It is possible, for example, to conceive a situation in which a drag performance raised existential questions about gender identity for one person, confirmed what a second already thought, and was consumed as a bawdy spectacle by a third. Whether we find ourselves raising doubts involves broad questions of context that the focus on a generic object (like drag or gender or woman) viewed by an individual subject tends to conceal. There will be contexts in which the word *woman*, for example, will not raise questions for me (for example, when I describe to my friend, a woman, the woman sitting next to me on the plane), and there will be contexts in which that same word will raise such questions (when I hear my male colleague describe the same woman).

Whether the doubts we do raise have any critical resonance beyond the merely subjective "it-seems-to-me," moreover, involves broad questions of publicity that the focus on a generic object (for example, drag as an artistic performance with inherent subversive effects) tends to occlude. As we will see in chapter 4, it is the spectators and their judgments that create the public realm in which (what Butler calls) performatives have critical political effects, or not. To see this, however, will require rethinking feminist critique outside the frame both of the subject question (in which the idea of the public hardly arises, save as the enforcer of a norm) and the skeptical problematic (in which the idea of critique is synonymous with the use of the understanding and the application of concepts in a pervasive practice of interpretation, "the essential possibility of deviant cases," and the ability to raise radical doubts).

Following Wittgenstein, it is not that we *cannot* doubt something, as if someone or something prevented us from doing so, but that under ordinary circumstances we do not doubt it. Certainty is a doing, not a knowing: "Why do I not satisfy myself that I have two feet when I want to get up from a chair? There is no why. I simply don't. This is how I act," writes Wittgenstein (OC §148). A day may come when I formulate my having two feet as an empirical proposition in need of verification, but within my present frame of reference I just get up and walk.[69] Wittgenstein does not rule out the possibility of doubting something like the existence of one's feet or hands, but instead struggles with the question of what conditions would have to obtain for our most deeply held beliefs to be invalidated.[70] In the process, however, he radically questions our (skeptically inflected) understanding of what a doubt is and under what conditions it can be raised (for example, doubting the existence of the external world or, for that matter, women while sitting alone in your study writing feminist theory). What has been at issue all along, after all, is not whether gender conventions are certain in the sense of being permanently beyond all dispute, but what disputing them would entail.

Wittgenstein's remarks about two-thirds of the way through *On Certainty* indicate the practice of doubting I have in mind. "After dismissing specific doubts as incoherent or unimaginable," as Jules Law observes, "he [Wittgenstein] almost inevitably turns around and asks if after all they are not imaginable in some bizarre way."[71] These doubts include everything from questioning whether he really lives in England to his name and his sex. They are raised not in the problematic form of critical reflection I have been discussing, but as imaginative exercises that involve trying to see from the perspective of another person: be it a king who believes he can make rain, a man who thinks his front door opens onto an abyss, or someone who claims he has no body.[72] Something similar, I want to suggest, can be said about Butler's critical account of drag. We may well see the performative character of gender when we see drag, just as Butler holds. That, however, requires not—not in the first place—the critical use of the faculty of concepts that allows us to doubt the existence of gender as "real," but something else: the productive faculty of figuration or presentation, namely, imagination.

Radical Imagination and Figures of the Newly Thinkable

I will discuss the importance of the faculty of imagination and the ability to see from other perspectives for a freedom-centered feminism in later chapters. For now, however, I want to introduce the idea of imagination as the faculty that enables a feminist critical practice that does not seek to occupy the external standpoint or entangle us in forms of reflection for which the strange is inevitably the exception that puts the rule into radical doubt. If it is the case, as Wittgenstein argues, that what stands fast for us does so not because it is convincing but because it is held fast by what lies around it; if certainty is not a matter of what is grounded but consists in an ungrounded way of acting, then whatever critical purchase we attain on our present social arrangements would have to involve something other than a theoretical judgment about (the "is" or "is not" of) an object made from a "self-consciously denaturalized position" (Butler). Whatever we can say about the true and the false, as Wittgenstein teaches, always takes for granted the ungrounded ground of our practices that "is not *true*, nor yet false."[73] Imagination allows us to think the possibility of something beyond the epistemic demand of deciding the true and the false, which I took to be Butler's critical feminist project in the first place.

The possibility of interrupting and altering the system of representation in which we decide the question of true or false involves the faculty of presentation or figuration, that is, the capacity to create forms or figures that are not already given in sensible experience or the order of concepts. Distinguishing between "the second [or reproductive] imagination," which has occupied the attention of most philosophers, and the "first [or radical] imagination," which was discovered (only to be covered over) by Aristotle, Kant, and Freud, Cornelius Castoriadis clarifies the difference between a recombinative activity and an original, creative "faculty of positing an object, of presenting it for the subject, originarily, of making it be an object, starting from X, starting from a shock coming from X, or starting from nothing."[74] Radical imagination does not substitute one concept for another, argues Castoriadis. Rather, it is the much more fundamental, nonconceptual capacity to present and order (that is, provide an elementary logic for) our experience, the very basis for concept application in the first place.

The figure furnished by imagination, observes Castoriadis, "entirely escapes the determination of the true-or-false."[75] That is because "the 'true' is thought starting from and by means of the presentation of its contradictory: the indeterminate from the determinate, the discontinuous with the continuous, the outside-time with time. What sense would there be in saying that the temporal figure furnished by the imagination, upon whose basis the outside-time is thought, is 'false' (or, moreover, 'true'), when, without this figure, there would be no thought of the outside-time?"[76] Not subject to the determinations of the true-or-false, the first imagination has been covered over by Western philosophers and political theorists who, foregrounding the capacity to think logically, have viewed imagination as a potential threat to the kind of critical thought that relies on the ability to form concepts and subsume particulars under them.

The capacity to create figures that do not come under the sway of truth, Castoriadis observes, animates radical social and political movements. Like Butler, Castoriadis is deeply concerned with the problem of the taken-for-granted, or what he calls "the instituted society" or "the institution, . . . [understood as the] norms, values, language, tools, procedures and methods of dealing with things and doing things, and, of course, the individual itself both in general and in the particular type and form (and their differentiations: e.g., man/woman) given to it by the society considered."[77] He sees that individuals do not choose but "are bound to reproduce the institution."[78] The compelling character of social norms and rules can lead us to treat our social arrangements as necessary, while the hidden nature of that compulsion can lead us to treat them as voluntary. The task of radical movements is to transform the instituted society by putting instituted representations into question (that is, the very presuppositions or foundations of our thought). The reflection such a task involves proceeds not by way of radical doubt but radical imagination: "the creation of *figures* (or of *models*) of the thinkable."[79] Such questioning of established truths cannot take place all at once, observes Castoriadis in the spirit of Wittgenstein, nor can it "occur . . . within a void, but is always paired with the positing of new forms/figures of the thinkable, which are created by radical imagination." More precisely, as such positing is not simply the activity of a solitary subject but of subjects engaged in a collective practice, these forms/figures of the thinkable are created by "the [radical] *social imaginary*, or the *instituting society* (as opposed to the instituted society)."[80] *Whatever doubts we may raise about an "established truth" such as gender, in other words, always begin with a productive or creative moment of figuration, not (as skepticism would have it) by revealing the ungrounded nature of belief.* Although we may arrive at the insight that a particular belief is ungrounded, our capacity to doubt has this productive moment of figuration as its condition. If what stood fast for us becomes unsettled, then, it is because we have created a new way of seeing, a different way of judging and organizing our experience.

Wittgenstein himself did not really explain how such a change could occur, for his primary concern was to show that we always see an object as something (that is, there is an "as-structure" in all prepredicative see-ing).[81] In aspect-dawning, we see a different object because we have an-other concept (for example, the rabbit instead of the duck). While allowing for those cases in which a concept has not yet been fixed, Wittgenstein's remarks on "seeing as," then, were concerned with this fix-ing of concepts and how it is that, ultimately, "[a] *concept* forces itself on one."[82] Before drawing deterministic conclusions about such a statement, however, we do well to consider, in tandem with Castoriadis's account of radical imagination, the possibility that some cases might arise in which "what is at issue is the fixing of concepts" rather than the substitution of one existing concept for another.

I've suggested that it requires imagination to see drag as the hyperbolic instantiation of gender norms rather than as, say, a man dressed as a woman. If we overemphasize the object itself, we lose sight both of imag-ination as the faculty that allows us to bring particulars into an unex-pected and potentially critical relation with each other—critical because we are able to see something new, something not given in the object itself—and of the context in which we engage other points of view in forming a judgment. Potentially valuable about a drag performance is not that it provides us with an instance of the strange that has the form of an empirical proposition that gives the lie to an established truth like natu-ralized sex difference. Valuable, rather, is that such a performance might be invoked to dramatize a figure of the newly thinkable that allows us to envision bodies anew. This figure of the newly thinkable does not inhere in the object itself. Rather, the object—for example, a drag performance—can be used or worked on by the radical imagination, the power of pres-entation or organization, to figure thinking anew. To take a well-known example, Freud reworked the hysteric's performance of the symptom into a figure that enabled him to think hysteria radically anew. And doesn't Butler rework the drag performance of femininity in such a way that it allows her to think gender anew? This, it seems to me, is the really insight-ful but easily overlooked achievement of *Gender Trouble*. When read as generative of a figure of the newly thinkable that breaks with the whole problematic of the true and the false, the most maligned aspect of that early work (that is, the account of drag as subversive) may well turn out to be its most creative and radical. The following chapters will show us other examples of the newly thinkable and its place in a critical feminism.

If the creative imagination is not only beyond the true and the false but also no longer enslaved to functionality, as Castoriadis argues, new ways of seeing bodies emerge beyond the economy of use (for example, reproduction, both social and biological) that defines the naturalized cou-pling of male and female in what Butler calls "the heterosexual matrix."[83]

As we shall see in chapters 3 and 4, this ability to posit an object outside the use economy is crucial to a freedom-centered feminism and to any noninstrumentalist politics whatsoever. For it allows us to release our judgment of objects and events from the causal nexus in which their appearance is prefigured as a potentiality whose actuality is expressed in their being a means toward an end.

To see, say, drag as a figure of the newly thinkable not defined by its use is both like and unlike seeing it as an instance of the strange. Like the strange, drag as a figure of the newly thinkable can have a radically defamiliarizing effect on our practices. It can help us see those practices as contingent and mutable, subject to change. By contrast with the strange, however, such a figure does not begin with radical doubt but offers a new way of seeing that allows us to gain a different perspective on an empirical object that has not (necessarily) changed. When we see an intersexed body, for example, we are confronted with what Butler calls the strange, but our tendency, as Fausto-Sterling shows, is to fold that act of seeing into what we have seen all along: sexed bodies. Thus if the exception to the rule rarely disrupts our tendency to subsume all bodies under the rule of sex difference, that may be because what we lack is not an appropriately denaturalized position from which to doubt what we think we see but an alternative figure of the thinkable with which to organize anew the very experience of seeing, that is, of meaning. Figures of the newly thinkable are crucial for a form of feminist critique that resists the lure of epistemology and the twin temptations of dogmatism and skepticism. Such figures are integral to a mode of judgment that is reflective and creative.

Toward a Freedom-Centered Feminist Theory

I began this chapter with the claim that feminism has an ambivalent relationship to the idea of theory as a set of hypotheses or models that aim to capture the systematic regularities governing human practices and to predict their effects. Such an idea of theory is premised on the attempt to occupy the external (Archimedean) standpoint. We have seen that this ambivalence has not deterred many feminists from attempting to produce something on the order of a total theory of sex/gender relations or trying to get behind our practices in order to criticize them. Even thinkers like Butler, who refute the epistemological assumptions behind the idea of a total theory, are tempted, nonetheless, by the conception of critical reflection that such a theory harbors. If we reject this conception, does that mean we are left with a mode of feminist critique that amounts to little more than the practice of description I mentioned at the outset of this chapter?

What if we were to reconceptualize theory as the creation of new figures of the thinkable?[84] These figures, as Castoriadis showed us, would bring particulars into relation with each other but be different from the hypotheses or models of speculative theory, which seeks to form and produce knowledge of a complete object. If Castoriadis is right, such figures are at the very heart of reflection, which is "the effort to *break closure*," that is, the domain of the instituted society in which we exist as subjects constituted by rules, norms, and laws.[85] Over time, these figures of the newly thinkable, too, come to create the closure they once questioned, which is to say that they, too, will have to be questioned by yet other figures generated by radical imagination. The sex/gender distinction that animated second-wave feminist theory, for example, was once a figure of the newly thinkable, though it was (mistakenly, in my view) interpreted as an epistemological category for producing knowledge of what was in any case already given. As such a figure, the sex/gender distinction did much more than produce knowledge; it provided a form, generated by radical imagination, for giving new meaning to women's experience and opened a space for thinking about how that experience could be created otherwise. And, like other such figures of the second wave, the sex/gender distinction, too, eventually hardened into a speculative theory used to discern systematic regularities and objective laws, which third-wave feminists such as Butler rightly rejected.

Conceptualizing theory as the ongoing production of figures of the newly thinkable, feminists might recast the relationship between theory and praxis. Praxis, as Castoriadis writes, "can exist only if its object, by its very nature, surpasses all completion; praxis is a perpetually transformed relation to the object" (*IIS*, 89). Whereas speculative theory seeks to complete its object, he observes, "the very object of praxis is the new, and this cannot be reduced to the simply materialized tracing of a pre-established rational order," akin to those rules as rails of which Wittgenstein spoke (*IIS*, 77). Providing the rules that guide our actions and predict their outcomes, speculative theory would keep praxis like a completed object "lock[ed] up in the strongboxes of its 'demonstrations,'" remarks Castoriadis (*IIS*, 89). The theory appropriate to politics, by contrast, is itself a doing, not a knowing to guide doing from a place outside it. Such theory would turn on the ability to form critical judgments from within the ordinary, that is, on the reflective ability to relate particulars to each other in unexpected (not necessary or logical) ways by creating new forms for organizing our experience. Above all, such a theory could not be given in advance of experience, including of course our political praxis, for it emerges out of our activity itself.

If the critical doing or figuration of the newly thinkable that Castoriadis calls theory has political purchase for feminism, it cannot be as a guide or maxim; it cannot function as a set of rules that tell us what to do when we act in concert. Rooted more in the faculty of imagination than understanding, such theory aims neither to produce concepts under which to subsume universals nor to attain the external standpoint from which to question those concepts. Creating new figures for organizing experience, it aims rather to alter our sense of the real—not of what we know but what we will acknowledge, that is, count in some significant way. As Cavell following Wittgenstein observes, "Acknowledgment goes beyond knowledge. (Goes beyond not, so to speak, in the order of knowledge, but in its requirement that I *do* something or reveal something on the basis of that knowledge.)" For example, "from my knowing I am late, it does not follow that I acknowledge I'm late," he writes.[86] This difference between knowledge and acknowledgment is what the skeptic does not see, for he or she assumes that what matters for human relations is what we can claim to know with certainty. And isn't that what leads feminists to assume that social change hinges on the doubts we raise about what others claim to know? But from knowing that there are empirical exceptions to the two-sex system, it does not follow that we acknowledge that there might be alternatives to the two-sex system. This is not—or not simply—a personal failure on our part, but symptomatic of a more general tendency to construe our relation to the world and to others in terms of knowing, as if more knowledge, and more doubt, would produce the nonepistemic transformation of what we count as real, as ordinary, and as part of the common world.

Castoriadis's account of radical imagination and Wittgenstein's critique of rule-following are valuable resources for developing a freedom-centered feminism that would take leave of the false security of epistemology and venture out into the world of action, where we simply cannot know what we do, at least not in the ways required by a means-ends conception of politics. Such feminism would be based on the faculty of presentation (imagination) and the creation of figures of the newly thinkable rather than the faculty of concepts (understanding) and the ability to subsume particulars under rules. Most important, such feminism would emerge as a historically situated and collective exercise of freedom, an exercise through which we change the conditions under which things are given to us; alter, that is, the relationship of the necessary and the contingent. As we shall see in the next chapter, this alteration neither involves nor requires attaining an external standpoint from which everything might be seen as non-necessary, contingent. Rather, it rests on the factical character of human freedom, the capacity to wrest something new from an objective state of affairs without being compelled to do so by a norm or rule. Changes in the meaning of gender, in other words, emerge not through the skeptical insight that gender as such is contingent and can therefore be changed (for example, we have the theory, now we can act), but through the projection of a word like *women* into a new context, where it is taken up by others in ways we can neither predict nor control. It is this act, and not any intrinsic stability (realism) or instability (deconstruction) in language itself, which has the potential power to change every political, worldly constellation.

As important as it is to dismantle the political pretensions of epistemology that have a way of creeping back into our thinking even after the linguistic turn, then, a freedom-centered feminism needs more than that. It needs also to affirm the transformative character of human practice in the absence of any external guarantees. To yield the armor of epistemology to the uncertainties of action, Arendt might say, is to find oneself face to face with the abyss of freedom. There is no objectively correct way of acting politically—say, speaking in the name of women—anymore than there is of following a rule. There are no "rules laid out to infinity," no "line in space" and no theory that could trace it, which, if only we would follow them, lead from the oppression of the past to the liberation of the present and into the freedom of the future. Terms of political discourse like *women* are not fixed by something that transcends their use in actual contexts, as the gender realist would have it, but neither are they intrinsically uncertain by virtue of the ever-present possibility of failure that supposedly inheres in language as the very condition of language itself, as Butler suggests. Rather, they are created *as* meaningful—or not—in and through political action—that is, what *we hold, we say*. In the following chapters we will try to develop this insight, which suggests both a less speculative and skeptical approach to feminist politics and a rather different way of thinking about claims to women as an irreducible element in such a politics. A freedom-centered feminism, after all, is concerned not with knowing (that there are women) as such, but with doing—with transforming, world-building, beginning anew.

CHAPTER TWO

Feminists Are Beginners:
Monique Wittig's *Les guérillères*
and the "Problem of the New"

Elles disent qu'elles partent de zéro.
Elles disent que c'est un monde nouveau qui commence.

—MONIQUE WITTIG, *LES GUÉRILLÈRES*

HOW DOES ONE start from zero? How does a new world begin? These questions arise rereading Monique Wittig's 1969 text within the time-space of third-wave American feminism, a feminism which, notwithstanding its constitutive diversity, seems unable to conceive of radical novelty, spontaneous beginning. Beginning means not utopia—feminism is clearly characterized by a utopic dimension—but an event that would not be what Kant called "the continuation of a preceding series."[1] Indeed, the idea of something without precedent must seem either naive or foreign to feminists, for whom the question of agency and social change has entailed the "resignification" of gender norms rather than emergence of the new. Therein lies the outrageous wager of Wittig's revolutionary text, *Les guérillères*: to break the series, to create the unprecedented—a new grammar of difference.

Feminist receptions of *Les guérillères* in terms of pre-existing categories—"science fiction," "lesbian literature," or "committed literature"—are testimony to what I have described as the general ambivalence that feminism has toward the idea of spontaneous beginning.[2] But such ambivalence is hardly unique to feminism. As Hannah Arendt argues, the "problem of the new" haunts the entire spectrum of Western philosophy as well as political theory and praxis. At bottom, she claims, the new confronts us with the problem of freedom, with radical contingency—the "*abyss* of nothingness that opens up before any deed that cannot be accounted for by a reliable chain of cause and effect and is inexplicable in Aristotelian categories of potentiality and actuality" (*LMW*, 207). Although thinkers like Kant knew that "an act can only be called free if it is not affected or caused by anything preceding it," writes Arendt, they could not explain it within what they saw as the unbreakable sequence of the time continuum, within which every act appears as the continuation of a series (*LMW*, 210).[3] So unable have philosophers been "to conceive of radical novelty and unpredictability," says Arendt (citing Henri Bergson), that "even those very few who believed in the *liberum arbitrium* have reduced it to a simple 'choice' between two or several options, as though these options were 'possibilities' . . . and the Will was restricted to 'realizing' one of them. Hence they still admitted . . . that everything is given" (*LMW*, 32).[4]

According to Arendt, the problem of the new has confounded not only "professional thinkers" but "men of action, who ought to be committed to freedom because of the very nature of their activity, which consists in 'changing the world,' and not in interpreting or knowing it." They, too, have covered over "the abyss of pure spontaneity" with "the device, typical of the Occidental tradition . . . of understanding the *new* as an improved re-statement of the old" (*LMW*, 198, 216). This device is at work in the paradigmatic act of freedom: the founding of a new body politic. Thus it was that the Romans turned to Virgil to explain the founding of their republic as a revival of Troy. Thus it was that the American Founding Fathers turned to the Romans when they, too, faced "the abyss of freedom" (*LMW*, 207). Desperate to anchor their free act in tradition and thereby legitimate it, they tried to solve the "riddle of foundation—how to re-start time within an inexorable time continuum" (*LMW*, 214)—in effect by denying that the sequence of temporality had been broken at all.

In light of these remarks on the ambivalence that philosophers and political actors have had toward radical novelty, one might be tempted to make an exception of Wittig's account of the new and call it fantasy or just literature. Who would not grant fiction's right to creation, whose instrument is radical imagination? But that concession is a restriction that repeats the denial of the new and thus of freedom. Is not that why philosophers and "men of action," otherwise busy denying both, have been quite willing to recognize the creative imagination of the artistic genius?[5]

Indeed, "fiction's right to creation" appears suspect once we recognize that the restriction of the radical imagination to the domain of art is deeply connected to the trivial status accorded to the fictive in philosophy, political theory, and other social discourses. According to Ernesto Grassi, the fictive is at best associated with rhetorical figures (for example, the noble lie), which function as an aid to reason, human beings being what they are—namely passionate creatures in need of images. Cornelius Castoriadis concurs: "The fictive has no status in ontology or in the preontology implicit in one's native tongue; it is only an inconsistent, enfeebled variant of what is not," that is, the positive expression of what every rational person knows is unreal. "A full recognition of the radical imagination is possible only if it goes hand in hand with the discovery of the other dimension of the radical imaginary, the social-historical imaginary," he observes.[6] Until we recognize the capacity for radical imagination as a fundamental human one rooted not in the subject but in praxis, and which animates the social, historical, and political domains, creative imagination will remain an empty concept limited to the uniqueness of the individual genius and to (supposedly) politically irrelevant domains such as art.

Radical imagination creates "phenomena," as Wittig puts it, "which as yet have no name, either in science or philosophy."[7] This unmotivated positing of new forms is what Grassi, following the Italian humanist tradition, calls *ingenium* ("the viewing of unexpected relationships between sensory appearances"). Like Castoriadis, Grassi sees this ingenious activity not as the privilege of the artist but as an ordinary human practice that enables us to "surpass what lies before us in our sensory awareness."[8] In contrast with reproductive imagination, the act of surpassing what is given in sensibility does not represent that which is absent in intuition or recombine already existing elements. It "finds the distinction of like and unlike within and from itself." In other words, says Grassi, "Only through this comparison [that is, analogical, metaphorical activity] do sensory phenomena acquire their meaning."[9] *Ingenium* is not the "other" of reason, language, and cognition. Providing the minimal order or logic necessary for the concept, ingenious activity, as Grassi writes, "outlines the basis or framework of rational argument; it comes 'before' and provides that which deduction can never discover." Imagination is the condition for thought, knowledge, and judgment.[10]

When Wittig writes of the radical creation of phenomena that have no name in existing social discourses, then we should think of that process as one which, by transferring [*metapherein*] meanings to sensory appearances (that is, metaphorically), builds the minimal structure of a "world." If it is the case that rational language—and the activities we associate with it, judging, thinking, and knowing—are parasitic upon this archaic language, as both Grassi and Castoriadis argue, then the archaic language of images and metaphors generated by radical imagination is of crucial importance for understanding what does and can appear as part of our world. That this language is able only to manifest (show by leading before the eyes) and not demonstrate (show something upon the basis of reasons) in no way alters its importance for feminists like Wittig or anyone else concerned with generating frameworks in which it would be possible both to create phenomena that have no name in our current system of reference and to affirm freedom, contingency, or the new. If "fantasy is defined as the activity of letting appear [*phainesthai*]," specifically, letting something unreal (nonphenomenal) appear by way of discovering *similitudines* among unrelated things, as Grassi argues, then *Les guérillères* is indeed a work of fantasy. It "leads before the eyes [*phainesthai*]" that which is not cognizable (that is, does not show itself in the concept).[11]

That which does not show itself in the concept, that which Wittig's fantasy text lets appear, is a space and form of human political association that has no reality under "the category of sex" and no voice in the "social contract" based on heterosexuality, the "it-goes-without-saying." Discovering that she can no more define what "the social contract is" than she can say "what heterosexuality is," Wittig observes, "I confront [in both cases] a nonexistent object, a fetish, an ideological form which cannot be grasped in reality, except through its effects, whose existence lies in the mind of people, but in a way that affects their whole life, the way they act, the way they move, the way they think." Within the frame of this "heterosexual social contract," she writes, "[h]omosexuality appears like a ghost only dimly and sometimes not at all."[12] Rather than denounce the social contract as a fraud, Wittig's surprising answer to the unreality of nonheterosexual practices in the social contract is to call for its creation anew as a genuine practice of freedom and voluntary association. The amazing achievement of *Les guérillères* is not to demonstrate (with concepts or arguments) but to lead before the eyes (with images and metaphors) the radical reformulation of the heterosexual social contract.

What interests me about *Les guérillères* as a work of fantasy, then, is not the appearance of the new as a radical act of artistic genius but the textual elaboration of freedom (understood as the human power of beginning) and the new social contract.[13] The question of what Kant called "the faculty of beginning spontaneously a series in time" (*LMW*, 158) concerns not the imaginative power of the artist (Monique Wittig) to begin anew but the potential space of freedom that her texts at once inaugurate and celebrate: a space in which to "reformulate the social contract as a new one," as she puts it, a space in which what is presently a mere "ghost" can appear and become part of our sense of the real.[14]

Reading Wittig in terms of the question of political freedom, I want both to interrupt the tendency of second- and third-wave feminism to conceive freedom as a property of individual will, which entails the subject question, and to relocate freedom in the public space as a practice of human association.[15] For Wittig, freedom is a political phenomenon—a property of what Arendt called the "I-can," not the "I-will"—that is inconceivable outside the realm of action and speech. Wittig's political essays sometimes voice the wish to retreat to the stoic position of the solitary subject and its putative inner freedom—"If ultimately we are denied a new social order, which therefore can exist only in words, I will find it in myself."[16] That wish, however, is more the expression of frustration at the anticipated defeat of the struggle for a very different kind of freedom.[17]

The freedom that concerns Wittig has an abyssal structure. It is not given in advance in the form of potentiality, it is not made necessary by something in the relations of oppression, and it is not legitimated by anything outside itself. It is a beginning that is completely arbitrary, contingent, and thus, in Arendt's words, "could just as well have been left undone" (*LMW*, 207). To appreciate Wittig's dramatization of this abyss—that is, "contingency, the price gladly paid for freedom" (*LMW*, 133)—we need to loosen the hold of past receptions of her work, most of which fail to take seriously—or even to see—the question of political freedom in it. This failure is testimony, not only to the general ambivalence that feminism has toward freedom, but also to the way in which the subject question has come to define our approach to some of the most important texts of second- and third-wave feminism.

Judith Butler's well-known critique of Wittig as a humanist, for example, focused exclusively on the question of subjectivity and neglected the problem of freedom (or, at best, redefined it in terms of subjectivity) in Wittig's texts.[18] Butler's reading served for many American feminists as the definitive verdict on Wittig's work, which is stunningly absent from 1990s feminist debates.[19] This dismissal of Wittig is not reducible to Butler's critique, let alone caused by it, but symptomatic of the dominant problematic of feminism at the time, namely, the subject question. Not surprisingly, then, to the extent that Wittig's work was not dismissed, it was assimilated to the feminist practice of radical doubt, which characterized the dominant strand of the category of women debates. This assimilation distorts the real promise of Wittig's work, which is not to put sex into doubt but to dramatize the space and practice of freedom, the power of beginning, and new modes of human association.

The Limits of Doubt

Let us approach Wittig's texts afresh, then, as texts that concern political practices of freedom and human association, collective attempts to begin spontaneously a new series in time. The series that Wittig would break goes under the name *normative heterosexuality*. Breaking this series amounts to restarting time for Wittig because "[h]eterosexuality is always already there in all mental categories." It is always already there in our founding myths "as something that *has* not changed, *will* not change." It is there in our language: "*fathers, mothers, brothers, sisters*, etc., whose relations can be studied as though they had to go on as such forever." Both a system of reference "we cannot think outside of" and a political relationship that originally had nothing ontological about it, heterosexuality is a "social contract" to which no one formally consented but to which we say yes every time "we talk a common language, as we do now."[20]

We should not be deceived by Wittig's straightforward account of sex as a politically constructed category.[21] What she calls the "'already there' of the sexes" is an exceedingly complex problem, one inadequately addressed by the feminist commonplace "sex/gender is constructed."[22] Once a radical response to the idea of sex/gender as natural, this commonplace, over the course of time, has led to the mistaken view that sex/gender, being constructed, can be seen as just that and revealed as contingent, usually, as I argued in the previous chapter, through an incredible act of intellection and skeptical doubt. This act turns on the mistaken idea that we could obtain an external standpoint from which to see cultural artifacts and practices like sex and gender as wholly constructed. In addition to highly problematic assumptions about the practice of doubting (for example, that we could doubt all gender all at once), the basic fallacy of this approach is to confuse truth with meaning. For feminism, sexual difference concerns meaning, not merely truth or cognition. What is cognizable under rules in a (determinant) judgment is called "sex difference," and it is the proper (and, in principle, knowable) object of the social and biological sciences. The criteria that support judgments of binary sex difference are not grounded in putatively apodictic first principles but rooted in relatively stable modes of human praxis. They are what Wittgenstein calls a prior agreement in judgments in our form of life. These criteria are not beyond question and, in fact, have been questioned by feminists. What persists once binary sex difference as an object of knowledge is destabilized (for example, once we "know" that there are at least five sexes, not two, as Anne Fausto-Sterling reminds us) is sexual difference as a question of meaning.[23] It is a question we do not stop thinking about and a condition we do not eliminate once we know that binary sex difference is a contingent social and historical construct.[24]

To engage sexual difference as a question and condition of meaning, understanding, and action rather than truth or knowledge, then, is to engage not one's cognitive abilities but one's capacity for imagination. If Ernesto Grassi is correct to argue that an imaginative, archaic language

FEMINISTS ARE BEGINNERS | 73

of metaphors and images—what he calls rhetoric—is the basis of all rational speech, then the cognition that produces (and contests) knowledge of binary sex difference is itself rooted in the faculties of *phantasia* and *ingenium*.[25] This archaic language is the necessary condition for proof of sex differences, the question of a true or a false. What is more, it is a language that "entirely escapes the determination of the true-or-false." That is because, as Castoriadis reminds us,

> The "true" itself is thought starting from and by means of the presentation of its contradictory: the indeterminate from the determinate, the discontinuous with the continuous, the outside-time with time. What sense would there be in saying that the temporal figure furnished by the imagination, upon whose basis the outside-time is thought, is "false" (or, moreover, "true"), when, without this figure, there would be no thought of the outside-time?[26]

As Wittgenstein puts this same point, "If the true is what is grounded, then the ground is not *true*, nor yet false." Not subject to the determinations of the true-or-false, the system of reference formed by that figure/phantasm, within which our arguments about or proofs of binary sex difference have their life, is "the inherited background against which I distinguish between true and false."[27] Here we are dealing with questions of meaning, not with truth.

On the face of it, Wittig's political essays would seem to be at odds with this question of meaning, if not wholly defined by the practice of doubt. Her point appears to be that "the category of sex" is a social and political construct that poses as a universal, necessary truth, one she sets out to debunk through the assertion of countertruths (for example, "Sex is empirical, contingent"). Against this dominant reception of her work, I will show that Wittig's writing, both fiction and nonfiction, is a beautiful example of the tenacity of the category of sex and the limits of doubt. The category of sex, Wittig recognizes, poses questions of meaning which cannot be addressed through the cognitive practices of knowing and doubting. On the one hand, the problem with sex is precisely its status as truth, for "truth," as Arendt writes, "compels with the force of necessity" (*LMT*, 60). In Wittig's words: "[T]he category of sex is a totalitarian one. . . . It grips our minds in such a way that we cannot think outside of it. This is why we must destroy it and start thinking beyond it if we want to start thinking at all."[28] Thus sex as truth and necessity or destiny is at odds with freedom. On the other hand, to counter the totalitarian category of sex with a countertruth such as "There is no sex" does not touch the framework within which the truth of sex is rooted, the figure/ phantasm that gives every proof within that framework its life. This recognition of the limits of doubt shapes the parameters of Wittig's revolutionary poetics: the free act that eschews truth in search of meaning and a new grammar of difference.

Understanding the limits of doubt when it comes to the always-already-there of the sexes can be deepened if we return to Arendt's account of the flight from radical contingency. The tendency to account for the new in terms of the old, Arendt argues, is accompanied by various forms of necessity, fatalism, and determinism. Following Bergson, she observes,

> [Difficulty in acknowledging human freedom is related to the] equally valid experience of the mind and of common sense telling us that actually we live in a factual world of *necessity*. A thing may have happened quite at random, but, once it has come into existence and assumed reality, it loses its aspect of contingency and presents itself to us in the guise of necessity. And even if the event is of our own making, or at least we are one of its contributing causes—as in contracting marriage or committing a crime—the simple existential fact that it now is as it has become (for whatever reasons) is likely to withstand all reflections on its original randomness. Once the contingent has happened, we can no longer unravel the strands that entangled it until it became an *event*—as though it could still be or not be. (*LMW*, 138)[29]

The difficulty we experience reflecting on this original randomness does not amount to a failure on our part, which could be corrected by better knowledge of contingency. As Arendt explains, "The impact of reality is overwhelming to the point where we are unable to 'think it away'; the act appears to us now in the guise of necessity, a necessity that is by no means a mere delusion of consciousness or due only to our limited ability to imagine possible alternatives" (*LMW*, 30). This difficulty lies at the root of many of the paradoxes of freedom, in Arendt's view. On the one hand, to assume that "everything real must be preceded by a potentiality as one of its causes implicitly denies the future as an authentic tense" (*LMT*, 15), she writes. On the other hand, that assumption and denial seem to be part of the fabric of human reality itself.

The difficulty of recognizing the contingency of something that exists and that has "*become* the necessary condition for my own existence," says Arendt, points to the fatal flaw in the notion of causality. "In other words, the Aristotelian understanding of actuality as necessarily growing out of a preceding potentiality would be verifiable only if it were possible to revolve the process back from actuality into potentiality, at least mentally; but this cannot be done. All we can say about the actual is that it obviously was *not* impossible; we can never prove that it was necessary just because it now turns out to be impossible for us to imagine a state of affairs in which it had not happened" (*LMW*, 139). Even if we *know* that truth claims are out of place when it comes to causality—a point Arendt never tires of repeating—that does not mean we will stop making them or thinking of human affairs in terms of causality.

The tension between what we know and how we act, according to Arendt, reflects the deep tension between the faculties of willing and thinking. "This is what made John Stuart Mill say that 'our internal consciousness tells us that we have a power [i.e., freedom], which the whole outward experience of the human race tells us that we never use'; for what does this 'outward experience of the human race' consist of but the record of historians, whose backward-directed glance looks toward what *has been—factum est*—and has therefore already become necessary?" (*LMW*, 139) Every story—not just fiction, but every account of what is—eliminates as the condition of its telling the "accidental elements." It is not that no one storyteller could possibly enumerate all the elements that composed an event but that "[w]ithout an a priori assumption of some unilinear sequence of events having been caused necessarily and not contingently, no explanation of any coherence would be possible" (*LMW*, 140). The question would be, could one tell a story that recognizes contingency, which shows not just what has been—*factum est*—but that "it could have been otherwise"? If Arendt is right, we cannot eliminate causality from the telling of a story, but perhaps we can give an account of what has happened which, although touched, framed, and animated by causality, shows causality itself to be contingent.[30]

Sustaining the tension between causality and contingency, Arendt suggests that the problem for feminists like Wittig, who would contest something (sex) that has "the quality of already-there," the *factum est*, and affirm freedom, is far more complicated than recent feminist affirmations of the contingency of sex would make it seem. Like Wittgenstein, Arendt helps us understand why we are mistaken to think we could obtain an external standpoint from which sex would be seen as "socially constructed," as contingent.

If we frame the problem of the new in a way that accounts for the genuine difficulty we have acknowledging contingency, while holding out the possibility that we might affirm something like contingent causality, we can begin to see that we need an alternative to the idea that sex is available to radical skeptical doubt. As already there, as part of what is given, as past, sex has *become* the necessary condition for my own existence. To think of myself and my actions as outside sex is the equivalent of jumping over my own shadow.[31]

Language as a "War Machine"

What Wittig calls "the already-there of the sexes" is an (albeit irreverent) example of Arendt's account of how contingency is transformed into necessity. Sex seems to exist as universal form in nature, "a priori, before all society."[32] "There remains within . . . culture a core of nature which resists examination." This core, which presents itself in, among other things, the "primitive concepts" and universalist pretensions of anthropology, sociology, and linguistics, says Wittig, "I will call the straight mind."[33] Organized around the ancient conception of form as the ultimate root or cause of the being of entities, the straight mind, as Wittig elaborates it, sets out sex as the necessary predetermination or boundary of the form of a possible cognition: "you-will-be-straight-or-you-will-not-be."[34] In phenomenal terms this means that what can appear is what is sexed, and that what is sexed is what is.

Wittig recognizes, more explicitly than Arendt did, that what is, and has therefore become, the necessary condition of my existence is less a phenomenal than a political fact that arises, to borrow Miguel Vatter's description of necessity, "from a certain employment of symbolic and political violence on the part of orders that in this way prevent the contingent and revocable character of their origins to appear in the light of day."[35] Political and social orders, in Wittig's view, conceal, in the necessity of nature, the contingency of the category of sex and with it their own origins, thereby denying both freedom and historicity. On the one hand, what occludes this question of origins, argues Wittig, are the cultural narratives created, in part, by linguists, historians, psychoanalysts, anthropologists, and the like, who "assume a quality of already-there, due to something exterior to a social order, of two groups: men and women. . . . This view has for them the advantage in terms of the social contract of doing away with the problem of origins. They believe they are dealing with a diachrony instead of a synchrony."[36] On the other hand, these accounts would have no credibility if they did not seem to describe the structure and practice of daily life, the lived reality of the heterosexual social contract, whose rules, conventions, and synchronic character are affirmed every time we move, act, or speak.

The origin of society and the nature of our "consent," in Wittig's telling, is not like the pact or agreement that Hobbes and Locke talked about. It is more like the social contract as it was elaborated by Rousseau, according to whom, she writes, "the social contract is the sum of fundamental conventions which 'even though they might never have been formally enunciated are nevertheless implied by living in society.'"[37] For Wittig, the objection of someone like Hume to the idea of the social contract as a historical document or pact is beside the point. The issue is not that we search in vain for this document, let alone affirm our obligations to each other in its absence, as Hume would have us do.[38] Rather, as Rousseau teaches, "Each contractor has to reaffirm the contract in new terms for the contract to be in existence." But isn't that what we do when we move, act, or speak? The contract is nothing apart from these ordinary human relations. But the very idea of the social *contract* also allows one to ask, is this consent to my advantage? "Only then does it become an instrumental notion in the sense that the contractors are reminded by the term itself that they should reexamine its conditions. Society was not made once and for all. The social contract will yield to our action, to our words," says Wittig.[39]

Recognizing with Stanley Cavell (against Hume) that "[t]he effect of the teaching of the theory of the social contract is at once to show how deeply I am joined to society and also to put society at a distance from me, so that it appears as an artifact," we can begin to see why changing the social contract, as Wittig would have us do, will be situated in the ordinary.[40] Like Hume, who understood that skepticism leads human beings to despair, Wittig implicitly sees the limits of radical doubt. In contrast with Hume's return to common life as the antidote to the loneliness of speculative thought, Wittig finds no solace in the "it-goes-without-saying" practices of the everyday. This de facto social contract is everywhere and nowhere, for it defines our existence as speaking beings. "[T]he first, the permanent, and the final social contract is language," Wittig declares. Language is not something each of us agreed to but a prior agreement in judgments we were born into. One can try to speak outside our language games, but then one would have nothing to say that others could understand, and with which they could agree or not. "*Outlaw* and *mad* are the names for those who refuse to go by the rules and conventions, as well as for those who refuse to or cannot speak the common language."[41]

Accordingly, the mode of critique for Wittig cannot be to posit a homosexuality that would be radically outside heterosexuality, as some readers interpret her project, for she sees that there is no outside to language and the heterosexual social contract. But perhaps there is a way to inhabit and disrupt the inside (the ordinary) without succumbing to the illusion of getting outside (the external standpoint). This possibility is suggested in Wittig's image of radical writing as akin to a "war machine," a "Trojan Horse."

> At first it looks strange to the Trojans, the wooden horse, off color, outsized, barbaric. Like a mountain, it reaches up to the sky. Then, little by little, they discover the familiar forms which coincide with those of a horse. Already for them, the Trojans, there have been many forms, various ones, sometimes contradictory, that were put together and worked into creating a horse, for they have an old culture. The horse built by the Greeks is doubtless also one for the Trojans, while they still consider it with uneasiness. . . . But later on they become fond of the apparent simplicity, within which they see sophistication. . . . They want to make it theirs, to adopt it as a monument and shelter it within their walls, a gratuitous object whose only purpose is to be found in itself. But what if it were a war machine?[42]

"Any important literary work is like the Trojan Horse at the time it is produced. Any work with a new form operates as a war machine, because its design and its goal is to pulverize the old forms and formal conventions," writes Wittig. A literary war machine is not "committed literature,"[43] that is, literature "with a social theme . . . [which] attracts attention to a social problem" and becomes "a symbol, a manifesto."[44] Committed literature is doomed to reproduce the very reality it questions, she claims; it can never bring forth something new. That is because it operates at the level of conceptual meaning, rather than at the level of letter or form.[45] "What I am saying is that the shock of words in literature does not come out of the ideas they are supposed to promote," she explains. "And to come back to our horse, if one wants to build a perfect war machine, one must spare oneself the delusion that facts, actions, ideas can dictate directly to words their form. There is a detour, and the shock of words is produced by their association, their disposition, their arrangement, and also by each one of them as used separately."[46] If one avoids this detour, says Wittig, one will produce a work populated with recognizable figures such as "the homosexual," which is "only interesting to homosexuals," and which fails to transform the system of reference in which that very identity appears "as a ghost or not at all."[47]

The two insights that shape Wittig's approach to changing the heterosexual contract, then, are first, a radical work must remain recognizable in the ordinary language it would disrupt; and second, the work must do more than represent, with recognizable concepts, arguments, and the like, the minority point of view. If the Trojan Horse is not recognizable as a horse, it will not be taken into the city. If it is too recognizable—not too strange, that is—it will not function as a war machine. Without in any way denying the importance of the strange in the disruption of the ordinary, Wittig shows that the ordinary is what allows us to recognize the strange in a way that is potentially subversive of those aspects of the ordinary that belong to our heteronormative system of reference. "At first it looks strange to the Trojans, the wooden horse, off color, outsized, barbaric. . . . Then, little by little, they discover the familiar forms which coincide with those of a horse." Recognition of the ordinary (the familiar forms of the horse) is what allows the strange to do its subversive work. Otherwise it remains strange (an off color, outsized, barbaric mass of wood to which no one would lay claim), nothing more.

As for the second feature of Wittig's approach, because heterosexuality as a system of reference is beyond questions of the true-or-the-false, the subversive potential of committed literature, which makes arguments and claims, is limited. This does not mean that the social ideas of committed literature do not matter but rather that how they matter will depend on that system of reference, on whose basis we decide what is true, what false, and what counts as a good argument in the first place. "A text by a minority writer is effective," writes Wittig, "only if it succeeds in making the minority point of view universal," which is to say only if it alters our system of reference. If a writer does not alter our point of view, minority characters such as homosexuals will be absorbed as exceptions that prove the rule: "the that-goes-without-saying of the straight mind."[48]

Wittig's literary "war machine" is outside the scope of the skeptical problematic that characterizes an important strand of feminist theory. The point here is not simply to question appropriations of her work as an example of radical doubt but to reconsider what it means to say, as she does, that sex is a political category. Emphatically stressing the *political* character of the category of sex, Wittig would have us recall both that a social contract requires consent and that the heterosexual social contract is contingent. What makes sex political, however, is not the mere fact of its contingency. Everything empirical is contingent, but not everything empirical is political. Eschewing arguments put in the mouths of minority characters, the war machine of *Les guérillères* will shift our point of view with a shock of words, both recognizable and strange. It will show that the whole question of what is necessary and what is contingent cannot be decided outside the space of action itself. If the social contract will yield to our actions, to our words, as Wittig declares, it is because, in her account, action (words and deeds), not radical doubt, alters the configuration of the necessary and the contingent. There is no point at which we can say: everything is contingent, nothing is necessary; or conversely, everything is necessary, nothing is contingent. What Vatter writes of Machiavelli's political theory could be said of Wittig's work: "Everything that is 'necessary' is endowed with an event-like character: things become necessary in and through the encounter of practices and times, not outside of them, and therefore can cease to be necessary in time."[49] With this in mind, let us turn to Wittig's famous war machine, *Les guérillères*.

Renversement

"TOUT GESTE EST RENVERSEMENT" [Every gesture/act/deed is overthrow/reversal]. This phrase opens Wittig's *Les guérillères*. It is repeated in a slightly modified form at its end: SANS RELÂCHE/GESTE RENVERSEMENT [Without respite/action overthrow].

Critics have rightly emphasized the importance of this phrase as a statement of the revolutionary character of Wittig's poetics.[50] The amazing achievement of what Wittig calls *renversement*, however, is lost if one approaches the text, as some readers have, in terms of the description found on the back cover of the English edition cited in this chapter: "Depicting the overthrow of the old order by a tribe of warrior women, this epic celebration proclaims the destruction of patriarchal institutions and language and the birth of a new feminist order." This description implies that *renversement* is a stage in a linear movement from female slavery to freedom, which accords with the temporal categories—past, present, and future—of narrative form. It reduces *renversement* to the destruction of the old order and the founding of the new, thereby distorting the fundamental achievement of Wittig's text, which lies not in the substitution of one (feminist) order for another (patriarchal) one, but in the creation of what Laurence Porter calls the "open structure" of freedom.[51] What is radical in Wittig's text, in other words, is not the overthrow of patriarchy, as most commentators seem to assume, but the refusal to install another (albeit feminist) political form in its place: one that would "found" freedom. Identical with action, freedom is a practice; it cannot be founded in the sense of being guaranteed by a certain set of institutions.[52]

Porter has argued in a short but important essay that Wittig breaks with the closed structure of traditional utopian literature and its tendency to promote a new orthodoxy, a new set of fixed values. "In her [Wittig's] fictional world, the women's oral and literary traditions form no fixed canons. The women become aware of unending semiosis: no symbol is an absolute. . . . And they refuse to worship their origins. In short, the women [in Wittig's own words] 'cultivate disorder in every form.'"[53] There is no founder and no founding text. We have "feminaries," texts whose author(s) is unknown and whose status is uncertain—"[They] are either multiple copies of the same original or else there are several kinds." Once necessary to an earlier generation of *guérillères*, the feminaries are read aloud for sheer amusement by a later generation. Composed of playful retellings of the dominant myths of the heterosexual order from a minority point of view, feminaries remain caught in the system of reference they would contest: revaluing what has been devalued (the feminine), they fail to universalize the point of view. The rhapsodies on the female genitals, for example, provoke laughter among the new generation, for they represent an inverted and outdated symbolic practice. "All one can do to avoid being encumbered with useless knowledge is to heap them [the feminaries] up in the squares and set fire to them. That would be an excuse for celebrations."[54]

Although Wittig's tale "begins with a clear hypothesis: What if women governed themselves?," as Porter writes, it does not end with anything like a stable political form such as a government (of women or any other recognizable political subject).[55] That raises the question of whether *Les guérillères* can be considered a text about the *founding* of a new social contract or whether it is not more properly read as a poetic account of liberation from the old, heterosexual one. That all depends on how you define the practice and the object of founding. It is true that Wittig's *guérillères* do not found a new order in the form of a government with a constitution, laws, and political bodies. What they do found is a mode of interacting with others in a wide array of settings whose sole principle is freedom.[56] This freedom consists in the desire not to be dominated— "They shout that it would be just as well to perish as to live in servitude" (*G*, 92/132). But it is not reducible to negative freedom. It is the desire not only for an end to slavery but for a space in which one can move in word and deed among equals.

If freedom cannot be founded and is present only as action, the problem for Wittig's tale would be how to sustain action, how to stall the solidification of the political event (revolution) into the political form (rule of law/government). I've argued that the persistent and irreverent questioning of origins is one way in which Wittig's warriors remain poised to unsettle established truths or, better, to keep opinions from becoming truths in the first place. But the problem of the new, with which I began this chapter, runs deeper. How can Wittig forestall the conclusion that the event (revolution) is the mere effect of a preceding cause and thus the continuation of a preceding series? How can she sustain contingency and save freedom?

Consider in this context the narrative structure of Wittig's text. As I said earlier, the back cover of the English edition of *Les guérillères* leads readers to expect a story told in conformance with a rectilinear notion of time: past (there was oppression), present (there is the struggle for liberation), and future (liberation will yield a new feminist order). This leads to the sense that the end is already contained in the beginning—the actuality (reality) of the new is already present as a potentiality (possibility) in the state of female servitude—and that the sole purpose of political action is to produce something that could be foreseen or strategically planned in advance. In that case, to cite Bergson, "the possible would have been there from all time, a phantom awaiting its hour."[57] If Wittig's tale is one of spontaneous beginning, how can it be squared with the "unbreakable sequence of the time continuum," especially as it is mapped by classic narrative form? If it is true that without the assumption of necessity the story would lack all coherence, as Arendt argued, how could one tell stories of freedom?

We might approach these questions by observing first that Wittig's story of a new social contract is unlike traditional tales of that kind. In contrast with social contract theory's solitary subject, whose move into political society is characterized by varying degrees of necessity (fear of death, protection of property), *Les guérillères* opens with scenes of collective association. The first fragment reads, "When it rains, they [*elles*] stay in the summer-house" (G, 9/9). There is no pact to be signed, which would then authorize someone or some agency to act on its signers' (or their posterity's) behalf—only horizontally structured practices of social interaction.

That is why, as Erika Ostrovsky observes, "[t]he verbs in *Les guérillères* [with the exception of the last sequence] are all in the present, mostly transitive, and in the active voice."[58] That is also why Wittig's warriors, always out of doors, are continually telling stories, both monumental and everyday, of their journey to freedom: "In Hélène Fourcade's story, Trieu has deployed her troops at daybreak"; "They persuade Shu Ji to tell them the story of Nü Wa"; "One of the women relates the death of Adèle Donge and how the embalming of her body was carried out"; and "Sophie Ménade's tale has to do with an orchard planted with trees of every colour" (G, 92/130, 80/112, 69/98, 52/72). And so on. Indeed, *Les guérillères* is a motley collection of stories, told by a variety of speakers about the struggle for freedom and about every imaginable event or object. The storytelling is a form of excellence or virtuosity. It is also—crucially, in fact—the primary mode of interacting with others, which enables a relationship to the past that is not defined by necessity.

The sheer multiplicity of stories told puts into question the necessity that obtains in every single version of a story. The same goes for the story of stories, the collective tale of freedom, in which are recorded the deeds and words of those who fought.

> The great register is laid open on the table. Every now and again one of them [*l'une d'entre elles*] approaches and writes something therein. It is difficult to inspect it because it is rarely available. Even then it is useless to open it at the first page and search for any sequence. One may take it at random and find something one is interested in. This may be very little. Diverse as the writings are they have a common feature. Not a moment passes without one of them [*l'une d'elles*] approaching to write something therein. Or else a reading aloud of some passage takes place. It may also happen that the reading occurs without any audience, save for a fly that bothers the reader by settling on her temple. (G, 53–54/74–75)

The "common feature" of these "diverse" writings is freedom. Although accessible, this collective text is "rarely available." When it is read, there is no sequence to be discerned, and in any case any possible sequence is disrupted by the random insertions of readers. Accordingly, there is little chance that the great register will turn into the kind of founding text that constrains future action on the basis of what an earlier generation found worthy of remembrance in the past.

The nonsequential character of the great register raises the larger issue of narrative structure as it bears on the question of freedom. Insofar as classic narrative form is a great contributor to the illusion of necessity, it seems significant that, as Wittig explains, "the chronological beginning of the narrative—that is, total war—found itself in the third part of the book, and the textual beginning was in fact the end of the narrative. From there comes the circular form of the book, its *gesta*, which the geometrical form of a circle indicates as a modus operandi."[59] Indeed, the phrase *TOUT GESTE EST RENVERSEMENT*, which closes the first page of *Les guérillères*, is immediately followed by the symbol **O**. This symbol "recalls the zero or the circle, the vulval ring" (G, 14/16) and thus the continual return to beginnings that characterizes the strategy of *renversement*. It takes up an entire page and appears three times in the text. It can

likewise be read as creating "a tri-partite structure" and an effort to negotiate the difficulties associated with rectilinear time.[60] If we consider that
gesta is the Latin word for "deeds," we can better appreciate how the circular form of the narrative responds to the problems posed by the time
continuum (that is, every act is a mere continuation of a series; the real
follows the possible) and enables Wittig to foreground the novelty of
action and thus freedom.

Wittig's tale neither locates an originary freedom in the past (for example, an ancient matriarchy) nor invokes the idea of a historical process (for
example, victory for the *elles*) to give meaning to the particular event. The
tendency to justify the particular, the event, in terms of its place in an over-
all process is distinctly modern. "The process . . . alone makes meaningful whatever it happens to carry along," writes Arendt, "bestowing upon
mere time sequence an importance and dignity it never had."[61] For us
moderns, worthy of remembrance is that which the "objective" judgment
of history has revealed to us in accordance with the criteria of victory or
defeat. *Les guérillères* does not celebrate the deeds of the vanquished
(men), but it does disrupt the rectilinear concept of time, bestowing on
the particular event a value that it would not otherwise have.

> They say [*Elles disent*], how to decide that an event is worthy of remem-
> brance? Must Amaterasu herself advance on the forecourt of the tem-
> ple, her face shining, blinding the eyes of those who, prostrate, put their
> foreheads to the ground and dare not lift their heads? Must Amaterasu
> raising her circular mirror on high blaze forth with all her fires? Must
> the rays from her slanting mirror set fire to the ground beneath the feet
> of those who have come [*de celles qui sont venues*] to pay homage to
> the sun goddesses? Must her anger be exemplary? (*G*, 28/37)

What decides this question is not history but the claim to freedom itself.

The circular structure of the narrative, symbolized by the **O**, does not
lend itself to a notion of historical process. But can't it be read as a cycli-
cal (ancient) theory of history? Wouldn't this circular structure imply that
beginning is really a return to beginnings, repetition in the traditional
sense of repeating an original? Isn't this just another version of thinking
the new in terms of the old (founding Rome anew, not a new Rome)?

The circular movement of *Les guérillères* is not a return to the pure
origin or principle of beginning. The notion that later generations of warriors are bound in some way to preserve the origin of the new society
would be inconsistent with the Wittigian practice of *renversement*. "They
say [*Elles disent*] that references to [the goddesses] Amaterasu or

Cihuacoatl are no longer in order. They say [*Elles disent*] they have no need of myths and symbols. They say [*Elles disent*] that the time when they started from zero is in the process of being erased from their memories. They say [*Elles disent*] they can barely relate to it. When they repeat, This order must be destroyed, they say [*elles disent*] they do not know what order is meant" (*G*, 30/38).

What must be destroyed and what is worthy of remembrance is not the same for every generation of *guérillères*, just as what is necessary changes with time. As a principle of beginning, *renversement* is at odds with any symbolic order that supports the sanctity of origins just as it demands the continual return to origins. This return is critical, for the free act that founds the new order is always in danger of taking on the appearance of necessity. The task of *renversement* is to reduce every order to its beginning and thereby reanimate the contingency of its emergence, its original randomness.[62]

No-More and Not-Yet

The radical understanding of the return to beginnings just described is what prevents Wittig's warriors from founding the new on the model of the old in the form of a return to a golden age before patriarchy. "Elsa Brauer says something like, There was a time when you were not a slave, remember that. You walked alone, full of laughter, you bathed bare-bellied. You say you have lost all recollection of it, remember. . . . You say there are no words to describe this time, you say it does not exist. But remember. Make an effort to remember. Or, failing that, invent" (*G*, 89/126–27). The return to beginning, in other words, is itself an invention, a creation. There is, finally, no pure origin of primary female freedom to which one could return (in memory), not least because, retrospectively seen, a free act tends to take on the form of necessity. If one cannot remember a time when one was free, that is because, as Wittig claims, woman and man are political forms that tend to present themselves to us as necessity, and as the necessary condition of what can appear and what is. Thus freedom emerges not through the rememoration of the past but through invention: the act of beginning anew.

The idea of a golden age of female freedom to which one could return assumes further that *elles* (they) form a primal community of sorts, a "we" that is already given in time. The emergence and character of this "we" is a primary problem for feminist politics and for all human communities. As Arendt notes, "No matter how this 'we' is first experienced and articulated, it seems that it always needs a beginning, and nothing seems so shrouded in darkness and mystery as that 'In the beginning'" (*LMW*, 202). The question of the "we" is at bottom a question of meaning. It cannot be answered adequately with scientific (biological, archeological, and anthropological) evidence because the "we," writes Arendt, like "[a]ll that is real in the universe and in nature," was once "an 'infinite' improbability" (ibid.).

The difficulty of telling the story of the "we" in non-necessary terms is the subject of Arendt's account of the two foundation legends of the occidental tradition—the one Roman, the other Hebrew.[63] What is striking about these legends, writes Arendt, is that in both "the inspiring principle of action is love of freedom" (*LMW*, 203). Moreover, each story relates a gap, or "*hiatus*," between "the freedom that comes from being liberated and the freedom that arises out of the spontaneity of beginning something new" (*LMW*, 204, 203). This gap between "a no-more and a not-yet" opens an abyss between the possible and the real, "the abyss of freedom" (LMW, 204, 207). As Arendt explains, "liberation, though it may be freedom's *conditio sine qua non*, is never the *conditio per quam* that causes freedom" (*LMW*, 207–8). Accordingly, "the end of the old is not necessarily the beginning of the new . . . the notion of an all-powerful time continuum is an illusion" (*LMW*, 204).

For Wittig the problem Arendt raises is how to articulate the emergence of the "we" as something constituted by a free act, that is, without naturalizing or predetermining its appearance in the possible, in the past. The idea that the new is the reestablishment of the old, a golden age when one was not a slave, amounts to denial of this free act. Not only is the "we" (the *elles* of *Les guérillères*) not the reemergence of a collective subject once unmarked by oppression, but it is also not reducible to or merely continuous with the subject that achieves liberation from oppression, for this liberation is not ever achieved once and for all. That is why the principle of *renversement* opens and closes the text of *Les guérillères*. Expressing both freedom and liberation but reducible to neither, *renversement* is an active principle without end.

The very title of Wittig's work, *Les guérillères*, indicates that the passage from liberation to freedom is marked by an abyss—a free act that brings about a new world. As Ostrovsky observes,

[G]*uérillères* is a poetic word in that it does not designate any existing thing. . . . While it is possible to interpret *guérillères* superficially as a term that merely indicates or accentuates women's bellicose role—that is, as a cross between *guerrières* or female warriors and the feminine plural of *guerilla*—thus reducing the subject of the book to a war between the sexes, on other levels of interpretation this title has far more complex meanings. The word itself can be compared to a "war machine" that destroys an existing order or a traditional view.[64]

The word *guérillères*, then, is irreducible to given significations.

The revolutionary effect of this poetic word, however, does not take place upon a tabula rasa. Wittig's way of presenting the free act does not amount to the creation ex nihilo. A work of language that recognizes that the heterosexual social contract lies in the linguistic practices of speaking beings, *Les guérillères* cannot escape the reality that precedes it. The common language of this contract is the very condition of having something (revolutionary) to say. Wittig recognizes that, to speak with Castoriadis, "*the old enters the new with the signification given to it by the new and could not enter it otherwise.*"[65] All social change, including the "absolute beginning" claimed by revolutionary actors, always presupposes the reality that preceded it. But that reality (the old) itself is available to us only as it is articulated by the new. We can never unravel the process of change back from an actuality (the new) to a potentiality (the old); we have the old only as it is given to us by the new. It is not the old that determines the new, then, but the new that shapes whatever meaning the old can have for us. Accordingly, the poetic word *guérillères* is a radical imaginary signification created through that dynamic, non-causal relationship between the old and the new. It points not toward the creation of a new concept (for example, a hegemonic lesbian "subject," let alone the "tribe of warrior women" described on the back cover of the English translation), but to the capacity for generating a new space of appearance and point of view.

Elles—A Fantastic Universal

If Wittig's masterpiece yields "new figures of the thinkable" (Castoriadis), it is not limited to the figure of the *guérillères*. Indeed, it is not quite right to say, as Ostrovsky does, that this word or figure functions as a war machine. What "destroys an existing order or a traditional view" is not the poetic word *guérillères*—which, in fact, does not appear in Wittig's text save in the title itself—but the ordinary pronoun *elles*. Deeply mistranslated as "the women" in the English edition of *Les guérillères*, the pronoun *elles* lies at the heart of Wittig's radical project to transform the social contract. One can significantly misunderstand the nature of that project if one does not appreciate the depth of the mistranslation. To comprehend what is at stake, let us turn first to what Wittig says in "The Mark of Gender" about her use of *elles*.

> As for *Les Guérillères*, there is a personal pronoun used very little in French which does not exist in English—the collective plural *elles* (*they* in English)—while *ils* (*they*) often stands for the general: *they say*, meaning *people say*. This general *ils* does not include *elles*, no more, I suspect, than *they* includes any *she* in its assumption. . . . The rare times that it is [used], *elles* never stands for the general and is never the bearer of a universal point of view. An *elles* therefore that would be able to support a universal point of view would be a novelty in literature or elsewhere. In *Les Guérillères*, I try to universalize the point of view of *elles*. The goal of this approach is not to feminize the world but to make the categories of sex obsolete in language. I, therefore, set up *elles* in the text as the absolute subject of the world. To succeed textually, I needed to adopt some very draconian measures, such as to eliminate, at least in the first two parts, *he* [*il*], or *they-he* [*ils*]. I wanted to produce a shock for the reader entering a text in which *elles* by its unique presence constitutes an assault, yes, even for female readers. . . . Word by word, *elles* establishes itself as a sovereign subject.[66]

Considering that the use of the pronoun *elles*, as Wittig states, "dictated the form of the book," we can begin to appreciate what is lost in the English translation. The translator lacked the lexical equivalent for *elles*, but his choice of "the women"—rather than "they"—had dire consequences: "the process of universalization is destroyed. All of a sudden, *elles* stopped being *mankind*. When one says 'the women,' one connotes a number of individual women, thus transforming the point of view entirely, by particularizing what I intended as a universal." What we have is a word, *women*, which appears "obsessively throughout the text." In addition, where there are "women" there are "men," and with these two groups the category of sex, or "the it-goes-without-saying" of the heterosexual social contract that was to be put into question in the first place.[67]

Wittig proposes the pronoun *they* for a new translation of *elles*. "Only with the use of *they* will the text [*Les guérillères*] regain its strength and strangeness."[68] This strength and strangeness belongs to what I call her "Trojan Horse of universalism," whose primary vehicle in *Les guérillères* is the pronoun *elles*.[69] The pronoun indicates not a subject whose freedom and relation to society would assume the problems and aporias associated with that category, but a point of view from which it becomes possible to act and see something new. More an image than a concept, *elles* inhabits and haunts Wittig's text. Should we ask, who belongs to the *elles?*, the closest thing approaching an answer would be the randomly inserted pages on which there are lists of names such as

DIONÉ INÈS HÉSIONE ELIZA
VICTOIRE OTHYS DAMHURACI
ASHMOUNIGAL NEPHTYS CIRCÉ
DORA DENISE CAMILLE BELLA
CHRISTINA GERMANICA LAN-ZI
SIMONE HEGET ZONA DRAGA (G, 67/95)

Nina Auerbach complains of Wittig's lists of names: "Though these names take on their own incantatory life, the empty resonance of their sound is also the death of the real people we used to read novels to meet."[70] Commenting on this remark, Toril Moi correctly observes that it is by no means clear that "the names are spoken by anyone," and that Auerbach's reading expresses the wish to attribute a subject or "unitary human voice" to Wittig's polysemous text.[71]

The names, international in character, I suggest, must be read in relation to Wittig's strange use of the pronoun *elles*. On the one hand, if the names *were* subject-centered, the translation of *elles* as "the women" would indeed make sense. It might even make sense to describe *Les guérillères* as "a blue-print for women in the future."[72] On the other hand, if *elles* itself were a hegemonic, unitary subject, there would be no sense in continually disrupting the text with lists of names. Whereas "the women" connotes particulars with no claim to universality, a unitary "elles" would connote a universal with no relation to the particular. Clearly, both the first and the second alternative are at odds with the practice of freedom in *Les guérillères*, whose central principle is not a timeless universality of being but an active practice of becoming, *renversement*.

What makes *Les guérillères* a truly radical text is neither its daring account of the "destruction of patriarchal institutions and language" nor its coinage of the neologism *guérillères* but its strange use of an entirely ordinary pronoun, *elles*. That pronoun functions not at the level of reference and the concept but at that of an archaic language of metaphor, which brings things before our eyes, allowing us to see something not obvious or given as an object of cognition (which is what "the women" suggests, although it, too, is based in that archaic language). Based in the human faculty of *ingenium*, Grassi, following Aristotle, writes that metaphor "is characterized by a unique strangeness [*to xenikon*] because it reveals something unusual and unexpected."[73]

Whereas the already-there character of the category of sex provided the basis for (a false) commonality among women, the similarities among *elles* are not given in sensory appearances but involve the creative act of transferal (*metapherein*) and fantasy or letting appear (*phainesthai*). What Wittig shows by combining two existing concepts that are normally not related (for example, the feminine gender and the universal voice) is not a new subject, let alone a hegemonic one, but a new enunciative position, a place from which to speak and act in concert (for example, *elles disent, elles regardent*, and *elles portent*). Her text articulates a relation between things that—speaking both logically and historically—have none. It lets something currently unreal (free social and political relationships not defined by the category of sex) appear by way of *ingenium*, the discovery not of identity but similarities.

What *Les guérillères* achieves is an alteration in our sense of reality by means of the archaic language of images. Wittig's text disrupts the heterosexual social contract, whose synchronic or always-already-there picture of two groups, men and women, holds us captive, to paraphrase Wittgenstein. And she does so not with argument or skeptical doubt but with the strange use of an ordinary pronoun, *elles*. Inhabiting the enunciative position of the universal voice (*ils disent*), the pronoun not only exposes the exclusion of women but also makes visible the fact that every locution on the order of what "everyone says," what goes unquestioned and what goes without saying, is itself the product of people speaking, acting: *elles disent*. Without the melancholy or pathos of radical skeptical doubt, *elles* shifts our frame of reference in which certain doubts never arise.

The image *elles*, then, is a radical creation in the ordinary. It addresses itself—as an image—to the question of meaning, not rational truth. The point here, once again, is not to set up a false opposition between meaning and truth, rhetoric and reason, or to deny the existence of logic and concepts in rhetorical texts but to reconceptualize their relationship and their source. As Grassi writes, "A logic that holds 'conveying meanings' and metaphor as the origin and basis of the interpretation of sensory phenomena is, in contrast to rational logic, a logic of images and metaphors. It will claim to be a logic of invention and not deduction. . . . Such a logic is 'fantastic' insofar as it shows a new world, that of humanity, and makes it open to view through metaphor."[74] Like rational logic, this rhetorical logic of images and metaphors also creates a universal, only it will be a "fantastic universal," not a logically deduced—that is, rational—one.

Elles is a "fantastic universal" that must be discovered in the practice of daily life, not an abstract rational universal that can be deduced from putatively timeless and apodictic first premises. As Grassi explains, "fantastic universals" have their source not in logical deduction but in *ingenium*, "because concrete reality is revealed through them."[75] Accordingly, *elles* is nothing apart from the various modes of human praxis in which it is engaged (for example, *Elles pleurent, couchées ou assises à l'écart; Elles disent que la déesse Eristikos a une tête d'épingle et des yeux jaunes; Elles sont montées tout droit dans leurs chambres.* And so on). The central activity in the text is speaking—*elles disent* is the most common locution—for the new social contract or world Wittig builds through the innovative use of an ordinary pronoun is based on a rhetorical practice. I have suggested that this practice is not "literary" in the narrow sense traditionally given to that term and to rhetoric. It is social and political.

Wittig helps us think about feminism as a rhetorical rather than a skeptical practice, and that means rethinking the relationship of thought to action. Whereas a skeptical practice suggests that we first reveal that sex is contingent and then act to change it, a rhetorical practice suggests that it is not thought but action that recovers the contingency of sex (or for that matter the original randomness of any social and political order). It is through the ingenious practice of action that we alter—and become aware, really, of the possibility of altering—the relationship of the necessary and the contingent.

Wittig has shown us the abyss of freedom that appears whenever we start something new. But she tends to treat given human practices as irredeemable for feminism insofar as they are permeated by the category of sex. Such worry leads critics such as Rosi Braidotti to interpret her work as "a voluntaristic attempt to tear women away from the crucial paradox of our identity [that is, the need both to claim and deconstruct it]." Although Wittig recognizes that she can no more jump outside those practices than the skeptic can put all in doubt, her writings could nonetheless be seen as advocating the idea that "we could dispose of 'woman,' shedding her like an old skin, ascending onto a third [postgender] subject position."[76] Braidotti's critique of Wittig raises the question of whether freedom-centered feminists might make a political claim to sexual difference, that is, a claim that exceeds the frame of the subject question which governs third-wave feminist thought. In the next chapter we shall see that it is possible to make such a claim without reinscribing "the myth of woman" or relinquishing the radical demand for freedom.

CHAPTER THREE

Feminists Make Promises:
The Milan Collective's *Sexual Difference*
and the Project of World-Building

It is more important to have authoritative female
interlocutors than to have recognized rights. An
authoritative interlocutor is necessary if one wants to
articulate one's life according to the project of
freedom. . . . The politics of claiming one's rights,
no matter how just or deeply felt it is,
is a subordinate kind of politics.

—MILAN WOMEN'S BOOKSTORE COLLECTIVE,
SEXUAL DIFFERENCE

THIS REMARKABLE CLAIM appears in *Non credere di avere dei diritti:
La generazione della libertà femminile nell'idea e nelle vicende di un
gruppo di donne* (Don't Think You Have Any Rights: The Engendering
of Female Freedom in the Thought and Vicissitudes of a Women's Group),
a text collectively written in 1987 by the Libreria delle Donne di Milano
(Milan Women's Bookstore Collective) and published in English under
the title *Sexual Difference* in 1990. Now out of print, *Sexual Difference*
is a deeply challenging work which never found much of an audience
among American feminists—it is virtually missing in the so-called category of women debates of the 1990s.[1] This absence is significant. As the
text's cotranslator and editor, Teresa de Lauretis, succinctly puts it, "A
freedom that, paradoxically, demands no vindication of the rights of
woman, no equal rights under the law, but only a full, political and personal accountability to women, is as startlingly radical a notion as any
that has emerged in Western thought."[2]

What does it mean for freedom to consist not in claiming equal rights,
but in developing a political and personal accountability to women?
And, if such a practice is indeed as radical as anything we might find in
the history of Western thought, why was *Sexual Difference* more or less
ignored by American feminist theorists? Reflecting on these questions,
feminists might consider their own entanglement in the conception of
freedom, inherited from the Western tradition, as a phenomenon of the
will, a property of the subject, and a means to an end whose name is sovereignty. On this account, dominant in liberal democracies like our own,
freedom is defined in highly individualistic terms, housed in constitutionally guaranteed rights, and experienced as something that begins
where politics ends.[3] For the Milan Collective, however, freedom is

something quite different: it is a creative and collective practice of world-building, fundamentally inaugural in character, which establishes irreducibly contingent, politically significant relationships among women as sexed beings who otherwise have none apart from their place in the masculine economy of exchange.

Rejecting the frame in which freedom has been claimed by most first- and second-wave feminists, the Milanese refuse to justify women's demand for freedom in terms of their likeness to men (sameness) or their special contributions qua women (difference) to the general welfare of society. Indeed, the Milanese refuse not only the fantasy of sovereignty that characterizes inherited understandings of freedom but also the logic of utility or expediency that presses women's claim to freedom into the service of their social function. It is a logic that, in their view, has fatefully governed historical iterations of the woman question and arguments for women's rights: namely, what is a woman *for*? Casting aside the logic of the social question in feminism, the collective's "unusual way of doing politics" (*SD*, 51) recasts the whole project of Western feminism in terms of "the practice of [engendering] free relations among women" (*SD*, 79) or what the Milanese call "the politics of sexual difference" (*SD*, 145).[4]

I've suggested that the Milan Collective's text may have been dismissed by American feminists due to our entanglement in a problematic view of freedom as sovereignty. But that assumes too much. Notwithstanding its Italian subtitle (The Engendering of Female Freedom in the Thought and Vicissitudes of a Women's Group), *Sexual Difference* was never received by American feminists as a political manifesto on women's freedom. Rather, it was received (in the context of the category of women debates) as an argument about the irreducible difference between the sexes, a symbolic asymmetry between masculine and feminine that trumps relations of class, race, sexuality, and national belonging.[5] Notwithstanding dissenting voices, which warned against the hasty dismissal of (mostly European) feminist texts as "essentialist," American feminists have by and large thought that claims to sexual difference, when they do not "lead us back to the myth of woman," as Monique Wittig caustically comments, foreclose serious discussion of other categories of social difference, their political origins and effects.[6]

My purpose in this chapter is not to rehearse the now familiar arguments that can be brought either for or against feminist accounts of sexual difference.[7] If we (feminists) have reached a point of exhaustion in this debate—as we clearly have in the one about foundations—that is not least because we have genuine difficulty in thinking about sexual difference as anything other than a subject question. Within the frame of the subject question it is hard to see sexual difference as anything other than the impossible choice of masculine or feminine that defines the very condition of subject formation within the social matrix of compulsory heterosexuality. Accordingly, we have thought sexual difference as either constitutive *of* the social (that is, quasi-transcendental) or as constituted *by* the social (that is, historically contingent).[8] Taking up the project of feminism in a freedom-centered frame that is focused on the problem of worldbuilding, the Milan Collective invites us to think sexual difference as *political*: that is, as a *claim* to sexed being that has to be articulated, that is, brought into a *public* relation with other such claims in a *public* space.

So as not to miss (yet again) the challenge posed by the *practice* of freedom whose name is sexual difference, we must remain attuned to the task of world-building that is at the center of the Milan women's politics.[9] This task is a response to what the collective calls the debilitating state of (symbolic) indifferentiation in which women find themselves in masculinist cultures: all women are the same. This sameness is not limited to the image of Woman that was the focus of Simone de Beauvoir's powerful critique of sex/gender difference, but carries over into the feminist politics organized around the principle of sex/gender equality, which is associated with her legacy. Within feminism, says the collective, equality strengthens "the female demand for a commonality based on gender"—"do not forget that you are a woman like all the others"—but neglects each woman's "need for her own personal distinction" (*SD*, 137, 135), her desire to be considered as more than an equivalent member of a set, that is, to be considered in her particularity. "A neutral justice ordered women not to compare themselves to one another, promising to bring them to equality with men, with the result that female experience stayed imprisoned in itself, without social translation" (*SD*, 113). What was lacking was the means to recognize, value, and mediate different experiences. Without "a space-time in which to locate [herself]" (*SD*, 26), each woman is trapped in her own experience, which is a radically subjective one: "with whom, after all, can she exchange [signs]?" (*SD*, 26).

Tearing Up the Social Contract

Naming the absence of interlocutors and a symbolic structure of mediation (a worldly in-between) entails "getting to the gendered foundations of the social contract" and discovering first that "there is no social contract between men and women," and second, that "women were a herd on the symbolic level," but in "social life . . . they were mostly isolated from each other" (*SD*, 134, 129, 134). The other face of the masculinist social contract is not simply men's property in women, as Carole Pateman has persuasively argued and the Milan Collective would agree, but also the "savage state of female humanity" (*SD*, 137), in which women lack the skills and "rules of social exchange" (*SD*, 134).[10] Relations among women, with the exception of those that interfere with the regulation of men's relations, constitute what the collective calls the "blind spot in male political thought" (*SD*, 136). It is no use to search "among the age-old male pronouncements on the relation between individual and collectivity for an answer to the problem each woman encounters in reconciling her wish for personal distinction with her sisters' demand that she not leave the women's commonality" (*SD*, 136).

The masculine social contract cannot serve as a model for free relations among women, the Milan Collective holds, because its central principle of equality traps feminism in the losing logic that Luce Irigaray reveals with her simple question: "Equal to what?"[11] That a masculine measure is the barely hidden standard behind women's historical struggle for equal rights is well known.[12] That this standard forces on them an impossible choice, equal *or* different, is a problem that has haunted feminism from the start.[13] It is a problem that has divided feminism into opposing camps (equality feminists versus difference feminists) and that seems to be irresolvable.[14] And perhaps it is. Within the frame of a feminism organized around the apparently contradictory principles of equality and difference, our only options would appear to be either (1) to follow one of these camps and make the impossible choice or (2) to accept the impossible choice, in Joan Scott's words, as "the constitutive condition of feminism" itself.[15]

But perhaps there is another option: what if instead of thinking about and practicing feminism under the banner of equality or difference (or both), we thought about and practiced it under the banner of freedom?

Wagering that feminism will not in any way advance, but rather be crushed under the weight of the impossible choice, the Milan Collective foregrounds freedom over equality, even makes a feminist practice of disparity, thus putting itself at enormous risk and at odds with our common understanding of Western feminism. The collective comes to this conclusion only after a long and failed attempt to realize the historical aspirations of feminism for equality. To suppress the principle of equality in the name of freedom, as the collective outrageously suggests feminists do, means "tearing up the social contract" (*SD*, 143), refusing its political form. But why would feminists, assuming that they may have good reason to question the principle of equality, want to tear up a contract which, after all, has also been a call to freedom?

The Italians are not deaf to the rhetoric of freedom that has been central to the idea of a social contract, but it is not a model of freedom they think worth emulating. Apart from its historical formulation as the freedom of (some) men, it is a freedom construed as a fantasy of sovereignty. This fantasy, uncritically adopted by many first- and second-wave feminists, has kept feminism tethered to a certain form of the social contract (liberalism), which tends to reduce political freedom to negative liberty and the constitutionally guaranteed rights of the individual (*SD*, 136–37). In the absence of the practice and symbols of free horizontal social-symbolic relations among women, liberalism gives rise to the "terrible invitation" to pursue freedom and equality with men by repudiating one's sexed body and one's affiliations with women. This repudiation of sexed being, far from enabling female freedom, destroys it. "[T]he woman who wants to leave [the] commonality, and who does not know, does not want to acknowledge, that she needs her fellow women" (*SD*, 135), the collective claims, ends up like the mythical Proserpine, "imprisoned in the realm of the petrified symbols of male power, in need of other women but incapable of negotiating with them for what she wants" (*SD*, 137). Recognizing that freedom as sovereignty is empty, an "I-will" without an "I-can," the collective holds that if women wish to be free, to paraphrase Hannah Arendt, it is precisely sovereignty they must renounce.[16]

"Tearing up the social contract" means refusing not only freedom as sovereignty but also any attempt to justify women's freedom in terms of its contribution to the community or the higher good (that is, in terms of the social question). "A female politics has been grafted onto this mental attitude, a politics planning to change the social order by invoking the values embodied in female, rather than male, behavior such as doing volunteer work, taking care of the weak, shunning the use of violent means, etc." (*SD*, 125). Rejecting the idea that women's freedom should depend on "the contents of an ethical nature, or, for that matter, on any other content," the collective declares: "Our politics does not aim at bettering society, but at freeing women and their choices—that is, freeing them from the obligation of justifying their difference, with all the forms of social servitude that obligation entails" (*SD*, 126). Female freedom is radically ungrounded: neither foundational nor consequentialist, its only raison d'être is itself.

The bold account of female freedom advanced by the collective emerges in a series of vignettes that recount the development of voluntary associations, "between 1966 and 1986, mainly in Milan," in which something new appeared: a groundless practice of free relations among individuals who had little or no social intercourse with each other apart from their traditional function in the male economy of exchange.[17] These associations, so crucial to the history of Western feminism, are vital to the constitution of a realm and practice of public freedom for women not exhausted by the realm of rights. Telling the mixed story of these associations, their successes and failures, the collective shows it is possible to have formal equality and constitutionally guaranteed rights without the experience of substantive political freedom. Indeed, it is deeply problematic, for democracy and for feminism, to confuse the constitution and practice of political freedom with formal equality and the institutionalization of rights. *Practices* of political freedom are fundamentally inaugural in character; they create, through speech and action, a subjective in-between that discloses differences and sometimes exceeds the institutional space of equal rights. I hasten to add, however, that to say as much is not to say that the practice of claiming one's rights cannot be a practice of freedom. Rather than set up yet another false choice (like equal *or* different) between rights and freedom, we must ask, how are the creative and disruptive features of political freedom and the quotidian practice of world-building, the creation of a new social contract, related to the struggle for, or exercise of, equal rights? To this question and its unusual answer in the politics of sexual difference I now turn.

The Desire for Reparation

The Milan Women's Bookstore Collective does not restrict the question of freedom to liberation from oppression. Rather, it is centrally concerned with freedom understood as the capacity to found new forms of political association. From the perspective of the Italians, however, these forms cannot be thought apart from the difference of sex, for "to be born a woman is an accident that conditions all of life" (*SD*, 128). A contingent fact that has the force of necessity, the difference of sex is not to be destroyed or transcended, but rather resymbolized, transformed "from a social cause of unfreedom into the principle of our [women's] freedom" (*SD*, 122). This transformation is always "constrained, to some extent, by the human condition of the female sex" (*SD*, 119–20). A human condition that must be changed yet cannot be gotten around, willed out of existence, or violently destroyed, sexual difference, as the Milanese see it, presents the problem of the new, only this "new . . . cannot be forced into being."

Social revolutions destroy in order to force one to think the new. But destroying is of no use to the revolution of female thought because the new to be thought is a difference. . . . Subversion has to do with the way things are arranged, that is, their meaning. There are new arrangements which render a given reality meaningless, and thus change it by making it *deteriorate*. . . . Physical destruction would not be as effective because there are arrangements which, even if destroyed, retain their meaning, and one can be sure that they will turn up again. (*SD*, 120)

The idea that "those individuals who are today defined as women must eradicate their own definition. . ., in a sense, commit suicide," as Ti-Grace Atkinson once famously declared, is utterly foreign to the Italian women's project of freedom.[18] If what is past is the condition of what is and thus of one's own existence, the wish to destroy can lead to what Nietzsche diagnosed as the self-loathing and enervating features of the impossible wish to will backwards. According to Nietzsche, the "It was" is crushing—for the past does not budge. The will's relationship to what is past is "I will and cannot." Because it can be neither forgotten nor changed, the past must be redeemed. To redeem the past one must alter one's relationship to it: "To redeem what is past and transform every 'It was' into 'Thus I would have it!'—that's what I take to be redemption."[19]

Like Nietzsche, the Italians hold that to redeem the past is to give one-self value, to create new values. But what would redemption look like in the context of a feminist practice of freedom, a politics of sexual difference? How might feminists affirm sexual difference without reinstating what Monique Wittig calls the "category of sex"? Wouldn't the affirmation of sexual difference entrap us in "the familiar deadlock of 'woman is wonderful'" or harbor what Wendy Brown calls "wounded attachments," that is, "attachments to unfreedom," to the historical injuries that constituted feminine identity in the first place?[20]

When read through the frame of the subject question, *Sexual Difference* exemplifies what Brown calls the "paradoxical" entanglement of modern struggles for freedom, like feminism, in "the very structure of oppression that freedom emerges to oppose."[21] The paradox of freedom, as Brown defines it, mirrors critical accounts of the paradoxical character of subject formation, which hold that the subject is, if not compelled, deeply constrained to reiterate the very social norms that constitute it as subject/ed. Absent such reiteration, the subject would have no sense of its own realness, no social existence at all. Drawing on Nietzsche's account of the reactive and reflexive structure of identity, Brown writes,

In its emergence as a protest against marginalization or subordination, politicized identity thus becomes attached to its own exclusion both because it is premised on this exclusion for its very existence as identity and because the formation of identity at the site of exclusion, as exclusion, augments or "alters the direction of the suffering" entailed in subordination or marginalization by finding a site of blame for it. But in so doing it installs its pain over its unredeemed history in the very foundation of its political claim, in its demand for recognition as identity.[22]

Caught in a vicious circle, the subject's political demand for recognition and reparation repeats, in the form of a compulsion, the very experience of injury that subjugates (but also constitutes) that same subject.

The Milan feminists, too, see the dangers involved in the desire for reparation when they write, "as long as a woman asks for reparation, no matter what she may obtain, she will know no freedom" (*SD*, 128). Like Brown, the Milan Collective sees how claims for reparation leave the past unredeemed, entrapping women in an endless pursuit of social recognition of their pain, which, in turn, only further constitutes "women" as an injury identity. Writes the collective,

[S]ociety has no problem in admitting that women are victims of a wrong, although it then reserves the right to decide according to its own criteria how they will be compensated, so the game may go on forever. But we well know that the demand is so indeterminate, the feeling of damage so deep, that there can be no satisfaction unless this consists precisely in the right to recriminate forever. (*SD*, 128–29)

That is what made second-wave feminism a "politics of victimization," which "need[ed] housewives, women with abortion problems, raped women—not flesh and blood women, desiring and judging, but figures of the oppressed female sex and, as such, avatars of everything female" (*SD*, 103). Is that not precisely what a "wounded attachment" is all about?

Although the collective agrees that the demand for reparation reinstalls injury as identity, the Italians notice something curious about feminism's politics of victimization: the position of the victim seems impossible for any flesh-and-blood woman to occupy. Accordingly, the one who figures "the wretchedness of the female gender" is always the "other woman," including the woman who came before, not least of all one's own mother.[23] "Projected onto another woman, the figure that no woman could make her own" became the core symbol of second-wave feminism, which needed those iconic "housewives, women with abortion problems, raped women."

In the collective's account, then, the "wounded attachment" Brown speaks about looks rather like an injury identity inhabited by none *and* "a mass identification with the suffering of some" (*SD*, 102).

According to the Milanese, the tendency to deny and affirm freedom at once is a political problem of symbolic practice: "free relations among women had no symbolic figuration" (*SD*, 70). Accordingly, writes the collective, what "the women's movement lacked [was] a representation of free female thought as that which comes *before* consciousness [of women's subjection] and makes it possible. [Instead] [i]t was believed that freedom came *from* consciousness" (*SD*, 103; emphasis added). What allows a woman to become conscious of oppression, in other words, is not the bare fact or truth of oppression but a symbolic representation of female freedom.

But not all figures of freedom are equally enabling for feminism. Consider the idea, important in early second-wave feminism, of an ancient matriarchy as the lost object of women's freedom. Such an object incites the desire for freedom only to turn that desire against itself in the impossible wish to will backwards.[24] Nothing compares to the absolute freedom of the past, and nothing but a return to the past can regain that absolute freedom. The present must be either transcended or destroyed. This idea of an ancient past, comments the collective, led certain Italian feminists to "falsif[y] the accounts of even the most recent and best-known events, such as the determining role that some women had in the formation of groups or common projects. This role was passed over in silence. Otherwise, it was resented as an impediment to the full expansion of each woman's freedom" (*SD*, 104). In other words, the free actions of women were either denied, for they paled in comparison to the absolute freedom of ancient women, or they were seen in terms of sovereignty: the freedom of the one or the few against the many.

What was missing, then, was not the experience of freedom (that is, the practice of forming new political associations with others through action and speech) in Italian feminism, but its symbolic figuration. In the absence of such figuration the experience of freedom was always beyond reach and incapable of serving as a resource to future innovation. This symbolic figuration of female freedom is crucial: to cast "women" as an injury identity *tout court* is, in the Milan Collective's words, to "end up delineating the problems of one category of women, obviously the most disadvantaged, and present them as typical of the female condition in general. This levels the condition of women to their least common denominator, keeps people from perceiving women's different choices as well as the real opportunities they have to improve situations for themselves, and thus denies the existence of the female gender—only a 'female condition' exists, with which probably no one really identifies" (*SD*, 68). Worse yet, such a condition is an uninhabitable subject position whose symbolic figuration is hegemonic: missing is an alternative to the iconic image of woman as victim.

What traps feminism in the logic of reparation is not an injury identity shared by all its members, then, but the absence of the figure of female freedom. Consequently, woman as victim provides the only figure around which to mobilize politically. The same society that is quite willing to recognize women as the victims of a wrong, so the game can go on forever, is less willing to recognize them as bearers of a desire that seeks social inscription but no reparation. And feminism, which has put forward representations of women as victims of a wrong, keeps the game in play, insofar as it offers no alternative symbols of female desire. Missing, in other words, is not the nonrecriminative desire itself—although *some* women at any given point in time may not have it, not all women are *always* without it—but the "symbolic authorization" of a female desire that does not "signify itself only in this negative form."[25]

If the problem of an injury identity, far from definitive of the actual desire of a whole social group, is a problem of a one-dimensional political representation, then what it calls for is not work on the subject—or not just that—but what the Italians call "political work on the symbolic" (*SD*, 106).[26] Rather than call for a return to a moment in the development of subjectivity prior to injury, as Brown herself does, the Italians call for the creation of a new symbolic practice, a practice "which sees outlined in failing or lack, not the wrongs of others [which call for reparation] but the something more which a woman wants to be and can be" (*SD*, 101). This "something more" is no mere desire for equality with men and thus no desire to be compensated for a harm. The Italians' wager is that feminist politics can be forged under the figure of freedom rather than injury, the desire for "something more" rather than equality. A reactive protest to eliminate forms of discrimination (addressed to men) could be transformed into a proactive practice to create a new social contract (addressed to women). Let us now see what this "practice of free relations among women" is.[27]

The Problem with Equality

As the name of the collective suggests, the stories told in *Sexual Difference* unfold primarily in relation to the space of the Women's Bookstore, which opened in October 1975 in Milan. The bookstore is described as initiating "the practice of doing," which builds upon the "speech groups" that were formed in the early 1970s around the practice of *autocoscienza*. Akin to the consciousness-raising of early second-wave American feminism, "[t]he practice of *autocoscienza*," writes the collective, "presupposed and promoted a perfect reciprocal identification. I am you, you are me; the words that one of us uses are women's words, hers and mine" (*SD*, 42). *Autocoscienza* was without doubt empowering, but its power was also its limit: "it could not show differences between women because 'I am you and you are me'" (*SD*, 45). Although many of the women who began the practice had turned their back on the possibility of equality with men, in reaction to continuing and pervasive sex discrimination (*SD*, 40), *autocoscienza* sustained the logic of equality, albeit among women: "If differences arose, they were noted insofar as they were able to bring about reciprocal change, so that reciprocal identification could be again set up" (*SD*, 44).

The problem of indifferentiation—all women are alike—and its reproduction in early feminism is the departure point for the practice of doing, which elaborates the "material side of the life of speech" and counteracts the tendency to practice feminism as a sisterhood, a mode of kinship in which commonalities are given in advance of politics. "For it [the practice of doing] gathered together women who were not necessarily bound to one another by affection or familiarity, or rallied by succinct slogans, but who were unified instead by a common project, to which each of them was committed for her own reasons, her own desires and abilities, putting them to the test of collective implementation" (*SD*, 86). Although the Italians, from early on, put the idea of "doing" at the center of their politics, they did not reject the importance of the exchange of personal experiences, which characterized the first speech groups, or the initial political value of *autocoscienza*, that is, the affirmation of "women's common identity" (*SD*, 42). Nor did they reject the examination of fantasy or issues of psychic life, "the practice of the unconscious," which also formed a moment in their history.[28] What gradually emerged, however, was an awareness of the limits both of the politics of equality and of work on the subject. They saw that the problem of an injury identity demands a transformation of the worldly conditions that keep women unable to symbolize their differences. In the practice of doing, "a new theme is introduced: the theme of a female politics no longer centered on access to consciousness and speech [that is, language]. . . . The new terms are *create* and *transform*—create female social spaces in order to transform the given reality" (*SD*, 84). This creation and transformation begins with developing the political skills to deal with the differences among women, which have heretofore been rejected as a threat to a form of feminism organized around the principle of equality and women's common identity.

Although there is nothing novel in the claim that feminism's greatest problem is its "not wanting, not knowing how, to come to terms with the differences which divide women from one another" (*SD*, 86), unique to the Italians is their discovery that differences among women are meaningless unless there is some way to relate them to each other, to evaluate or judge them. Not *wanting* to acknowledge differences is, on their account, a problem of not *knowing how* to acknowledge them. Learning how will require developing the political ability to relate and judge differences among women, which, in turn, requires another political skill: the feminist symbolization of sexual difference. Like the Italians, American feminists have seen the symbolization of differences among women as the needed corrective to the politics of identity that was associated with consciousness-raising and early feminism. Whereas American feminists have tended, by and large, to associate the symbolization of sexual difference with the effacement of differences among women, the Milan Collective holds that such differences will be effaced in the absence of the political symbolization of sexual difference.

The Milan women develop a politics of sexual difference as a quotidian practice of doing in the space of the bookstore itself. A central project in the practice of doing, the bookstore is conceived as one of several "*luoghi delle femministe*": feminist spaces, at once "physical and symbolic," in which free relations among women can take shape (*SD*, 96, 93).[29] Describing a poster announcing its opening, the collective writes, "The Bookstore is a shop open to the street. . . . Anyone can enter. It was made for women by other women. The women who enter are not asked who they are or what they believe. Here they can establish relations with others, 'if they so wish.' The bookstore is a political space because in it, women meet publicly and freely. 'To be among women . . . is the starting point of our politics'" (*SD*, 92). It was there that "a new practice was . . . elaborated: it was called the practice of relationships among women" (*SD*, 50). This practice "was an unusual way of doing politics, which revealed to many women that the system of social relations could be changed—not in the abstract, as we have all learned is possible, but in the concrete, inventing new ways to spend our own energy" (*SD*, 51).

A space where women who share similar interests (for example, in texts, authors, genres, criticism, and so on) can get together, the bookstore functions initially as the minimal condition of politics. It is a shared worldly interest which, as Arendt puts it, "constitute[s] in the word's most literal significance something which *inter-est*, which lies between people and therefore can relate and bind them together."[30] On Arendt's action-centered account of politics, this in-between has the double function of binding men together *and* separating them at once. This "physical, worldly in-between along with its interests is overlaid and, as it were, overgrown with an altogether different in-between which consists of deeds and words and owes its origin exclusively to men's acting and speaking directly *to* one another. This second, subjective in-between is not tangible," writes Arendt, "[since] the process of acting and speaking can leave behind no such results and end products. But for all its intangibility, this in-between is no less real than the world of things we visibly have in common. We call this reality the 'web' of human relationships."[31] The Milanese call it the "practice of relationships among women."

The subjective in-between, political relations themselves, "owes its origin exclusively to men's acting and speaking *to* one another," observes Arendt.[32] This is a simple but important point, one of which we are forever in danger of losing sight. Speaking *to* another person requires, of course, the presence of other people—another simple point—which is to say, it requires interlocutors. But an interlocutor is someone who sees from a standpoint not my own. An interlocutor is only possible on the condition of human plurality. Within the context of American feminism, it is has been assumed that this plurality is "the differences among women." On this account of plurality, then, one would discover one's interlocutors by recognizing the social differences (for example, of class, race, sexuality, and so on) that appear like significant demographic facts prior to their political articulation.

The Italians, too, had thought that recognizing social differences was the answer to feminism's identity politics. That was the whole point behind "the practice of doing." But the practice of doing, learning how to deal with the differences among women, had failed. Why? Posing this question, the Milan Collective turns to another practice of doing, the Women's Library in Parma, and analyzes its founding document.

To explain their project more clearly, the founders of the Library chose to "transcribe every woman's opinion," to report, that is, some portions of a debate leading to the "document" which would present their venture. The reason given for this choice is the need to [in the Parma women's words] "compose a political document which may reflect all our points of view," for, as one woman said in the course of the debate, "the diversity of the women in the group and their nonhomogeneity is a political guarantee that no one will be erased and everyone will 'exist.'" (*SD*, 94)

But that egalitarian way of framing the project ran into problems: the guarantee failed. The Collective explains: "It is here that an intricate problem appears. The theory is that differences are necessary for the existence of the female sex, but making judgments is not allowed" (*SD*, 94).[33] The unspoken taboo on judgment allowed certain differences to be spoken, but left them meaningless. In fact, says the collective, the Parma document (and others of its kind) "reduc[es] to nothing the heap of speeches about the value of differences among women" (*SD*, 99). In the absence of judgment, a way to evaluate and articulate or relate those differences, the latter will not amount to anything. Duly noted, even celebrated, but not judged, differences are no more significant for feminism as a "practice of doing" than they were for the practice of *autocoscienza*, in which they were either ignored or denied.

Recognizing how the "differences among women" became, as in American feminism, an empty slogan that, albeit paradoxically, concealed "the really significant differences," so much so that they "became sources of guilt" (*SD*, 99), the Italians come face to face with the limits of the practice of doing: "without relation to the other than herself, female desire [is] without interlocutor" (*SD*, 99). It is not the social differences among women, which are there from the start, that constitute the plurality necessary for the existence of an interlocutor. Plurality is not a demographic or existential fact, but a political relation to social differences; it requires that I do something in relation to such differences, that I count them in some politically significant way. The presence of female interlocutors is irreducible to the indiscriminate recording of each and every woman's opinion. Such recording appears to take account of differences but actually holds them in a crushing equality. The idea that to "transcribe [and refuse to judge] every woman's opinion," far from providing "a political guarantee that no one will be erased and everyone will 'exist,'" as the Parma feminists assumed, destroys the space in which such existence could attain reality: the worldly in-between of feminist politics itself.

"A woman can and must judge other women. A woman can and must face the judgment of other women" (*SD*, 142), declares the collective. The suspension of judgment in early feminism (for example, *autocoscienza*, the practice of doing) was in no way liberating: on the contrary, if the need for approval prevails, if women dare not subject their desires to the judgment of other women, female desire will wane. Unable to judge the various opinions, the Parma feminists could not say why a women's library was a better project of doing than any other project. The Milan Collective comments, "What remains, as a foundation, is that we like doing this" (*SD*, 95). That the foundation is nothing but a desire (rather than, say, a well-grounded argument) is not the political problem, as far as the collective is concerned. "But a desire that is exhibited along with the fear of judging and being judged generates a feeling of superfluousness that damages the foundation [which is desire]." What remains is little more than a female desire which is hither and thither, "without ever attaching itself to anything" (ibid.). Unable to "force female desire out of its reticence and induce it to put itself at stake" (ibid.), let itself be judged, the politics of doing had created the spaces in which different desires could in principle be expressed, only to be leveled by the taboo on judgment. That failure would lead the Italians to put something at stake: they broke with the logic of equality and discovered the political value of disparity.

Discovering Disparity

Chapter 4 of *Sexual Difference* describes the turning point in the collective's history. It opens with a section titled "From women's literature, the first figures of freedom" and relates the "story of the Yellow Catalogue [*Catalogo giallo*]—because of the color of its cover, this was the name given to a pamphlet entitled *Le madri di tutti noi* [The Mothers of Us All] published in 1982 by the Milan Bookstore and the Parma Library." This pamphlet "is about disparity, about the simple fact that women are not equals even among themselves, and about the possible social interpretation of this fact by women themselves" (*SD*, 108). In terms of its project, "the Yellow Catalogue was unlike others of the kind because it privileged literary writing, especially novels, and because it took the reader's side" (*SD*, 109). It was focused, in other words, not on the artistic genius who produces the creative work, but on the readers who judge it.

Although it was expected that this engagement with women's literature would reveal a distinctive literary form, it turned out that what could have been seen as "an example of women's contribution to human culture" was of almost no interest. The search was for something that could not be defined, that had no name: "what human culture does not know about the difference in being a woman" (*SD*, 109). With "the need to find a meaning for the things that concerned us most directly" (*SD*, 110) and nothing but a vague sense "that women writers could help us in one way or another," writes the collective,

[we] began with our choice of women writers and novels to be read. We immediately decided to read our favorites. It was the only decision possible, since more objective criteria [that is, rules of aesthetic judgment] did not exist. But it was not the innocent decision it seemed to us at that moment. . . . The fact of one woman's preference for another woman outside a relationship of friendship or love was not something for which we were prepared. (*SD*, 109)

On the contrary, such preferences were virtually forbidden insofar as they revealed differences that were dangerous to the identity of the group. "The act of preferring, with its latent 'harmfulness,' was destined to unbalance that schema of female politics which kept every female desire in a tormenting equilibrium, as if crucified." Not all readers had the same preferences, some had no preferences, and some had strong preferences. "It was precisely this circumstance, which one would tend not to consider at all, that brought about the crisis" (*SD*, 110). The crisis broke out in the midst of a quarrel over the figure of Jane Austen.

This happened when the number one opponent of Austen, in the middle of a discussion where she was again in the minority . . . stopped arguing and said, as if she were making an observation: "The mothers [who prevent their daughter's freedom] are not the writers; they are really here among us, because we are not all equals here." When this simple truth was put into words that first time, the words had a horrible sound. . . . But their meaning was crystal-clear. No one doubted that they were true. . . . It did not take long to accept what for years we had never registered, though we had it in front of our eyes. We were not equal, we had never been equal, and we immediately discovered that we had no reason to think we were. The horror of the first moment changed into a general feeling of being a bit freer. (*SD*, 110–11)

Why would a sense of freedom result from the discovery of inequality among women? And, further, what if anything does this have to do with the practice of making aesthetic judgments?

The moment of being a bit freer is initially associated with liberation, the collective observes, from "an ideal of equality which neither grew out of our history nor corresponded to our interests" (*SD*, 111). This ideal crushed every nonrecriminative female desire (that is, not expressive of an injury identity) and articulation of difference in the name of a commonality based on membership in an oppressed group. Because of this neutral, genderless ideal, "[W]e had forced ourselves to imagine what did not exist and had forbidden ourselves to take advantage of what did. As if our problem had ever been that of finding a remedy for a possible rivalry between strong competing desires. Our problem was, on the contrary, the uncertainty and the reticence of our desires, which were recognizable underneath the so-called power conflicts between women as that which made them painful and endless" (SD, 111).

What did exist were differences of talents, abilities, and social position among women, which, if feminists had the political skills to deal with them, could enrich their practice even while also sometimes throwing it into crisis. What did exist were differences of taste, which were not reducible to social differences. All women are not alike, not only because they are members of different social groups that divide them from each other—which is how recent American feminism has typically understood the idea of differences—but also because they have different likes and dislikes, which, though related in some way, are not exhausted by their membership in any particular social group whatsoever.

The debate over Austen made visible a mode of difference that is irreducible to social differences (for example, gender, race, class, sexuality) and that was occluded in the practice of doing. The "practice of doing" had generated no alternative to the representation of universal female wretchedness; not because feminists were blind to these differences, but because they did not know how to deal with them, how to evaluate and judge them. Lacking this political skill, they tended to suppress differences and deep conflicts of opinion. Perhaps they never developed this skill, speculates the Milan Collective,

> because they thought that in order to signify the female difference, in order not to be assimilated by men, every woman had to be the same as every other—more exactly, as every other woman in the movement. In this way, diversity, quarrels, and different levels of consciousness could exist among women, but not contradictions, or radical objections like . . . "I don't care at all about the women who must deal with the problem of abortions." (SD, 69)

Without a space for strong conflicts or disagreements, there was no space for strong desires and no possibility of genuine politics. At that point in their history—each woman "without relation to the other than herself, female desire without interlocutor" (SD, 99)—the Milanese foreclosed the need for judgment with "a feminist point of view": an "ideology" or "a pre-constituted, ready-made discourse" which "no longer has ties with reality" (SD, 85). Ideology provided the rules for judgment. But following rules, exemplified in syllogistic reasoning, are of no use in aesthetic or political judgments, where we are faced with the particular qua particular. As Arendt puts it, "If you say, 'What a beautiful rose!' you do not arrive at this judgment by first saying, 'All roses are beautiful, this flower is a rose, hence this rose is beautiful.'"[34] Likewise, you do not move in the other direction, as it were, from the judgment "*This* rose is beautiful" to a general claim about other roses or all roses. The same goes for the political realm, argues Arendt, in which we are confronted with the singularity of objects and events.

It might be merely fortuitous that the discovery of disparity among women emerged only once the Milan Collective had turned to works of literature. Or it might be significant: in the expression of preferences and exchange of opinions about authors like Austen, one discovers the "it-pleases-or-displeases-me," which has no anchor in truth (or truth discourse: ideology) and cannot in this way compel agreement. Unlike ideological (syllogistic) reasoning (for example, all women authors are wonderful, this author is a woman, hence this woman author is wonderful), which secures the monologic of a "proper" feminist viewpoint and with it the unity of the group, judgments of taste reveal differences of opinion that cannot be subsumed under a rule. In the practice of (aesthetic or reflective) judgment, one becomes aware of the existence of *significant* differences among women. This awareness positions others to become genuine interlocutors: those women who have preferences like and unlike mine, who see from a standpoint not identical with my own, and whose opinions I am called upon to judge or by whom my own dearly held opinions will be judged and perhaps unsettled even to the point of crisis.

Discovering differences of opinion that cannot be adjudicated by a rule, the Milanese discovered disparity. They discovered that they were not equal among themselves. But to discover disparity is one thing, to practice it is another. There are, after all, numerous forms of social disparity, many of them unjust. "The practice of disparity is a necessary test," they declare. "It will make it possible to distinguish unjust forms of disparity from others which are in any case unavoidable" (*SD*, 132).[35] The practice of disparity is a necessary first step for "making the difference speak in free social forms" (ibid.). Although we do not yet know what this practice would look like, we might nonetheless wonder how it could be consistent with the democratic ideals of feminism.

Let us return to the problem of equality. The Milan feminists take up the deeply skeptical view of equality held by many third-wave Western feminists, including American feminists who have by and large accepted a rights-based legal strategy of social change. Apart from the obvious gap

that exists between the ideal of equality and the reality of pervasive discrimination, the principle of equality appears to establish sameness, in
relation both to men and to other women, as the condition for women's
political and social rights. But sameness is not what the political principle
of equality is supposed to achieve, for sameness, observes Arendt, is
"antipolitical." Arendt writes, "The equality attending the public realm is
necessarily an equality of unequals who stand in need of being 'equalized'
in certain respects and for specific purposes. As such, the equalizing factor
arises not from human 'nature' [nor from man's] but from outside."[36]

In historical practice, however, the political principle of equality has
tended to level all social and sexual differences and to force the assimilation of women to a masculine standard disguised as neutral and universal. But this way of thinking about equality, as Ute Gerhard reminds us,
is based on the Aristotelian principle of "treating likes alike." Like
Arendt, Gerhard inspires us to think about equality as a political principle that must *relate* different beings, not make them the same. Rather than
think about equality as sameness or identity ($a = a$), she argues, we can
think of it as a relational concept ($a = b$). Seen as relational rather than
fixed or static, equality is a political principle that, far from denying differences (only likes can be treated alike), takes them for granted as things
that must be brought into a certain kind of relation with each other
(unlikes must be treated alike) for specific purposes. The important question becomes, "who or what decides which characteristics or particulari-
ties suggest comparison or equal treatment?"[37] This is a political question,
argues Gerhard, the answer to which "cannot be determined at the level
of doctrinal formulas or 'argumentative logic'; it can only be determined
by taking into account the conditions under which the question of equality is posed."[38]

This simple but decisive move entails a change in perspective, for now
we are asked to focus not on the (social) objects being compared (for example, *a* and *b*; men and women), as if they alone determined the standard of
comparison in a logical operation, but on the subjects making the comparison, their capacity for reflection (that is, thinking the particular in the
absence of a universal) and the sociohistorical context of their judgments.
To emphasize the importance of standpoint and context to feminist
accounts of equality, in other words, is to consider the specific circumstances in which a claim is made as well as the social location both of those
who make it and those who decide what shall count as the standard of comparison. If that standard does not inhere in the object itself, then every claim
to equality calls for a political judgment, that is, a judgment that relates particulars (things which are unlike). A feminist practice of equality, then,

requires the introduction of a third term or party, a *tertium comparationis*, which, as Gerhard writes, "can never simply be 'man' or the status of men; it must be a standard that is fair to both genders."[39]

In the next two chapters we shall see what it means to think about equality as a problem of political judgment rather than, say, "argumentative logic." For now, however, we might consider how thinking about a practice of equality as requiring a third term allows us to make sense of what appears to be the profoundly anti-egalitarian practice of disparity. Although the Italians do not really see the possibility of refiguring equality such that it would not reduce to sameness, that is exactly what their practice of disparity achieves: it enables the development of the third term just mentioned.

In the Italians' account, the third term begins to emerge in relation to women authors, like Austen, "who . . . were named 'prototypes.'" The purpose of these prototypes was "to characterize the position of that which comes first and offers us the means by which to know and differentiate ourselves" (*SD*, 112). It would not be difficult to see the prototype as an iconic female figure whose stature no flesh-and-blood woman could begin to approach. Keenly aware of this problem, the Italians observe that the figure of the superior woman is the other face of the iconic figure of the victim, with which no flesh-and-blood woman could identify, and both are symptomatic of a missing "female social economy." Both of these ways of symbolizing (horizontal and vertical) relations among women indicate that they are no real relations at all, but only an unmediated link to what is the same (and wretched) or what is different (and superior). Neither of these iconographic positions (the victim or the superior woman) is inhabitable by flesh-and-blood women themselves.

The tendency to idealize, then, is one practice of disparity that is *not* enabling for feminism. The possibility of giving oneself value required a power, a "female plus" (*SD*, 127), that valorized *both* the female gender and the individual woman in her difference from other women. What the Italians were looking for, and found initially in prototypes, is better understood as an example with which to relate particulars, rather than a rule (or ideal type) with which to subsume them. Unlike the superior women that the politics of equality has also, however paradoxically, generated, prototypes authorize those women who authorize them: "Attributing authority and value to another woman with regard to the world was the means of giving authority and value to oneself. . . : 'In defending [Gertrude] Stein, I am defending myself'" (*SD*, 112). If what authorizes a feminist practice of freedom is nothing but women themselves, as the Milan Collective declares, then such a figure must remain part of the practice, that is, subject to judgment, argument, and debate. Otherwise, it threatens to become a transcendent source of authority that denies freedom. That risk was minimized when it came to prototypes, which were numerous (Austen, Stein, Morante, Woolf, Bachman, Plath, etc.). But what happens when the "gendered figure of origin" and freedom is named "the symbolic mother" (SD, 113)?

On the face of it, the "symbolic mother" as a figure of missing female authority can seem like the "female duplicate of the authority of male origin" (SD, 111). How could the figure of the *mother* possibly organize a feminist practice of freedom? Wouldn't this figure symbolize the relations of kinship that have crippled feminism from the start? Taking up Luce Irigaray's claim that within masculinist cultures the relationship between mothers and daughters is missing ("the mother always carries a son in her arms"), the collective asserts that "there are no forms of symbolic bond between a woman and the woman greater than herself, who is her mother. Only a natural relationship exists between the two, variously overlaid with affect . . . but without symbolic translation" (SD, 127). The very idea of a *symbolic* mother, therefore, could be at once radical—whatever a mother is in masculinist cultures, she is never symbolic—and ordinary.

A symbolic mother is a gendered figure of origin around which to organize a feminist practice of freedom, a new social contract. A central problem identified by the Italian feminists, we recall, is "the real difficulty which a woman encounters in acknowledging the immensity of a desire she has no way of putting forward, openly, in full sight of society, without the disguise of some female virtue" (SD, 115). In politics this disguise takes the form of claims to make society better. These claims resonate within the larger frame of the social question, which requires that women express their political demands in the language of social utility or expediency. Some of the Italian feminists, for example, were unable to distinguish "a new, freer social interpretation of female difference" from what "is consonant with the social good." Confusing "being different with being better," they "objected that this plus is not qualified; it does not express positive values, and hence it cannot qualify, give value, either to female difference or to a female politics" (SD, 124). Caught in the economy of use, they are still trying to provide a raison d'être for the female sex and for female freedom: the betterment of society. They cannot imagine a social practice that seeks the freedom of women without investing it with "some positive social quality" (SD, 125). The Milan Collective responds: "[T]he female plus expresses nothing but the concept of the irreducible difference owing to which being a woman is neither subordinable nor assimilable to being a man" (SD, 124). That is to say, it expresses no social value, no social use whatsoever, but only a desire for freedom that seeks no reparation and cannot be subsumed under the banner of equality.

The new social contract called feminism "must give a foundation to women's freedom" (*SD*, 32), declares the collective. This foundation is no ground composed of rational premises upon which all would-be members of the feminist community would have to agree. Organized around a trope, the symbolic mother, this contract authorizes women in their desire for freedom not by appealing to rationality or timeless principles, but presenting the appeal "in the context of political practice through the words and gestures of daily life, in one's relationship with this or that woman, in the quickening of desires, in proximity to everyday things" (*SD*, 111). No totem like the primal father—who must be killed in the "other" story of the social contract, whose murder is the condition of relations of political equality among men, and whose immanent return haunts them—the symbolic mother, the collective writes, comes "to indicate the source of social legitimacy for female difference, as concretely embodied for a woman by those women who validate her desire and support it in the face of the world" (*SD*, 107). That is another way of saying that this figure of gendered mediation cannot be an absolute: it will have no existence apart from the material and symbolic practice of free relations among women.

A Political Practice of Sexual Difference

The name of the practice that puts the plus of female origin, the symbolic mother, into circulation, so that it may become collective wealth, is *affidamento*, or entrustment. Discovering *examples* (not rules) of entrustment in the biblical story of Ruth and Naomi, in the relationship between the poet H. D. (Hilda Doolittle, 1886–1961) and Bryher (a pseudonym) in Greece (as described in H. D.'s *Tribute to Freud*), in the friendship between Virginia Woolf and Vita Sackville-West, among other exemplary relationships between women, the collective declares, "[T]he entrustment of one woman to another is the stuff of political struggle" (*SD*, 31).

In its most crystallized form, the person to whom one entrusts oneself is the woman (or women) who supports one's desire for freedom, who says, "Go on" (*SD*, 33–34).[40] "It [this experience] gave H. D. the feeling that she had a poetic vocation, together with the certainty that all this was possible because of the woman who was beside her and who, at the decisive moment, said to her: 'Go on'" (*SD*, 33–34). "Clearly, we do not think that to give oneself authority is an individual act. Authority is received originally from another human being who is in the position to give it, who has the authority to give it. But she cannot have it if the person who needs to receive it does not acknowledge it in her. 'Go ahead,' answers Bryher to H. D. [in Hilda Doolittle's *Tribute to Freud*], giving back to her, in the form of symbolic authorization, the maternal authority which H. D. had attributed to her by turning to her" (*SD*, 126). In contrast with the idealized figures of early feminism, the vertical relation of entrustment is also a horizontal, reciprocal one: the authority that legitimates women's desires is nothing without the acknowledgment that confers it. (Besides, "the woman who is truly respectful of entrenched hierarchy . . . entrusts herself to a man or to the male enterprise" [*SD*, 133].)[41]

Entrustment is not a private matter: "That is why we say that the relation of female entrustment is a social relation, and we make it the content of a political project. The symbolic debt toward the mother [that is, the women who support us in our desires] must be paid in a visible, public, social manner before the eyes of everyone, women and men" (*SD*, 130). Entrustment is not sisterhood: "Entrusting oneself is not looking to another woman as in a mirror to find in her a confirmation of what one actually is. . . . In the relation of entrustment, a woman offers to another woman the measure of what she can do and what in her wants to come into existence" (*SD*, 149). Entrustment is not a rule or a timeless political form: "There probably are, or will be, other possible answers, better ones, for that matter" (*SD*, 121). Entrustment is a contingent political practice, which developed as one possible response to women's symbolic homelessness and their lack of relation among themselves, in Milan, between 1966 and 1988. It is a contingently necessary practice, for it could have been otherwise, yet it answered to a need that was experienced as necessary: the absence of authoritative interlocutors.

If "feminism must give a foundation [of sorts] to women's freedom" (*SD*, 32), but no rational or social justifications for that freedom (for example, the betterment of society, and so on), entrustment is that foundation. In the practice of entrustment, "female freedom is guaranteed by [nothing other than] women themselves" (*SD*, 142). What authorizes a woman's actions and claims, then, is neither an absolute, a figure whose authority is self-evident and requires no agreement or action on one's own part, nor (as second-wave feminist theory tended to assume) a political epistemology, a defense of political claims as truth claims. Rather, it is the women whose desire for freedom one authorizes and who in turn authorize one's own desire, daily—who say, "Go ahead."

This phrase, in its utter simplicity and multiple, quotidian articulations, symbolizes, however modestly, an exit from the impasse of feminism's freedom of the will. It symbolizes the transformation of the empty freedom of "I-will" into the worldly freedom of "I-can." To say or to hear "Go ahead," and *to act publicly* in accordance with that phrase, is to take leave of feminism's injury identity, its politics of victimization, without denying one's membership in a group called women. The woman who could not find herself represented in the image of "a homogenous, socially oppressed group," we recall, is easily tempted by that denial, caught in a fantasy of sovereignty. The woman "who does not know, does not want to acknowledge, that she needs her fellow women" (*SD*, 135) ends up "imprisoned in the realm of the petrified symbols of male power, in need of other women but incapable of negotiating with them for what she wants" (*SD*, 137).

Rereading this sentence now, we can see that acknowledging is not a mere synonym for knowing. From my knowing I owe a debt, it does not follow that I acknowledge I owe a debt—otherwise the relations among women would be different than they are (to paraphrase Stanley Cavell). "One could say [with Cavell]: Acknowledgment goes beyond knowledge. (Goes beyond not, so to speak, in the order of knowledge, but in its requirement that I *do* something or reveal something on the basis of that knowledge.)"[42] That is why the debt to other women must be paid in a visible, public manner. It is not enough to carry silent knowledge of that debt around in my head: thoughts alone do not alter the texture of reality—actions do. Thus, the Milan Collective boldly declares, "Simple gratitude in the relation between women is what female freedom is practically founded on. Everything else, in theory as in practice, is either a consequence of that or has nothing to do with freedom. One woman who is grateful to another for giving her something is worth more for the liberation of the female sex than a group or a whole feminist movement in which this kind of gratitude is missing" (*SD*, 130). Gratitude is an expression not of hierarchy but reciprocity; it is a mutual acknowledgment of the nonsovereign conditions of female freedom, the imbrication of claims to community and claims to individuality. The woman who refuses to pay this debt "will never be free," for "[t]he world will always be for her a thing thought up and governed by others from whom she can extort one advantage or another, but in the forever subordinate position of one who petitions" (*SD*, 129). For a woman, then, the only way out of the apparent impasse of the logic of reparation or woundedness as the condition of modern political subjectivity described by Wendy Brown is to acknowledge what one owes to other women, to acknowledge, that is, community.

"The female price for freedom is the payment of this symbolic debt" (*SD*, 129), the collective claims. And such acknowledgment can never obtain if a woman relinquishes her ability to make judgments or her claim to individuality.

When read as a *political* claim to membership in a genealogy of women, sexual difference is a means of reconciling oneself to what has been given without in any way condoning how it has been given. It is an attempt to escape the *ressentiment* that attends the wish to rid oneself of "the 'causal' datum of being female," to will backwards. "In the social-symbolic order thought up by men, to be born a woman is an accident that conditions all of life. She has no personal destiny in life; there is no way for her to make freedom and necessity coincide. For her necessity means to submit to the social use of her anatomy (maternity, virginity, prostitution . . .), while her freedom merely means to evade all of this" (*SD*, 127–28). Sexual difference is not "the factual premise that our belonging to social life is determined by our belonging to its female component." It is the "political practice . . . [that] transform[s] this factual premise from a social cause of unfreedom into the principle of our freedom" (*SD*, 122). "In other words, a woman is free when she chooses to signify her belonging to the female sex, well knowing it is not an object of choice" (*SD*, 138).

The politics of sexual difference as the Italians understand it, then, would transform the I-will that remains bound to necessity, caught in a fantasy of self-sovereignty, and filled with *ressentiment*, into the I-can that experiences freedom in a community at once conditioned and chosen: "a social contract . . . based on the principle of gratitude and exchange with other women" (*SD*, 142). This new social contract is based not on a set of rationally agreed upon principles that are supposedly apodictic but on a *promise* to make good a claim to community and acknowledge a debt. Articulated around a figure (the prototypes, the symbolic mother), the basis of this kind of feminist community is not a compact rooted in certain truths that would bind its signers and their posterity forever, and whose legitimacy reduces to little more than what the social contract theorists tactfully called "tacit consent." Sexual difference has no existence whatsoever, and no guarantee, apart from the daily practice, in a visible and public manner, of acknowledging the women who come before one and who say, "Go ahead." It is a quotidian political practice of making and keeping promises.

The ability to make and keep promises, as Arendt argues, is crucial to a nonsovereign practice of freedom. For this ability attenuates the unpredictability that characterizes human action, the fact that we act in ways whose consequences we can never foretell with certainty. The faculty of promising, she writes,

> is . . . the only alternative to a mastery which relies on domination of one's self and rule over others; it corresponds exactly to the existence of a freedom which was given under the condition of non-sovereignty. The danger and the advantage inherent in all bodies politic that rely on contracts and treaties is that they, unlike those that rely on rule and sovereignty, leave the unpredictability of human affairs and the unreliability of men as they are, using them merely as the medium, as it were, into which certain islands of predictability are thrown and in which certain guideposts of reliability are erected. The moment promises lose their character as isolated islands of certainty in an ocean of uncertainty, that is, when this faculty is misused to cover the whole ground of the future and to map out a path secured in all directions, they lose their binding power and the whole enterprise becomes self-defeating.[43]

The faculty of making and keeping promises, far from a way of overcoming contingency and unpredictability, is a way of making them more bearable, lest we be tempted "to turn away with despair from the realm of public affairs and to hold in contempt the human capacity for freedom."[44] Like a "force" that keeps people together even when they are not acting in concert, promising gives sovereignty a certain limited reality. The very peculiar kind of "sovereignty of a body of people bound and kept together, not by an identical will which somehow magically inspires them all [as contract theorists like Rousseau held], but by an agreed purpose for which alone the promises are valid and binding," writes Arendt, is far superior to the supposed sovereignty of "those who are completely free [in the traditional sense], unbound by any promises and unkept by any purpose."[45] It is the limited sovereignty of an I-can achieved through the promises that bind rather than the illusory sovereignty of the I-will that acknowledges no debt or community at all.

The ability to make and keep promises transforms the bare fact of differences among women into something politically significant: authoritative interlocutors. It transforms a notion of equality based on the "unfortunate mirroring among women" (*SD*, 126) into something more dangerous but less spectral—reciprocity. Insisting that a feminist transform what she knows into what she acknowledges, the Milan Collective brazenly asserts, "It is more important to have authoritative female interlocutors than to have recognized rights." Does that mean feminism, once it has created authoritative interlocutors, should no longer be concerned with rights?

Refiguring Rights

At the beginning of this chapter I suggested that *Sexual Difference* may have been ignored by American feminists because, when read through the frame of the subject question, the text could easily be mistaken for an argument about an essential sexed difference. We are now in a better position to see why that critique is off the mark. In the resolutely political formulation given by the Italian feminists, sexual difference is a practice of freedom centered not on the production or destruction of an identity, but on entrustment and acknowledgment, the making and keeping of promises, and the capacity to make judgments. Focused on world-building, on feminism as a new social contract, the political practice of sexual difference seeks to bring about a change in the texture of worldly reality. When understood as the creation of a political space—that is, a worldly in-between defined by relations of distance and proximity, organized around figures of the newly thinkable (for example, "the symbolic mother"), and subject to reorganization and judgment—sexual difference does not apply across the board to all women qua women (however one defines membership in that class). It only applies to those individuals who make a political claim to membership in a genealogy of women. That political claim is the acknowledgment of a debt, that is, the signification of the nonsovereign conditions of female freedom in a public, visible manner.

But even if we grant that *Sexual Difference* is not an essentialist text—or, at the very least, not *simply* so—there is yet another concern that might lead us to discount it: namely, what appears to be a wholesale rejection of feminism's historical struggle for equal rights. Indeed, within our rights-based framework, *Sexual Difference*—leaving aside the scare of essentialism—was almost destined to be received as a feminist text non grata. The politics of freedom (sexual difference) *versus* the politics of equality (sexual indifference) could easily be read as a zero-sum game: equal rights *or* female freedom. Deeply critical of the former, the Milanese seemed to choose the latter, eliminating the possibility of both.

There is, however, another way of reading this text, one which foregrounds the practice of freedom as the condition of claiming one's rights and the claiming of rights as a practice of freedom. "The politics of sexual difference does not come *after* the equality of the sexes has been achieved; it *replaces* the much-too-abstract and often contradictory politics of equality in order to fight against every kind of sexist oppression from the place of an achieved female freedom, founded on social relations between women" (*SD*, 145; second italics added). Although we could take that sentence to mean that the politics of equality is a dead end for feminism, we could also interpret it to mean this: The belief that the politics of sexual difference comes *after* the equality of the sexes has been achieved is mistaken, not because the politics of equality ought to be *replaced* by the politics of sexual difference, but because the former will remain substantively elusive in actual practice without the latter.

When read through the lens of the subject question, this alternative interpretation would appear to be a claim about the need to inscribe sexual difference in law. And Luce Irigaray, probably the most important feminist thinker for the Italians, has argued just that.[46] But both Irigaray and the Milanese also call our attention to another feature of rights, namely their tendency to deteriorate into dead legal artifacts and even dangerous political instruments when they lose their connection to practices of freedom.[47] Indeed, the deeply juridical and institutional orientation of much contemporary feminism, like that of American society at large, shows how we have lost track of the idea of political freedom which the radical claim to rights once encoded. If, as Irigaray argues, women require sexed civil rights, that is because those rights, like equal rights, are a demand for both participation (not mere representation, political or juridical) and the entrustment of citizens to one another ("not to some leader, male or female").[48] When rights become institutionalized, we tend to forget their origin in a radical, ungrounded claim to freedom, to nondomination and to equal participation in public affairs. We tend to become invested in securing them as such, rather than in maintaining our investment in the sometimes less stable practices that created them in the first place. The call for the return to civil rights is a reminder of that origin: political struggles such as feminism, Irigaray writes, "did not wait for legal judgment, nor even that of state representation, in demanding changes to rights."[49] Freedom lies in the exchange of words and deeds that may or may not issue in a demand for rights. Freedom does not consist, not as such, in the political representation that follows from the successful institutionalization of such a demand.

There is an ineliminable tension between the political representation that rights secure and political freedom, argues both Irigaray and the Milan Collective. Feminism is a deeply diverse political movement, organized around a gender rich in diversity, which no notion of "women in general" can possibly represent (*SD*, 74). This is no more an argument against representation than it is one against rights, being, rather, a sharp reminder that it is deeply mistaken for feminists to confuse the experience of freedom with representation and the institutionalization of rights. The Italians have shown us the cost, for women, of having representation and institutionalized rights without genuine political freedom. In the absence of freedom, equal rights tend to come at the cost of assimilation or what Irigaray calls the "law of the same." But equality, as Arendt reminds us, is a political and therefore humanly constructed principle that ought to support the experience of human plurality, that is, the experience of moving freely among one's peers, hearing and judging different points of view. To foreground freedom and the subjective in-between that sustains it, as both Arendt and the collective in their different ways do, is to reject not equal representation or equal rights, but rather a notion of both that seems to demand sameness because it has hardened into an abstract principle or rule and thus detached from its origin in practices of freedom.

When brought back into relation with their origin in practices of freedom, rights may be used to do more than affirm *what* we already are (that is, members of various groups with ascribed social identities). They can and should affirm our desire to be something more. Understood in this way, rights are political instruments of freedom that say, "Go ahead." "It is more important to have authoritative female interlocutors than to have recognized rights," then, not because rights don't matter, but because they only matter if we can claim them, use them, move beyond them to new claims and new freedoms. They only matter if, like those interlocutors, they inspire us to go ahead. Indeed, rights, as Ute Gerhard argues, "cannot be imported or prescribed; they apply only if the people involved are in a position to claim or defend them as rights."[50] The creation of such a position, the Milan Collective shows, assumes practices of freedom, a worldly in-between, and authoritative interlocutors. "An authoritative interlocutor is necessary if one wants to articulate one's own life according to a project of freedom and thus make sense of [produce meaning for] one's being a woman [a contingent fact]," something "[n]either laws nor rights can give" (*SD*, 31). Rights claims addressed to the state, in other words, can never substitute for the political claims feminists address to one another.[51]

Thus, when read not through the subject question but through the practice of freedom that was its original home and aspiration, a claim to rights is not—or not simply—a demand for recognition of *what* one is; it is a demand for acknowledgment of *who* one is, and, more important, of who one might *become*. So understood, equal rights are not legal artifacts that can be applied in a rule-like fashion to all subjects who fall into a certain identity category. Rights are not things to be distributed from above, but a demand for something more made from below.[52] Rights are not things, but relationships. As such they are not something we *have* but something we *do*, they not only constrain but also enable us in our relations with others.

To think about rights in this way is to question accounts of women's historical claims to equal rights which foreground claims to equality over practices of freedom. Perhaps feminists do well to turn the story around, recalling rights' original home in a radical claim to freedom. This claim is irreducible to the struggle for women's liberation, which is typically construed in social terms and as something that rights are taken to encode. There is nothing inevitable about the extension of rights to disenfranchised groups like women, for the claim to rights as a practice of freedom does not flow necessarily from the liberation from oppression. Rather, freedom, like rights, is something that can only be guaranteed by those people who claim it. As the Milan Collective observes,

> For female freedom to be guaranteed by itself—without which it is not freedom, but emancipation, as it is rightly called—it is indispensable that the historical circumstances which favored our [women's] liberation from the outside be rendered superfluous, so to speak; that they be translated into, or replaced by, a freedom which reproduces itself parthenogenetically and produces the material conditions necessary for its exercise. If, as has been written, it is true that the pasteurization of milk contributed more to giving women freedom than did the struggle of the "suffragettes," we must act so as never again to let it be true. Similarly for medicine, which reduced infant mortality and invented contraceptives . . . or for the progress in societal life which induced men no longer to consider women inferior beings. *Where does this freedom come from that arrives in a bottle of pasteurized milk?* What roots has the flower which is offered to me as the sign of a superior civilization? Who am I if my freedom lies in this bottle, in this flower someone placed in my hand? (*SD*, 144; emphasis added)

Neither bestowed nor inherited, freedom can only be claimed by women themselves. And what will secure it, ground it, justify it? "[F]emale freedom is guaranteed by women themselves" (*SD*, 142).[53]

What appeared to be the Milan Collective's deep skepticism if not outright rejection of rights and the politics of representation has allowed us to see the limits of a principle of equality that is not part of a practice of freedom. The Milan feminists needed, perhaps, to state their case in such uncompromising terms in order to open our eyes—which tend increasingly to be blinded by juridical and state-centered answers to political questions—to what women can and cannot achieve in their struggle for, and exercise of, rights. Whether rights can be part of such a practice must be decided in context and in relation to the particulars of the case in which rights are at stake. Insofar as the demand for rights is a claim to equality, it is not a demand based simply on argumentative logic, for such a demand can only be answered by taking into account the contingent conditions under which it is posed. Demands for equality need not—as logic would have it—exclude demands for difference. As Gerhard argues, once we see that equality is neither a firm standard (with man as the measure) nor an absolute principle (a logical truth we are bound to accept) but a dynamic, evolving concept that entails the articulation of two terms by means of a third, a *tertium comparationis*, we will see that the precise meaning of equality depends on what *we hold*. Indeed, deciding what shall count and what not for the means of comparison is "by no means a logical operation, but is instead the result of an assessment, a value judgment," writes Gerhard, and this will vary on the basis of time and place. Irreducibly contingent, "the respect in which people are to be considered equal depends on the 'reflective standpoint.'" It is neither a logical matter nor (simply) a legal problem but rather "a political issue."[54] What rights call for, then, is neither our blind acceptance nor rejection, but rather, our political judgment. In the next chapter we will see what this faculty of (reflective) judgment is and why it is crucial to a freedom-centered feminism.

CHAPTER FOUR

Feminists Make Judgments:
Hannah Arendt's *Lectures on Kant's Political
Philosophy* and the Affirmation of Freedom

The loss of [inherited] standards . . . is only a
catastrophe for the moral [and political] world when
one assumes that individuals are not capable of
judging things in themselves, that their power
of judgment is not adequate to an original judgment;
one cannot expect of them anything more
than the application of known rules.

—HANNAH ARENDT, *WAS IST POLITIK?*

IN THE LAST chapter we saw that the practice of political freedom
entails not only spontaneity but also world-building: the creation, and
continual reinvention, of institutions that sustain a worldly in-between, a
space that both relates and separates those individuals gathered together
in it. *Sexual Difference* showed us the emergence of such a practice in
Italian feminism. That was no small achievement. Looking back at "the
events . . . that took place between 1966 and 1986, mainly in Milan," the
Women's Bookstore Collective had to make sense of "things that had no
names" and no place in the world: free relations among women. What
allowed the authors of *Sexual Difference* to see those relations as free
rather than necessary? How were they able to replace the traditional
image of female wretchedness with the radical figure of female freedom?

Although the events that transpired between 1966 and 1986 were the
basis for the collective's unconventional account of women's political
relationships, the story told in *Sexual Difference* is in no way driven or
exhausted by those empirical events. Looking at the very same events in
which others had found a community of women based on a common
identity forged through the experience of shared suffering, the Milanese
saw the emergence of something new, something to which both post-hoc
accounts of Italian feminism and even the actors involved in those events
had been blind. It was in their role as spectators that past events and
things first appeared to members of the collective as nameless, that is, as
lacking figuration or not subsumable under an existing category or rule.
In the process of reflection they came to see that the persistent temptation
to narrate the new practice of free relations among women in terms of the
old practice of bonding around pain was a denial of freedom, and that
without freedom feminism itself made no sense. There was something

numbingly predictable about an account centered on victimization, yet it provided a strange comfort. The familiar story of women demanding reparation for past crimes concealed the far more unfamiliar story of women demanding freedom for no reason other than the desire for freedom itself.

Refusing to justify women's demand for freedom in terms of the scripts available to them (for example, the creation of a better society, the triumph of social justice, and so on), the Milan Collective had to learn to tell a different story. In this alternative account of Italian feminism, the radical demand for freedom is not attenuated by the logic of a narrative that renders events meaningful in virtue of their relation to an overarching process such as historical progress. We might interpret this departure from causal and teleological modes of interpretation as the discovery of an "objective fact," namely the reality of female freedom. In that case, however, we would miss what is most important: the Milan women discovered not the "real fact" of freedom or, for that matter, any other fact of Italian feminism, but rather a certain relation to those facts. Their celebratory account of freedom and contingency was an artifact of their own practice, and one name for that practice is political judgment.

To say that freedom is an artifact of judgment is not to deny the presence of freedom in human action. It is, rather, to be reminded that the freedom present in action, as Arendt argues, is both fleeting (without the artifacts of remembrance, such as stories and narratives, action would vanish without a trace) and frightening (action without a cause seems unpredictable in terms of its effects and inconceivable in terms of the rectilinear time concept which organizes our sense of meaning and purpose).[1] Political freedom is neither a substance we possess nor an object we cognize; rather, it is exhibited in action and affirmed by the faculty of judgment. As we saw in chapter 2, however, "philosophers and men of action" alike have been more likely to deny than to affirm freedom. Faced with what Kant called the "melancholy haphazardness" of action, they have time and again converted contingency into necessity: they have sought meaning in human action by converting single deeds into necessary moments of some larger whole, like the unfolding of social progress, and they have denied what is irreducibly new in action by subsuming those deeds under a given category or rule.[2]

For the Milan women, as for Arendt, the very idea of a historical process, which alone gives meaning to whatever it happens to carry along, carries the risk of becoming a denial of freedom and an escape from the task and burden of political judgment.[3] In the Italians' view, feminism has not been immune to this risk. One way in which feminism has denied freedom and the demand for judgment, they argued, took the specific if paradoxical form of asserting a constitutionally based guarantee of women's rights as if it were the very instantiation of women's freedom and historical proof of attained democratic values. Rejecting constitutionally guaranteed rights or any other legal artifacts as the rule according to which to judge the existence of women's freedom, the Milanese questioned the almost automatic equation we tend to make between rights and freedom. What they refused was not rights as such but the kind of political thinking that mistakes legal artifacts of freedom for a practice of freedom. Although their refusal of rights as a yardstick by which to measure women's freedom risked foreclosing the radical potential of rights, as I suggested in the last chapter, that refusal also led the Italians to foreground the faculty of judgment and its importance for a freedom-centered feminism. But what exactly is this faculty of judgment and why is it important to a freedom-centered feminism?

Judgment and the "Problem of the New"

In the widest sense of the term, judgment is the faculty that allows us to order or make sense of our experience. Be it the particulars of objects that need to be related to concepts for the purposes of cognition or the particulars of events that need to be organized into narratives for the purposes of political life, judgment gives coherence and meaning to human experience. Whether what I see over there is a "tree," what I hear on the radio is a commentary on "the latest famine in Africa," or what I read in the paper is an editorial on the "war between the sexes," I am at once engaged in and a witness to the practice of judgment. The ubiquity of the judging faculty in all human activities, however, makes it almost invisible to us *as* judgment, as something *we* do. This is especially true in the case of cognitive judgments, where we seem only to report a fact that stands there quite independently from how we judge (for example, I see that tree over there because there really is a tree over there; I see two sexes because there really are two sexes, and so on).

Kant—and later Wittgenstein—called into question the idea that cognition turns on the mere physiological fact of something like perception and emphasized the crucial role of judgment in anything that has meaning for human beings. For judgment, generally speaking, is the ability to think the particular as contained under the universal or, writes Kant, "the faculty of subsuming under rules; that is, of determining whether something stands under a given rule . . . or not."[4] Without the faculty of judgment we could have no knowledge, he famously argues, for in the absence of concepts that function as rules for subsuming or classifying particulars, we would have only "this" and "this," but not anything that we could call an object of experience (for example, this "woman" or this "man"). Every "object" comes into being as such through recognition in a concept, Kant holds.[5]

According to the logic of recognition at work in what Kant calls a "determinant judgment" (that is, logical and cognitive), it is hard to see—as the philosopher himself recognized—how there could be a new object or event, that is, something that cannot be explained as the continuation of a preceding series and in terms of what is already known. The empirical judgments of sex difference that we examined in chapter 1, for example, subsume particulars under the rule of male or female in a way that misses what is potentially novel about intersexed bodies, for they too are cognized by being brought into conformity with the rule of binary sex difference. In a determinant judgment, then, following a rule seems to transform the new into the old as the condition of knowledge and meaning.

For freedom-centered feminists, however, what Arendt calls "the problem of the new" is more than an epistemological question about how we have knowledge of particulars; and it is more than a moral question about how to save the freedom of the subject in a phenomenal world that can only be cognized through the law of causality. The problem of the new is a political question about how we, members of democratic communities, can affirm human freedom as a political reality in a world of objects and events whose causes and effects we neither predict nor control. Arendt vividly captures the difficulty we have in so affirming: "[W]henever we are confronted with something frighteningly new, our first impulse is to recognize it in a blind and uncontrolled reaction strong enough to coin a new word; our second impulse seems to be to regain control by denying that we saw anything new at all, by pretending that something similar is already known to us; only a third impulse can lead us back to what we saw and knew in the beginning. It is here that the effort of true [political] understanding begins."[6] At stake in the kind of judgment that is relevant to politics is not knowledge but understanding, or rather the understanding, as Arendt says, that "makes knowledge meaningful." At stake is trying to be at home in a world composed of relations and events not of our own choosing, without succumbing to various forms of fatalism or determinism—whose other face is the idea of freedom as sovereignty.

Our ability to come to terms with what is given (that is, the past that can be neither forgotten nor changed) in a way that affirms a nonsovereign human freedom (that is, freedom that is based in the I-can, not the I-will; freedom that begins in political community, not outside it) can only be achieved through a critical practice of judgment. Such a practice cannot be based on the "autonomy principle" that Hume disrobed as a philosophical conceit (that is, the idea that reason judges critically by emancipating itself completely from the customs or prejudices that compose our preliminary understanding).[7] There is no place outside this understanding from which we can judge. When not seen as something to be leapt over in our reach for the external standpoint, this groundless ground of our judging practices, I argued in chapter 1, is too often treated as if it determines what we can encounter in the world or it were somehow immune to revision.[8] In that case, our precognitive understanding of meaning is transformed from an enabling condition of feminism and our critical orientation in an ever-changing world into what Arendt called a "worldview" that works to "protect us against experience [and the new] insofar as everything real is already given in [it]."[9] If this was what second-wave feminism had become in the opinion of the Milan women, it was not because feminists made a claim to rights, but because they failed to develop the practice of judgment that would have given them critical purchase on their own rights claims.

A feminist practice of judgment, then, cannot be modeled on the rule-following that characterizes what Kant called a determinant judgment. To obtain critical purchase on our social arrangements and the ungrounded ground of our form of life, but without yielding to the temptation of the external standpoint, feminists need to develop a practice of judgment that is not rule-governed, at least not in the philosophical sense of following a rule that Wittgenstein shows to be a deep misunderstanding of what we do. Developing such a practice is far from easy and—as the ongoing sense of crisis in contemporary feminism shows—requires vigilance on our part. Inherited concepts that function as rules for ordering particulars (for example, male, female, man, woman, and so on) may no longer be credible in the way that they were for most second-wave feminists, but we have yet to understand or accept the consequences for feminist politics today. Judging without the mediation of a concept is a quotidian skill we would do well to learn and practice. It always carries the risk that we will fall back on known concepts or rules for making sense of political reality out of our own sense of frustration or inadequacy. And yet if we want to come to terms with objects and events that have no place within our system of reference save as curious anomalies to the rule that merely preserve the rule (for example, five sexes), we need to develop the faculty of judgment. And developing this faculty involves more than the affirmation of contingency that third-wave feminists have stressed. Or, better, it involves the creation of coherence and meaning that does not efface contingency and thus freedom.

The new strains our capacity for judgment and understanding—if only we will let it—for it "calls forth forces in thought which are not the forces of recognition, today or tomorrow, but the powers of a completely other model, from an unrecognized and unrecognizable *terra incognita*," as Gilles Deleuze observes.[10] Rather than deem whatever cannot be subsumed under rules or attain objective validity as irrelevant to the faculty of judgment, Arendt and Deleuze hold that precisely whatever is not an object of knowledge is an occasion for developing the critical aspects of the faculty of judgment itself. That is to say, it is in cases where what Kant called determinant judgment strains or fails that true judgment begins. In cases where a judgment can produce no knowledge (as a concept is not already given), the common sense or harmony of the faculties that obtains in a judgment is no longer under the legislation of the understanding (that is, the faculty of concepts according to Kant), but attains a free accord. In the "free play of the faculties," as we shall see later, imagination in particular is no longer bound to the logic of recognition, which requires that it re-produce absent objects in accordance with the concept-governed linear temporality of the understanding. Imagination, *when it is "considered in its freedom"*—nothing compels us to consider it as such—is not bound to the law of causality, but is productive and spontaneous, not merely re-productive of what is already known, but generative of new forms and figures.

Foregrounding the productive role of the imagination in the faculty of judgment, I at once take up and depart from Arendt's own unfinished project to develop a theory of political judgment. Despite her heavy reliance on Kant's third *Critique*, she never really considered the imagination in its freedom, for she never thought of it as anything more than reproductive. Arendt's limited view of imagination is all the more curious when we recognize that the reproductive imagination is bound to what Kant called the "faculty of the understanding" and thus to concepts in a way that is difficult to square with her own vigorous refusal of cognition as relevant to political judgment. Such neglect of the free play of imagination in a practice of judging without a concept is one reason that Arendt's scattered reflections on the topic have lent themselves to both the appropriation and criticism of philosophers such as Jürgen Habermas, who famously accuses her of failing to answer to the all-important requirement of validity. For Habermas (as for most commentators on Arendt's writings on judgment), validity looms as the single unanswered question that threatens to render her entire account incoherent. Any renewed attempt to bring Arendt's reflections on judgment into critical dialogue with feminism cannot evade this charge of incoherence, not least because feminism, as we shall see, has not been exactly immune to demanding from an account of judgment the same measure of truth.

Presupposed in such a charge is a conception of politics that, in contrast with Arendt's action-centered conception, sees the very work of politics almost exclusively in terms of the adjudication of an otherwise "impenetrable pluralism" (Habermas) of political claims and opinions. It is a conception of politics that has likewise governed most of second-wave feminist theory and that persists in the work of many feminist political thinkers today. Politics as a practice of adjudication requires an account not simply of validity but validity of a certain kind, namely objective validity. Although Arendt's critics strongly distance themselves from the philosophical legacy of objectivism or any metaphysical notion of truth, they never consider the possibility, elaborated by Arendt, that there could be a form of validity or objectivity specific to democratic politics that would not be based on the application of rules to particulars. They thus never see, really, that Arendt does in fact have an answer to the question of validity, with one important caveat: she does not think that validity in itself is the all-important problem or task for political judgment—the affirmation of human freedom is.

The Old Problem of Objectivity

Although feminists have become cautious about the logic of recognition that guides cognitive judgments about things like sexed bodies, we still find it difficult to imagine how political claims that do not subsume a particular under a universal could be valid. This difficulty reflects the rule-governed theorizing that characterized second-wave feminism. Accordingly, the (immanent) loss of the category of women has been, and continues to be, interpreted in terms of a crisis concerning the supposed inability not only to act collectively (in the name of women) but also to make political judgments that are universally communicable, accepted as valid by others. Once we question the idea that there are rules for judgment that would function like objective criteria upon which all "women as women" would have to agree, however, we seem to be left with a question: what could possibly make a judgment valid for someone who does not share the judging subject's particular social location? Insofar as social location includes membership in a group increasingly narrow and defined by multiple categories (for example, race, class, ethnicity, sexuality, age, nationality, and so on), the once critical idea of "differences among women" appears, at a certain point, to yield a radically subjectivist conception of political judgment. At that point a judgment based on the subject's particular experience seems almost as hard to contest or confirm as an avowal like "I am in pain." What could there be to dispute?[11]

Subjectivism haunts contemporary feminism, but in a way that is deeply entangled with a certain understanding of politics. If the work of politics is to pursue an end—such as the betterment of society or a group and its members (the social question) or the transformation of feminine subjectivity (the subject question)—then it appears to require an agreement as to what that end is and in whose name it is to be undertaken. Second-wave feminism more or less took for granted the idea that the objectives of politics could be discerned through a knowledge-producing practice. Exemplified in standpoint theory (discussed below), this practice attempts to sort out true from less true or patently false opinions about the common world, which could then be used to guide social change. As feminists must "know what they do" according to this conception of politics, the loss of the categories of understanding and standards of judgment associated—rightly or wrongly—with third-wave feminism could be experienced as nothing other than a crisis: a virtual free-for-all in political opinions and judgments that can produce no knowledge whatsoever threatens to destroy the very possibility of coming to an agreement about what the proper ends of politics are.

The subjectivism that haunts contemporary feminism, then, confronts us with the old problem of objectivity. Although feminism has taken a deeply critical stance toward the Archimedean idea of objective truth as "the view from nowhere," the problem of objectivity persists, as Kirstie McClure suggests, in the form of the question, "What is it that authorizes the discourse of a feminist?"[12] This question can be understood, with McClure, in terms of the claims of feminist theory, but it can also be raised in relation to political judgment. What makes political judgments different, on the one hand, from the kind of knowledge/truth claims that feminists criticize as belonging to a fantasy of (Archimedean) objectivism and, on the other hand, from the avowals that we fear as mere subjectivism?[13] According to what criteria and on what basis can we evaluate judgments if such judgments do not claim validity and universality based on objective concepts (such as "women") that function as rules for subsuming particulars? Can judgments that are not based on subsuming particulars under universal rules be universally communicable? And if they are not communicable on the basis of universal rules, can they be communicable or valid nonetheless?

Judging without a Concept

In her *Lectures on Kant's Political Philosophy*, Arendt offers a way to begin thinking about a practice of political judgment that would bring together the demand for objectivity and the recognition of plurality, a practice for which plurality itself would be the basis for apprehending and understanding new objects and events in their freedom. Kant's account of judgments of taste is illuminative for a theory of political judgment, Arendt argues, because politics, like aesthetics, calls upon us to judge the particular without subsuming it under a concept. Although judgment in general "is the ability to think the particular [sensible intuitions] as contained under the universal [law, rule, concept]," according to Kant, it is "reflective judgment" that interests Arendt.[14] Distinguishing between judgments that are "determinant" (for example, logical and cognitive) and judgments that are "merely reflective" (for example, aesthetic and teleological), Kant elaborated, respectively, the difference between a judgment that subsumes a particular under a universal that is given and a judgment in which only the particular is given and the universal is sought.[15] Arendt captures this difference when she writes, "If you say, 'What a beautiful rose!' you do not arrive at this judgment by first saying, 'All roses are beautiful, this flower is a rose, hence this rose is beautiful.'"[16] The aesthetic judgment, "*this* rose is beautiful," is not grounded in the universal nature of roses.[17] There is neither cause nor necessity in it. That is why it might be relevant for thinking about politics, a realm in which we are concerned with contingency and freedom.

The possibility of judging the particular in the absence of a concept without relinquishing the claim to intersubjective validity is the central problem raised in Kant's *Critique of Judgment*. If judgments were not universally communicable, writes Kant, "they would one and all be a merely subjective play of the presentational powers, just as skepticism would have it" (*CJ*, §21, p. 88). Kant's account of aesthetic judgments raises the problem of subjectivism and thus the question of validity in a particularly acute way, for such judgments are based on nothing more than the subject's feeling of pleasure or displeasure. Such feeling makes no reference to concepts because it is not "referred to the object," says Kant, but "solely to the subject and is not used for cognition at all, not even for that by which the subject *cognizes* himself" (*CJ*, §3, p. 47; emphasis in the original).[18] Rather than anchor validity in some property of the object, which necessarily and universally causes certain feelings in subjects (as some of his intellectual predecessors had done), Kant argues that feelings of pleasure or displeasure "designate nothing whatsoever in the object, [such as its ability to satisfy a purpose or use, but only how] he [the subject] is affected by the presentation" (*CJ*, §1, p. 44). This rose *is judged* to be beautiful and thus pleasing.[19] "[B]eauty is not a property of the flower itself" (*CJ*, §32, p. 145).

Accordingly, aesthetic judgments presuppose an ability to support them as claims that are universal, not merely subjective, but not in the manner of establishing objective proof. Asserts Kant: "[T]here can be no rule by which someone could be compelled to acknowledge that something is beautiful. No one can use reasons or principles to talk us into a judgment on whether some garment, house, or flower is beautiful" (*CJ*, §8, p. 59).[20] In judgments of taste, which depend on our pleasure, "[w]e want to submit the object to our own eyes, just as if our liking of it depended on that sensation" (*CJ*, §8, p. 59). No one can judge for us; and no judgment can serve as evidence that another judgment is correct or incorrect (*CJ*, §34, p. 149). In the absence of concepts, there is nothing that could determine the correctness of a judgment in the manner of proof that could compel others to agree with a particular judgment. "And yet, if we then call the object beautiful, we believe we have a universal voice, and lay claim to the agreement of everyone," adds Kant (*CJ*, §8, p. 59). To claim "This rose is beautiful" is different from claiming "I like canary wine." Whereas the latter claim is *merely* subjective, a matter of what is "agreeable to me" (and thus in no need of agreement nor subject to dispute), says Kant, it would be "ridiculous" to say that this rose "is beautiful *for* me," for a judgment of beauty takes for granted that others, too, ought to agree (*CJ*, §7, p. 55). Acknowledging the irreducibly subjective structure of feeling that defines aesthetic judgments, the task and burden of the third *Critique* is to demonstrate that judgments based in nothing but affect could be posited as universally valid despite not being objectively true.

The irreducibly subjective experience of pleasure or displeasure that characterizes "a pure judgment of taste" (*CJ*, §13, p. 69), Kant argues, claims intersubjective agreement a priori, that is, in the absence of the actual (empirical) assent of other subjects. But if the validity of a judgment does not depend on such assent and cannot compel it on the basis of proofs, why bother exchanging views at all? Kant's answer is to distinguish between two argumentative interlocutions: to dispute (*disputieren*) and to quarrel (*streiten*). Whereas *disputieren* assumes that one can reach an agreement through arguments that follow the rules of conceptual logic and objective knowledge (as is the case with determinant judgments), *streiten* occurs when concepts are lacking and agreement cannot be reached through the giving of proofs (as is the case with reflective judgments). And yet, despite the absence of the objective necessity of an agreement reached by proofs, the debate lives on, for each judging subject makes a claim that posits the agreement of others and, if necessary, attempts to persuade others of her view.

Aesthetic judgments have "subjective validity": making reference to others, they anticipate communication and agreement with them. There is necessity in judgments of taste, but this necessity is not "objective . . . , allowing us to cognize a priori that everyone *will feel* this liking for the object I call beautiful," but "subjective" and "exemplary": "necessity of the assent of *everyone* to a judgment that is regarded as an example of a universal rule that we are unable to state" (*CJ*, §18, p. 85). Such necessity points not to the empirical fact that "everyone judges like that . . . [but only] that we *ought* to judge like that, which amounts to saying that they [judgments of taste] have for themselves an a priori principle" (*CJ*, First Introduction, 10, p. 428; emphasis in the original). This "ought," Kant writes, is still uttered only conditionally. "We solicit everyone else's assent because we have a basis for it that is common to all" (*CJ*, §19, p. 86). What supports our claim that everyone ought to agree with our judgment are our shared feelings and use of the faculties (that is, reason, understanding, and imagination): "The necessity of the universal assent that we think in a judgment of taste is a subjective necessity that we present as objective by presupposing a common sense" (*CJ*, §22, p. 89).[21]

The deduction of a common sense (*sensus communis*) as the ground for the validity of judgments of taste is at the core of Kant's attempt to develop a critique of aesthetic judgment along transcendental lines. According to critical interpretations of Arendt's rereading of Kant, the conception of common sense as the condition of possibility for the validity of aesthetic judgments is far too abstract (entangled as it is in the formalism of his transcendental philosophical method) to be of much use for a theory of political judgment.[22] Interested in the universal conditions for judgment, comments Ronald Beiner (editor of Arendt's Kant Lectures), Kant not only ignores "the substantive features of this or that judgment," which matter very much in politics, he gives hardly "any attention to the kinds of knowledge involved in judgment and . . . any specification of epistemic capacities that render men qualified, in greater or lesser degree, to judge."[23] From the perspective of politics, says Beiner, we should worry that Arendt, following Kant, "states quite categorically that judging is not a cognitive faculty" and therefore can involve no claims to knowledge/truth.[24] Arendt's refusal to provide a "cognitive foundation" for politics, as Habermas puts it, leaves "a yawning abyss between knowledge and opinion that cannot be closed with arguments."[25] And Arendt does in fact say that in aesthetics, as in politics, "one cannot dispute" claims in the manner of giving proofs, "but only quarrel/fight [*streiten*] and come to an agreement [*übereinkommen*]" through persuading speech.[26]

One Concept of Validity

The idea that cognitive discriminations and cognitive insights play an irreducible part in political judgments seems, on the face of it, so obvious that it is hard to understand why Arendt insisted upon their noncognitive character.[27] In the view of her critics, Arendt uncritically adopted Kant's notion of a (noncognitive, non-rule-governed) reflective judgment as the model for political judgment because she shared what they take to be his far too rigid understanding of a (cognitive, rule-governed) determinant judgment.[28] And it is easy to see that if determinant judgments are construed in the manner of a mindless kind of rule-following, reflective judgment will immediately appear as deeply appealing to anyone concerned with attending to the particular qua particular.

Arendt did not think any mode of judgment easy, and neither should we. Even determinate judgments, which entail the application of rules to particulars, always require reflection and skill "because no rule is available for the *applications* of the rule," as Arendt observes of a famous passage from the first *Critique*.[29] Any rule that is given to explain the application of another rule requires, in turn, a rule to explain it, and so on in an infinite regress.[30] For Arendt, as for Kant, judgment of any kind must be spontaneous and creative because there are no rules governing the application of rules to material. Arendt was drawn to Kant's account of aesthetic judgments in particular because, as reflective judgments, they call our attention to the creative and "autonomous nature of judgment."[31] In the absence of a rule under which to subsume a particular, the faculty of judgment uses, for its activity of reflection on what the imagination presents, a "principle of its own," writes Kant (*CJ*, Introduction, 3, p. 16), rather than borrowing the rules or principles of reflection from either the faculty of understanding or that of reason. Consequently, such judgment, though unique in this respect, exhibits the skill required but otherwise concealed in the faculty of judgment more generally.[32] As I argued in chapter 1 about empirical judgments of sex difference, our grasp of objects is generally so quick and intuitive, so rooted in habit and worldview, we are practically blind to what we do. As Wittgenstein observed, such judgments seem to accord with the philosophical conception of following a rule, where the rule is like a line in space that we cannot but help to follow or trace. When we reflect upon what we do, we tend to see not freedom, the contingency of our own practice, but rather the necessity of following that line. Hardly visible to us is the possibility that we could not follow the rule or, alternatively, the possibility, present at every moment of following it, that we could stop—or follow it otherwise.

Questioning the association we tend to make between the application of concepts and the ability to judge, Arendt's point is not to exclude arguments from the practice of political judgment—as if something or someone could stop us from making arguments in public contexts—but to press us to think what we are doing when we reduce judgment to the contest of better arguments. Arendt is struggling with a difficult problem to which her critics, focused as they are on the problem of validity and the adjudication of political claims, are blind: how to save freedom in the face of our deep sense of necessity in human affairs.[33] If Arendt is deeply suspicious of the "process of reaching agreement in practical [political] questions as rational discourse" (Habermas), it is because she sees in some of our practices of justification a strong tendency to compulsion, which, in turn, destroys the very space in which the contingent objects of political judgment, the particular qua particular, the words and deeds of human action can appear. She sees how we tend to run the space of reasons into the space of causes: logical reasoning is transformed from a dialogic tool of thought, with which we aim at agreement, into a monologic tool of thought, with which we compel it. What Habermas calls "the rationality claim immanent in speech" risks becoming what Wittgenstein calls "the hardness of the logical *must*."[34]

It would be easy for a feminist to be pulled in the direction of Arendt's critics, for validity is at the center of standpoint theory, surely the most influential feminist epistemological framework of the late twentieth century. According to Susan Hekman, "feminist standpoint theorists have recognized that feminist politics demand a justification for the truth claims of feminist theory, that is, that feminist politics are necessarily epistemological." Above all, standpoint theory seeks to "justify the truth of the feminist claim that women have been and are oppressed."[35] Hekman rehearses the criticism of the initial formulations of standpoint theory, which focused on the tendency to treat women as a homogenous group with shared experiences and perspectives. These critiques gave rise to refinements of the theory, which seek to take account of the differences among women. But acknowledgment of these differences, in turn, created what she describes as an impasse. If standpoint theory cannot talk about women as a group, how can it make the political judgment that women are oppressed and defend that judgment as valid?

Hekman refuses the answer given by liberal thinkers like Susan Okin and Martha Nussbaum, who claim that there is an objective truth of women's oppression. These thinkers, says Hekman, wrongly assume "that we need a concept of how the world *really* is, a metanarrative that provides standards for cross-cultural judgments, if we are to fashion a feminist, or any kind of, politics."[36] Although Hekman is appropriately critical of the idea that there is some objective reality that could ground feminist judgments, it is not clear how an alternative practice of judgment could emerge if we construe, as she clearly does, the political problem of women's oppression, or any political problem, exclusively in terms of the epistemological problem of justification.[37] This epistemological or cognitive framing of judgment leads Hekman to pose the problem of judgment as if the recognition of differences *necessarily* undercuts feminism's political ability to make a claim to truth *and in this way* to articulate a wrong. And yet, she concedes, feminism must take account of differences. We then face an impossible choice: acknowledge differences (and risk a subjectivism that effaces truth) *or* articulate a wrong (and risk an objectivism that effaces difference). Although Hekman clearly refuses this choice, she also scripts it, in exemplary fashion, as intrinsic to the collapse of women as a political category. But what is her way out of the impossible choice?

What Hekman is in effect calling for in her critique of Okin and Nussbaum is a practice of judgment that would allow feminists to articulate a wrong (oppression) without subsuming particulars under universals, attempting to occupy an external standpoint, or underwriting the liberal political logic that construes a wrong strictly in terms of an absent right whose guarantor is the state. But Hekman goes no further. She cannot see that a *reflective* practice of judgment is the issue at stake for feminism because, haunted by the specter of subjectivism that differences seem to carry with them, she is entirely focused on the problem of how to claim (objective) validity, without of course falling prey to objectivism. Settling on the force of "rational argument" as a tool of the social transformation she has defined in epistemic terms, Hekman concludes, "We may not be able to persuade nonfeminists that the institutions of patriarchy are evil and should be dismantled. But we may be, and indeed have been, able to persuade them, through the use of skillful arguments, that sexual harassment, marital rape, and wife battery should be defined as crimes."[38] (To some extent, yes, but how—with logical proof or more compelling evidence?)

As it turns out, however, standpoint theory lacks not a means for generating more compelling evidence or claims to truth but an account of feminist opinion formation and judgment that is world-building and freedom-centered. The need for this account is implicit in the claim, initially made by Nancy Hartsock, that a feminist standpoint is a *political* position that is *achieved*, not given. Recognizing that experience is crucial for understanding the practice of political judgment and, further, that women's experience alone does not translate into a feminist practice of judgment, standpoint theory had an important insight. Because it construed our relation to the world in strictly cognitive terms, however, standpoint theory could never deliver on this insight. Focused on the problem of (objective) validity, the theory was blind to everything that might be relevant for politics if it did not take the form of a knowledge claim. Consequently, competing perspectives among women could never appear as the material of feminist opinion formation or world-building, but only as competitors for epistemic privilege. To appreciate this alternative conception of perspectives, however, we must first loosen the hold that the entire problematic of validity has on our political thinking or, better, try to imagine, with Arendt again, a different kind of validity—the kind of validity that political judgments should have.

A Political Concept of Validity

Arendt suggests how we might rethink the work or nature of validity claims in politics when, in her discussion of the importance of the exchange of opinion in ancient Greece, she first relates, then distinguishes, learning to form an opinion from honing the skill of argument. What really mattered for the creation of the public realm, she finds, is not "that one can turn arguments around and assertions on their head, but that one developed the ability really to *see* things from multiple perspectives, and that means politically."[39] The origins of this political way of seeing, she argues, lie in "Homeric objectivity" (that is, the ability to see the same thing from *opposite* points of view: to see the Trojan War from the standpoint of *both* of its greatest protagonists, Achilles *and* Hector).[40] What transforms Homeric impartiality, "still the highest type of objectivity we know," into the ability to see from multiple points of view is the daily practice of public speech, "citizens talking with one another."[41] Arendt explains,

> In this incessant talk the Greeks discovered that the world we have in common is usually regarded from an infinite number of standpoints, to which correspond the most diverse points of view. In a sheer inexhaustible flow of arguments, as the Sophists presented them to the citizenry of Athens, the Greek learned to exchange his own viewpoint, his own "opinion"—the way the world appeared and opened up to him . . . —with those of his fellow citizens. Greeks learned to *understand*—not to understand one another as individual persons, but to look upon the same world from one another's standpoint, to see the same in very different and frequently opposing aspects.[42]

Despite her critics' charges, Arendt in no way excludes the role of argument in learning to see politically. In contrast with many of her critics, however, Arendt does not treat arguments (or speech) as a means to an end, specifically as the means to separate out what Habermas calls the otherwise "impenetrable pluralism of apparently ultimate value orientations" (that is, opinion based on "particular interests") from what is universal because it is rationally defensible (that is, opinion based on "generalizable interests").[43] Although Arendt, like Habermas, is deeply concerned with the formation of opinions that are political rather than merely subjective or private, she does not construe the diversity of opinions as threatening an "impenetrable pluralism," which it would then be the heroic task of rational argument to illuminate and ultimately settle. For her, political arguments belong to the argumentative interlocution Kant called *streiten*, not *disputieren*, that is, the kind of interlocution that generates agreement on the basis of persuasion rather than irrefutable proofs. Arguments are valuable not in the adjudicating form of conversation stoppers but in the ongoing, world-building form of "incessant talk." Arguments are valuable not when they produce agreement—though they may well do so—but when they enable us to see from standpoints other than our own and deepen our sense of what is shared or real. This shared sense of worldly reality is the condition of anything we could call communicable and valid, and it is unthinkable apart from the plurality of viewpoints from which an object or event is seen.

Whereas Arendt's critics and many feminist theorists tend to see plurality as something that threatens validity, giving rise to relativism and decisionism in politics, Arendt holds that there is no validity (no sense of worldly reality) without plurality. Subjectivism in her view is a consequence not of multiple perspectives but of a failure to take them into account, a consequence of being imprisoned in one's own viewpoint. No single perspective can match the sense of reality that arises out of "the sum total of aspects presented by one object to a multitude of spectators," she writes. Although this may sound as if Arendt were locating plurality in the object that "presents" its aspects to us, she goes on to observe that, "under conditions of mass society or mass hysteria, where we see all people suddenly behave as though they were members of one family, each multiplying and prolonging the perspective of his neighbor," that very same object can lose its multiple-aspect quality.[44] When that happens, she argues, we no longer have a world in common. We have the world in common *because* we view it from different perspectives. Absent those perspectives we lose "the sameness of the object," its realness or "objective" quality. Rather than threaten our shared sense of worldly reality, in other words, plurality generates it. Plurality—if we take proper account of it—saves us from both objectivism and subjectivism, and therefore from risking dogmatism or skepticism, Arendt suggests.

By contrast with the strongly cognitivist approach of philosophers like Habermas, Arendt's account of worldly reality is not driven by the idea that there is one truth behind the many interpretations of it. Rather, the common world itself—not the earth or nature as such, but the human artifact—comes into existence only through plural perspectives.[45] Although such perspectives may well yield a sense of a thing's existence (*that* it is), they do so by way of communicating its essence (*what* it is)—that is, what it is *for* us. This is another way of saying that plural perspectives on the same object are exercises in the application of criteria. As Stanley Cavell showed us in chapter 1, when I describe how something seems to me, I at once take for granted and test the limits of our agreement in judgments and thus our criteria. Criteria are criteria of judgment: we use them to indicate that something counts as something for us (for example, judging someone to be in pain on the basis of her groans). "Criteria are 'criteria for something's being so,'" writes Cavell, "not in the sense that they tell us of a thing's existence, but of something like its identity, not of its *being* so, but of its being *so*. Criteria do not determine the certainty of statements but the application of the concepts employed in statements."[46] Our ability to apply criteria takes for granted shared routes of feeling, interest, and valuing; criteria manifest what counts *for* human beings.

Like Cavell, Arendt is concerned with the ways in which, when we speak, we say what counts for us. We affirm that something *is* so by claiming that it is *so*. This claiming or counting, we recall, is not exhausted by classical accounts of knowledge, but always entangles us in questions of acknowledgment: I have to be willing to count that groan as an indication that you are in pain or—as Jacques Rancière will show us—count your speech as political speech rather than just a subjective expression of discontent. Aesthetic and political judgments, in which there is no concept to be applied, raise the question of criteria in an acute way, for saying what counts involves something other than the activity of subsumption. Unique to such judgments is that the subject does not recall the grounds upon which things can be rightly judged, but is called upon to elicit, in relation to specific interlocutors, the criteria appropriate to the particular at hand. "At the end of reasons comes persuasion," as Wittgenstein puts it.[47] As we shall now see, this involves a very different understanding of what it means to make an argument.

From World-Disclosure to World-Opening

To attempt to persuade with argument in the political realm, says Arendt, is "'to give an account'—not to prove, but to be able to say how one came to an opinion, and for what reasons one formed it" (*LKPP*, 41). She does

142 | CHAPTER FOUR

not dispute the idea, precious to Habermas's notion of the practical kind of rationality presupposed in communication "oriented toward mutual understanding," that speakers should—he would say must—be able, if asked, to justify their own speech acts. What she disputes, rather, is the idea that agreement among interlocutors follows necessarily from our acceptance of certain arguments and principles of argumentation.

Arendt takes up Kant's insight that we can well follow and even accept the arguments brought to defend a particular aesthetic judgment without having to accept the conclusion. "It is this—the fact that anyone who can follow an argument need not accept the conclusion, even if she doesn't find anything definitely wrong with it—that leads Kant to claim that the imputed universality of aesthetic judgment does not spring from (the application of) a concept, that it cannot be thought of as objective universality," writes Stephen Mulhall.[48] Disagreement—even deep disagreement—is possible, though neither side is making a mistake or failing to grasp that a particular judgment is well supported. For example, I can accept your argument about why a certain painting is beautiful (such as its unique place in the history of art, its artist's vivid use of color, or the representation of perspective) and still disagree with your judgment of beauty. That refusal may make my sense of taste deficient in your eyes, but not in the sense of being mistaken.

To conclude that, in such a case, my judgment is not rational would be to concede (with Arendt's critics) a rather narrow understanding of what rationality is, namely, a form of thinking based on giving proofs. This includes not only the scientific rationality Habermas accuses Arendt of uncritically inheriting from Kant's first *Critique* but also the practical rationality associated with the central role of arguments in a discourse ethics. Cavell takes up the Kantian notion of the subjective validity of aesthetic judgments to call our attention to the notion of "pattern and support," rather than agreement in conclusions, as the crucial element in rational argument. Stephen Mulhall parses Cavell's view thus:

> Cavell is not suggesting that logic or rationality is a matter of the existence of patterns (of support, objection, response) *rather than* of agreement (in conclusions); he is suggesting that logic or rationality might be more fruitfully thought of as a matter of agreement in *patterns* rather than agreement in *conclusions*. Whether the particular patterns or procedures are such that those competent in following them are guaranteed to reach an agreed conclusion is part of what distinguishes one type or aspect of rationality from another; but what distinguishes rationality from irrationality in any domain is agreement in—a commitment to—patterns or procedures of speaking and acting.[49]

The issue, then, cannot be that aesthetic judgments lack rationality. In the third *Critique*, Kant no more ruled out giving reasons for our aesthetic judgments than does Arendt in her reading of him. Someone who is unable to support her judgments is not engaging in aesthetic (Kant) or political (Arendt) judgment at all, but merely stating a subjective preference (for example, "I like canary wine"). Criteria are to be considered when choosing between competing judgments, but these criteria can never function as proof. Consequently, there is no single argument that can or should persuade everyone capable of reason, regardless of standpoint or context, of a particular aesthetic or political judgment.

Political and aesthetic judgments are arguable, in other words, but in a very specific way. They belong to the interlocution Kant calls *streiten*. We try to persuade others of our views and in this sense attempt to reach agreement. But the failure to reach agreement, for Arendt as for Kant, in no way signals a failure to communicate rationally or to follow agreed-upon conventions for rational argumentation. As we have seen, I may well follow and even accept your argument and still not agree with your conclusion. This sounds strange only because we are so accustomed to thinking that agreement in conclusions follows from agreement in premises and procedures, follows in such a way that anyone who accepted the premises and procedures but not the conclusion is either making a mistake or is mentally deficient. And in the case of judgments in which concepts are applied, that is more or less the case.

But the poet who judges his poem beautiful, contrary to the judgments of his audience, says Kant, may well accept their criticisms based on the conventions (for example, rhyme, meter, and so on) of poetry—yet stubbornly hold to his view.[50] The signers of the 1848 Declaration of Sentiments, who judge men and women to be created equal, contrary to the judgments of the Founding Fathers and most nineteenth-century Americans, may well accept the criticisms that men and women are different by nature—yet stubbornly hold to their view. What we hold to in the face of this apparent contradiction is neither illogical nor irrational, but rather a value that has not yet found expression in the sense of a determinate concept. To anticipate the argument that follows, what we hold to in political as in aesthetic judgments (as the claim to gender *equality* suggests) is not necessarily something that is irreducibly nonconceptual (as Jean-François Lyotard will argue), but rather something that is an imaginative extension of a concept beyond its ordinary use in cognitive judgments and knowledge claims, that is, beyond its characteristic role, which is to introduce interests. Whether we eventually abandon an earlier judgment on the basis of sharpening our own power of reflective judgment (as Kant's poet does) or hold to it in the face of a world that once declared us scandalous (as the signers of the Declaration did), we must judge for ourselves and try to persuade others of our views. And this may well involve not—or not simply—the ability to judge in the absence of a concept which we have been discussing but an imaginative "exhibition of the concept [for example, of equality]," to speak with Kant, that "expands the concept itself in an unlimited way" (*CJ*, §49, p. 183).

This ability to persuade others of one's views does not depend on facility in logic. One may well have the so-called force of the better argument and fail to convince one's interlocutors (and not because they lack competence, that is, fail to understand what a good argument is). The ability to persuade depends upon the capacity to elicit criteria that speak to the particular case at hand and in relation to particular interlocutors. It is a rhetorical ability, fundamentally creative and imaginative, to project a word like *beautiful* or a phrase like *created equal* into a new context in ways that others can accept, not because they (necessarily) already agree with the projection (or would have to agree if they are thinking properly), but because they are brought to see something new, a different way of framing their responses to certain objects and events. Arguments are put forward like the *examples* that Kant holds to be the irreducible "go-carts" of an aesthetic judgment: they *exhibit* connections that cannot be rationally deduced from given premises. If an argument has "force," it is more as the vehicle of an imaginative "seeing" (to stay with Arendt's own language) than an irrefutable logic. And its force is never separable from the person making the judgment and the context into which she speaks. There can no more be *the* final or conclusive argument for the equality of the sexes than there can be *the* final and conclusive argument for the beautiful. Every political or aesthetic argument must be articulated in relation to a set of particulars.

With this in mind we can better grasp what Arendt means when she describes seeing politically as involving the exchange of arguments that allow us to see something new insofar as they work on the basis of something other than logical compulsion. Logic alone cannot help us see something new, but only what is already given in the premises; it does not touch the preunderstanding or past judgments that now serve as principles of judgments, but rather takes them for granted. Arendt herself never rejects the (Kantian) maxim of logic as the condition of coherent thought; what she disputes, rather, is the idea that thinking logically is ipso facto thinking politically, for the latter form of thinking, though logical in some very general sense, requires something else. Arendt writes, "Kant insisted upon a different way of thinking, for which it would not be enough to be in agreement with one's own self, but which consisted of being able to 'think in the place of everybody else.'"⁵¹ Political thinking, in other words, requires that *we take account of plurality*, that we *count* the different standpoints and opinions ("it-seems-to-me") described above as the condition of an expansive notion of objectivity or worldly reality, and this may well involve challenges to, and changes in, our criteria. We shall examine this counting practice—what Arendt calls "representative thinking"—in detail below; at this point it is worth asking why plurality is something of which we need take active account.

Although Arendt sometimes speaks of plurality as if it were exhausted by a state of being in which we find ourselves as human, plurality is much more than that. No mere existential concept—like most feminist accounts of the "differences among women" or like the particular interests that make up Habermas's account of an "impenetrable pluralism"—plurality is a *political* relation that is irreducible to empirical differences.⁵² It is perfectly possible for such differences to exist in the absence of plurality (for example, members of different social groups could start acting, as Arendt said above, like "members of one family," "each multiplying and prolonging the perspective of his neighbor"). It is also perfectly possible for judging subjects to deny plurality in the face of empirical differences (as if "Man and not men inhabited the earth"). Like all political relations, plurality is external and irreducible to its terms: it is not given in the "objects" themselves (that is, the differences of perspective based on the different standpoints associated with membership in different social groups), but is a creation.

If plurality is more than an ontological condition of human differences, then it is no mere condition of being human ("men not Man"), which we have a tendency to deny—though we do tend to deny that human condition of finitude, as both Cavell and Arendt in their different accounts of modern subjectivism and skepticism show. Rather, plurality requires that we *do* something in relation to whatever empirical differences may exist: plurality names not a *passive* state of ontological difference but an *active* and, as I show below, *imaginative* relation to others in a public space. Plurality, as a political relation external to its terms, is based in the faculty of presentation (imagination) and not—or not initially—in the faculty of concepts (understanding). I can *know* that empirical differences exist as part of the human condition, yet fail to *acknowledge* them, for the latter act involves more than cognition or the application of concepts to particulars (or, more precisely, *where* cognition is involved, acknowledgment requires that I *do* something on the basis of what I know).

By making plurality the condition of, rather than the problem for, intersubjective validity, Arendt shifts the question of opinion formation and judgment from the epistemological realm, where it concerns the application of concepts to particulars and the rational adjudication of knowledge/truth claims, to the political realm, where it concerns opinion formation and practices of freedom. Politics involves the exchange of arguments in the sense of the opening up of the world that has been disclosed to us through language, our criteria, or concepts. However one understands the attempt to give reasons, it takes for granted a prior "opening up [of] the world where argument can be received and have an impact," as Jacques Rancière reminds us.[53] The poetic, rhetorical, and world-creating capacity of language, which Habermas sets at odds with the proper communicative use of language that makes possible the "intersubjective recognition of criticizable validity claims," is, in Rancière's view as in Arendt's, the very condition of anything that we might count as validation by proofs.[54] Proofs work on the basis of deduction from accepted premises. Opening up creates the context in which a change in perspective may happen—perhaps by means of proofs, perhaps not—and things we may have known all along get counted differently.

Opening up the world in a political sense requires a public space defined by equality. Not equality simply as a formal condition of citizenship under law (*isonomia*); not equality as a procedural rule that is linked to that other empty rule of argumentation in a discourse ethics; but equality as a political relation that we create and sustain in and through taking account of plurality, daily.[55] The "opening up of common (which does not mean consensual) worlds," writes Rancière, entails *acknowledging* what we may already *know*: for example, *counting* the subject who argues "as an arguer," that is, as someone whose speech is no mere avowal but makes some universal claim that we would call political.[56] Prior to anything that we might count as a dispute is this act of counting one's interlocutors *as* interlocutors. Persuasion, Arendt observes, "presupposes equality and works through argumentation."[57] Conversely, argumentation works as a form of persuasion to the extent that it presupposes equality. This is a simple but important point. As Rancière explains, "The problem is knowing whether the subjects who count in the interlocution 'are' or 'are not,' whether they are speaking or just making a noise [uttered in perfectly grammatical sentences—then the issue is not linguistic competence]. It is knowing whether there is a case for seeing the object they designate as the visible object of the conflict. It is knowing whether the common language in which they are exposing a wrong is indeed a common language."[58] The issue, of course, is not what we know but what we will acknowledge, count as political.

What makes language common in this distinctly *political* sense is not the shared linguistic ability that allows us to understand the words someone speaks. Rather, it is our counting those words *as* (political) speech (with subjective validity) and not noise (merely subjective). This counting is not reducible to seeing, finally, "the force of the better argument." Just as one can well understand and even accept the terms of an argument without accepting the conclusion when debating an aesthetic or political judgment, so too can one understand what is being said without counting it as political speech and the one who says it as a political speaker. Homer's account of the Trojan War was a paradigm of the impartiality proper to politics, to return to Arendt's example, not because it presented both sides of the conflict as socially given positions laden with opposing interests (Greek versus Trojan), which is how a validity thinker might see it, but because it presented the Trojans like the Greeks as speaking beings, not as barbarians who make no recognizable claims. It is only then that the kind of objectivity that is proper to the political realm can emerge.

"Being and thinking in my own identity where actually I am not"

We have seen that Arendt refigures the validity that is appropriate to democratic politics as unthinkable apart from plurality. For her critics, by contrast, validity obtains when impartiality is achieved through the discursive adjudication of rationality claims, that is, the separation of particular from general interests (for example, the feminist standpoint). Consequently, impartiality obtains when opinions and judgments are purified of interests that are strictly private—but what remains is a form of interest nonetheless, only now this interest is said to be rational and universal in a nontranscendental sense.

Although Arendt, too, holds impartiality to be the condition of a properly political opinion or judgment, what she understands by impartiality is akin to what Kant means when he says that concepts cannot play any role in an aesthetic judgment because they refer to objects and introduce interest, that is, the pleasure or liking "we connect with the presentation of an object's existence" (*CJ*, §2, p. 45). This interest is related to the object's purpose, its ability to serve an end: "interest here refers to usefulness," observes Arendt (*LKPP*, 73). Concepts are to be excluded, according to Kant, because they entangle aesthetic—Arendt would say political—judgments in an economy of use and in a causal nexus. The "inability to think and judge a thing apart from its function or utility," writes Arendt, indicates a "utilitarian mentality" and "philistinism."[59] She continues, "And the Greeks rightly suspected that this philistinism threatens . . . the political realm, as it obviously does because it will judge action by the same standards of utility which are valid for fabrication, demand that action obtain a predetermined end and that it be permitted to seize on all means likely to further this end."[60] For Arendt, who held means-ends thinking to be a denial of the freedom exhibited in action and speech, the introduction of interests, be they private or general, introduces the instrumentalist attitude.[61] Her critics cannot think the idea of disinterestedness in terms other than objective validity and never see any need to relinquish the object as ground zero of every judgment. Accordingly, the relation among subjects is, for them, mediated through objects and thus through the faculty of the understanding and its application of concepts.

As no concept determines the formation of opinion according to Arendt, such formation cannot entail—not in the first place—the subject's relation to the object, which defines cognitive judgments in Kant's view. Rather, the relation to the object is mediated through the subject's relation to the standpoints of other subjects or, more precisely, by taking the viewpoints of others on the same object into account. Arendt describes this intersubjective relation as "representative thinking":

> I form an opinion by considering a given issue from different viewpoints, by making present to my mind the standpoints of those who are absent; that is, I represent them. This process of representation does not blindly adopt the actual views of those who stand somewhere else, and hence look upon the world from a different perspective; this is a question neither of empathy, as though I tried to be or to feel like somebody else, nor of counting noses and joining a majority but of being and thinking in my own identity where actually I am not. The more people's standpoints I have present in my mind while I am pondering a given issue, and the better I can imagine how I would feel and think if I were in their place, the stronger will be my capacity for representative thinking and the more valid my final conclusions, my opinion.[62]

The Kantian name for representative thinking, Arendt writes, is "enlarged mentality" or, more exactly, an enlarged manner of thinking (*eine erweiterte Denkungsart*) whose condition of possibility is not the faculty of understanding but imagination.[63] This faculty, at work in seeing from the standpoints of other people, keeps enlarged thought from becoming either an enlarged empathy or the majority opinion. Imagination is a means, writes Arendt, "to see things in their proper perspective, to be strong enough to put that which is too close at a certain distance so that we can see and understand it without bias and prejudice, to be generous enough to bridge abysses of remoteness until we can see and understand everything that is too far away from us as though it were our own affair."[64] Imagination mediates: it moves neither above perspectives, as if they were something to transcend in the name of pure objectivity, nor at the same level as those perspectives, as if they were identities in need of our recognition. Rather, imagination enables "being and thinking in my own identity where actually I am not."

To unpack this curious formulation of enlarged thinking, let us consider more closely the special art upon which it is based, what Arendt calls "train[ing] one's imagination to go visiting" (*LKPP*, 43). Commenting on this art of imaginatively occupying the standpoints of other people, Iris Marion Young argues that it assumes a reversibility in social positions that denies structured relations of power and ultimately difference. "Dialogue participants are able to take account of the perspective of others because they have heard those perspectives expressed," writes Young, not because "the person judging imagines what the world looks like from other perspectives."[65] Likewise, Lisa Disch is critical of the notion that "a single person can imaginatively anticipate each one of the different perspectives that are relevant to a situation. It is this presupposition that reproduces an aspect of [the very] empathy [Arendt otherwise rejects in her account of representative thinking]; it effects an erasure of difference."[66] Both Young and Disch agree, then, that a feminist (or any democratic) appropriation of the idea of enlarged thought must be based in actual dialogue, not imaginative dialogue. This "*actual* dialogue between *real* (rather than hypothetical interlocutors)," as Beiner likewise observes, sets the parameters for the kind of validity or universality that is proper to political judgment and whose condition is common sense.[67]

We could qualify this critique and say that imagination is no substitute for hearing other perspectives but nonetheless necessary according to Arendt because, empirically speaking, we cannot possibly hear all relevant perspectives. To do so, however, would be to accept the conception of imagination implicit in the critique, namely, that this faculty is at best a stand-in for real objects, including the actual opinions of other people, and at worst a distortion of those objects, in accordance with the interests of the subject exercising imagination.[68]

This limited view of imagination is not entirely the fault of Arendt's critics. Arendt herself failed to develop Kant's notion of productive imagination and its relationship to freedom, and yet both the problem of freedom and the faculty of imagination are central to her account of judgment. Treating imagination as if it were a "mere" substitute for absent objects (for example, actual dialogue), the account of imagination as empirical and reproductive neglects the place of the imagination in first, giving us the objects of judgment themselves (for example, in the form of schemata and examples) and second, giving us those objects in a manner consistent with freedom (that is, outside the causal nexus). Missing is an understanding of imagination as freed from the charge of knowledge. This alternative understanding entails a non-concept-guided view of imagination or better, as Sarah Gibbons observes, "the broader function of imagination as grounding the possibility of concept-application in the first place."[69]

In contrast with the emphasis on actual dialogue and an "interpersonal relationship" (centered on mutual understanding or recognition) in a discourse ethics, Arendt invokes imagination to develop reference to a third perspective from which one observes and attempts to see from other standpoints, but at a distance. Arendt does not discount the importance of actual dialogue any more than did Kant, but, again like Kant, she emphasizes the unique position of outsideness from which we judge. It is this third perspective that Arendt had in mind when she claimed in the passage cited above that imaginative visiting involves not the mutual understanding of "one another as individual persons" but the understanding that involves coming to "see the same world from one another's standpoint, to see the same in very different and frequently opposing aspects." At stake here is the difference between understanding another *person* and understanding the *world*, the world not as an object we cognize but "the space in which things become public," as Arendt says.[70]

For Arendt, the kind of understanding made possible by exercising imagination concerns our ability to see objects and events outside the economy of use and the causal nexus. "Being and thinking in my own identity where actually I am not" is the position achieved not when, understanding another person (as in a discourse ethics), I yield my private interest to the general interest, but when I look at the world from multiple standpoints (not identity positions) to which I am always something of an outsider and also something of an outsider to my self as an acting being.[71] This is the position of the spectator that Arendt describes in her Kant lectures. The spectator is the one who, through the use of imagination, can reflect on the whole in a disinterested manner, that is, a manner free not simply from private interest but from interest *tout court*, which is to say from any standard of utility whatsoever. Were the imagination merely reproductive and concept-governed (as Arendt herself seems to assume or at least never questions), it might be possible to attain the kind of impartiality that Arendt's readers associate with the position of the spectator, namely, the impartiality of the general interest. But would one be poised to apprehend objects and events outside the economy of use and the causal nexus—to apprehend them in their freedom?

Being so poised, Kant could express enthusiasm about the new, the world-historical event of the French Revolution, though from the standpoint of a moral acting being, Kant said he would have to condemn it. From the standpoint of the spectator, however, he could find in this event "signs" of progress. These "signs of history" are not facts to be presented by the reproductive imagination in accordance with the understanding and judged according to a rule of cognition. Rather, David Carroll observes, such signs "have as their referent the future which they in some sense anticipate but can in no way be considered to determine."[72] To the spectator, the French Revolution does not provide cognitive confirmation that mankind is progressing; rather, it inspires "hope," as Arendt writes, by "opening up new horizons for the future" (*LKPP*, 56). As a world-historical event, the revolution indicated what cannot be known, but must be exhibited, presented: human freedom.

The freedom-affirming position of the spectator "does not tell one how *to act*," writes Arendt of Kant's enthusiasm (*LKPP*, 44; emphasis in the original). What one sees from this impartial standpoint, then, is not the general interest or anything that could be considered a guide to political action or to further judgment, Arendt observes. The judgment one makes as a spectator is in no way connected with an end. Indeed, "even if the end viewed in connection with this event [the French Revolution] should not now be attained, even if the revolution or reform of a national constitution should finally miscarry," says Arendt, citing Kant, nothing can destroy the hope that the event inspired (*LKPP*, 46). For a new event, from the perspective of the spectator poised to apprehend it in its freedom, is not a means toward an empirical end of any kind, and thus the validity of the judgment in no way turns on the realization of an end. Rather, validity is here tied to an affirmation of freedom that expands the very peculiar kind of objectivity that Arendt associates with the political sphere, namely, the objectivity or sense of reality that turns on seeing an object or event from as many sides as possible. Like "the highest form of objectivity" that arose when Homer, setting aside the judgment of History, sang the praise of both the Greeks *and* the Trojans, so too does Kant's judgment of the French Revolution expand our sense of the real, for it refuses to judge on the basis of victory or defeat, of any interest or end whatsoever.

The judgment that at once expands our sense of reality and affirms freedom is possible only once the faculties are "in free play," as Kant puts it.

Only where the imagination is not restrained by a concept (given by the understanding) or the moral law (given by reason) can such a judgment come to pass. And the French Revolution was for Kant a world-historical event for which we have no rule of cognition. In free play, the imagination is no longer in the service of the application of concepts. But the application of a concept was not the task Kant had in mind when he expressed enthusiasm for the French Revolution, which provided no concepts and no maxim for acting whatsoever. To judge objects and events in their freedom expands our sense of community, not because it tells us what is morally or politically justified and thus what we should do, but because it expands our sense of what is real or communicable. This affirmation of freedom would not be possible in the absence of productive imagination.

Imagination and Freedom

In Arendt's reading of Kant, the imagination is subordinated to the conceptual functions of the understanding: it has the task, outlined in the first *Critique*, of gathering representations in the successive order that is necessary for the temporal nature of inner sense and the possibility of concept application.[73] In that text, Kant famously describes the need for a synthesis of reproduction in the figure of a line. If I cannot reproduce the first parts of a line as I advance to those that follow, he argues, I cannot obtain a complete representation. But reproduction itself would be in vain if I could not recognize that all the different parts of the line belong to one total unit. Imagination allows for the production of the synthetic connections among discrete representations that the mind needs to conform to this temporal nature, without which there would be no cognition of objects but only a series of particulars: *this* and *this* and *this*. But if imagination were limited to the recognition of what we see now as what we saw before, why would Kant and also Arendt associate it with freedom, which requires us to recognize not the sameness of particulars but their singularity and contingency?

Another way to put this question is to ask how the role of imagination in judgment raises the problem of knowledge as a form of recognition. In chapter 1 we saw that in empirical judgments of sex difference, the understanding applies concepts that transform the "[s]omething in the world [that] forces us to think," to borrow Deleuze's felicitous phrase, into something that is known.[74] That there are bodies that do not correspond to one of two sexes is an empirical fact, I argued, the denial of which sounds like a failure of cognition but is actually a refusal to allow this something to disturb the faculty of the understanding and its application of concepts to particulars. It is a refusal to count something, for which there is no rule of cognition, as part of our common world and, instead, to present it (by means of reproductive imagination) and to subsume it (by means of determinant judgment) under the rule of our two-sex system and thereby render it "knowable" through an act of recognition.

The problem, then, is how to present something to the judging faculty for which we lack a concept and the linear temporality of reproductive imagination in concept application. Such temporality was the source of what Arendt, citing Kant, called "the embarrassment of 'speculative reason in dealing with the question of the freedom of the will . . . [namely] a power of *spontaneously* beginning a series of successive things and states.'"[75] In the second volume of the *Life of the Mind* (discussed in chapter 2), Arendt shows how the association of freedom with the will leads to an impasse: within the rectilinear time order every act of the will, the moment we reflect upon it, seems to come under the sway of causality. Whether they could not reconcile this power of beginning a new series of acts and states with the time continuum that this new series interrupts; feared the awesome responsibility that the notion of free will imposed on human beings; or could find no meaning in the contingency that defines willed acts, philosophers and "men of action" alike, says Arendt, have been led to deny the will due to its inevitable connection with freedom. The point, of course, is not to save the idea of free will but rather to affirm free action, that is, our capacity to begin anew.

In the *Critique of Judgment*, freedom is portrayed as a predicate of the power of imagination and not of the will, and the power of imagination is linked with that wider manner of thinking, which is political thinking par excellence, in Arendt's view, because it enables us to think from standpoints not our own. But if this ability is to yield the freedom-affirming view of the spectator; if it is not to end in an enlarged empathy or be little more than a poor substitute for actual dialogue, then surely imagination must be creative, not reproductive. In the third *Critique*, Kant describes such a power of imagination as the faculty of presentation (*Darstellung*), not merely reproduction (*Vorstellung*). He writes, "This power [imagination] is here not taken as reproductive, where it is subject to the laws of association, but as productive and spontaneous (as the originator of chosen forms of possible intuitions)." Indeed, Kant asserts, "in a judgment of taste, the imagination must be considered in its freedom" (*CJ*, §22, p. 91), that is, not as in any way tied to empirical laws of association. Unconstrained by "a determinate concept of an object," the faculties of understanding and imagination are in "free play" (ibid.).

Imagination is not autonomous, but neither is it subordinate. Its role is still that of mediating between intellect and sensibility, but this is better understood in the broadest terms as that of presentation or exhibition rather than schematization and representation.[76]

Nowhere in Kant's work is the productive force of imagination more visible than in book 2 of the *Critique of Judgment*, the "Analytic of the Sublime." Mostly missing from Arendt's account, the Kantian sublime shows the limits of the reproductive imagination for thinking about that which has no rule of cognition and no promise of form under existing concepts.[77] "In relation to the [mathematical] sublime," as Rudolph Makkreel observes, "the imagination is claimed [by Kant] to institute a 'regress' that annihilates the conditions of time and is related not to concepts of the understanding, but to ideas of reason."[78] The imagination, striving to comprehend the infinite, is threatened with loss of itself, for it cannot do what reason demands: present totality.[79] Reaching the limits of its reproductive power to present absent objects in a time progression, the imagination "is induced to strive for . . . a reconsideration of its relation to time," writes Makkreel.[80] This reconsideration involves "the possibility of negating the mathematical or linear form of time," which strikes a blow at that which is most important for the reproductive imagination and thus for recognition in a concept: the very possibility of succession.[81]

The failure of reproductive imagination, in turn, opens up the possibility of a different use of imagination in judgment, namely comprehending as a whole what is normally apprehended as temporally discrete and causally related. The regress makes visible a temporality that tends to be occluded from our view, that is, whenever we use the imagination strictly in its reproductive capacity, as we do whenever we make logical or cognitive judgments: namely, the noncausal, nonlinear temporality of the new.[82] Meaning or order in the sublime emerges as comprehension in an instant, rather than subsumption to the whole, which characterizes the idea of historical progress discussed at the beginning of this chapter.

Jean-François Lyotard, too, stresses the new perspective opened up by the regress of the imagination in the Kantian sublime, but in a manner fully at odds with the hermeneutical orientation of Makkreel's reading and, indeed, with any sense of coherence or meaning whatsoever. In contrast with the idea that the free play of the faculties produces coherence and meaning of a different kind, Lyotard asserts, there is a "differend" (what Kant calls a *Wiederstreit*) "at the heart of sublime feeling," namely the absolute power to conceive (reason) and the absolute power to present (imagination).[83] The heterogeneity and excessiveness of these powers in the sublime makes visible the moment—seemingly occluded in the

"Analytic of the Beautiful" and the various accounts of political judgment based on it (for example, Arendt's)—in which we are confronted with something that is unpresentable because it transcends given forms of discourse.

Thus in the aesthetic of the sublime, says Lyotard, the (reproductive) imagination's failed attempt to *exhibit* what is foreclosed or denied cultural articulation in our system of reference testifies to the presence of the unpresentable.[84] This attempt, in turn, disrupts the illusion of communicability that underlies every empirical idea of the *sensus communis*, in his view. Foregrounding the sublime over the beautiful, Lyotard not only sets the art of *streiten*—which Kant held to be proper to any interlocution over aesthetic judgments—against all communicative theories of the political, he also sets the *Wiederstreit* (or differend) that "cannot be resolved" against *any* possibility of a politically mediated agreement about community. In this way Lyotard excludes more than the *disputieren* that Habermas takes to be constitutive of a politics oriented toward mutual understanding. He excludes as well the kind of agreement or validity peculiar to democratic politics, namely, the agreement, or *übereinkommen*, reached through *streiten* and persuasion, which Arendt, too, found in Kant and took to be the form of interlocution proper to political and aesthetic judgments alike.

What Arendt sees as the very nature and contingent achievement of political speech (that is, agreement reached through persuading speech, not proofs) is for Lyotard just one more dangerous illusion of a communicative theory of politics. Indeed, Arendt's reading of Kant, claims Lyotard, is one among many "sociologizing and anthropologizing [mis]readings of [Kantian] aesthetic common sense." She mistakes Kant's notion of communicability (*Mitteilbarkeit*) for the "assent that empirical individuals give one another in regard to the beauty of an object"—as if the "universal voice" of taste were "based on a collection of votes."[85] Missing the properly transcendental meaning of the Kantian *sensus communis*, Arendt (like Habermas), contends Lyotard, fails to see that "the community required as a support for the validity of such judgment must always be in the process of doing *and* undoing itself."[86]

It is not incorrect to see in Arendt's reading of the *sensus communis* something like a *tendency* toward an empirical reduction—such a tendency also exists in Kant's own text, as Lyotard notes. What minimally supports Lyotard's reading is Arendt's neglect of the productive imagination. This neglect tilted her interpretation in an empirical direction (though she clearly never reduced the universality of a judgment of taste to anything like a vote, nor did she ever see in it a community based on consensus). This empirical reduction of community reappeared in the work of her feminist critics (Disch and Young), who, contra Lyotard, accused Arendt in effect of not being empirical enough (that is, not taking proper account of the full range of actual empirical opinions but relying instead on imaginative dialogue).

Lyotard sees something crucially important that Arendt's other critics tend to miss: the imagination, considered in its freedom, opens a *question* of community that cannot be settled by a communicative practice of politics centered on the exchange of proofs. Such a practice tends to conceal how we misunderstand precisely at those moments when we understand and also occlude from view the source of the misunderstanding. But Lyotard offers little in the way of an alternative conception of community, other than saying that it is always in process, always anticipated but never reached. This is a familiar idea taken up by feminist theorists in the wake of the collapse of women as a coherent category for constituting the political realm of feminism. Although it is clearly important to expose the exclusions that constitute community, the question remains as to how a more democratic feminist (or any other political) community based on practices of freedom might be formed. On what basis are we in community with others, and what role is played by judgments that affirm freedom in the creation of community? If Arendt's reading of Kant cannot be dismissed (with Habermas's) as yet one more example of "empirical realism" (Lyotard), it is because her interpretation of *sensus communis* is not exhausted by the notion of the empirical (sociological or anthropological), but neither is it transcendental. Rather, it is political.

Sensus Communis and the Practice of Freedom

Lyotard's critique of communicative theories of politics challenges us to rethink feminist community as that which is at once presupposed and created anew in the practice of judgment. It would be hasty to conclude that a critical practice of judgment must be articulated in relation to the aesthetic of the sublime rather than the beautiful, or that it must center on objects that are irreducibly adverse not only to cognition (conceptual determination) but also to the imagination's nonconceptual power of presentation. On the one hand, the vast majority of the objects of political judgment, like those of aesthetic judgment, are not radically resistant to presentation and representation; on the other hand, there is something that we might wish to call unpresentable in the sense that it is foreclosed, denied cultural intelligibility in our system of reference.

But then it seems—as it often does in what Ewa Ziarek calls "the rhetoric of failure," to which Lyotard's critique belongs—like the presentable and the unpresentable are our only choices, and the problem with any attempt to present the unpresentable is that it inevitably leads to the subsumption under a concept and the entire logic of recognition described above.[87] The critical literature on political community that works with the idea of the radically excluded tends to cast our choice in just these terms, while simultaneously advocating the political and cultural recognition of unintelligible lives and subjects, albeit without the normalizing gesture of recognition. But it is not clear as to how such a non-normalizing practice of recognition could obtain, that is, be in any way actualized without committing the sin of "empirical realism." Indeed, community is equated in "the rhetoric of failure" with communicability and seen as something that is by definition closed the moment it attains any sort of empirical actuality. That is why Lyotard insisted that, to remain open, community must remain an unrealizable ideal.

And there surely is something important about the argument that community must remain an unrealizable ideal, for it keeps us vigilant about the ways in which community, even at those moments when it seems most open, is constituted through some form of exclusion. In their separate critiques of gay marriage, for example, Judith Butler and Michael Warner strongly argue that the inclusion of lesbian and gay people in this institution, far from being a clear advance in their status as citizens, forecloses possibilities for sexual freedom, which has been a long-standing goal of the movement, and remarginalizes people who do not live or wish to live in couple-like relationships.[88] Whereas for liberals like Susan Okin and Martha Nussbaum, rights give the rule that leads to the progressive extension of the principle of equality to excluded groups, for Butler and Warner rights subsume a wide variety of gay and lesbian sexual practices under a rule that makes all cases look alike: the desire for marriage. The political demand for sexual freedom that is *not* a demand for the extension of marriage rights (or anything like it) is not heard as a demand for freedom, for liberal political culture can hear such a demand only in the idiom of rights. At best the demand for sexual freedom is heard as a demand for a certain kind of "lifestyle," the "freedom to be me," that is, as a claim to some kind of identity that, needless to say, has already been protected under some kind of right (for example, privacy). Outside the idiom of rights, in other words, the demand for sexual freedom appears nonsensical.

To describe these conflicting ideas of sexual freedom as radically heterogeneous, as a differend or *Wiederstreit*, is valuable insofar as such description forcefully questions the idea, central to most communicative theories of the political such as liberalism, that all conflicts are in principle resolvable—that is, so long as they put forward rational arguments which establish, by means of proofs, that a certain empirical concept corresponds to an object present in experience. The idea that one can dispute different points of view in this way fully occludes the very question of what could possibly count as proof of an empirical concept. Luce Irigaray's account of sexual difference, Butler's account of nonheterosexual practices, and Ann Fausto-Sterling's account of intersexed bodies are all examples of why such proofs fail in the absence of the shared premises (framework or paradigm) from which they are deduced. The idea that we need more evidence of practices and subjectivities that are outside the norm begs the question of what counts as a fact or as the factuality of what is said. Consequently, the resolution of such disputes tends to take the form, as each thinker shows, of recognition in a concept, which is another way of saying existential oblivion, with social and political consequences, for whatever does not fall under a concept.

This critique suggests again the limits of thinking about politics in terms of knowledge claims. "Knowledge is based on acknowledgment," as Wittgenstein showed us in chapter 1—that is, on a mode of counting something as something, which is the condition of knowledge, but also doing something in relation to what one knows (taking account of plurality, for instance). To say, for example, that the demand for sexual freedom calls for our judgment is not to foreclose cognitive or empirical questions. Rather, it is to say that a cognitive judgment of a thing's existence (that is, its function or purpose or ability to satisfy an end or a use) is not what we are being called upon to make, any more than a botanist, as Kant said, is called upon to explain the flower as a reproductive organ of a plant when he declares the flower beautiful. One can well know such things about plants, just as we know certain things about nonheterosexual practices. To judge aesthetically or politically, however, requires that we count what we know differently, count the flower as beautiful quite apart from its use, count nonheteronormative sexual practices as part of the common world, quite apart from whatever social function they might serve. Contrary to her critics' charge, Arendt's position on cognitive claims in the political realm was not: never make a cognitive judgment when you judge politically. It was: do not confuse a cognitive judgment for judging politically. Something else is required, for a political judgment reveals not some property of the object, but something of political significance about the judging subject, about "who" someone is.

As Arendt explains, "Whenever people judge the things of the world that are common to them, there is more implied in their judgments than these things. By his manner of judging, the person discloses to an extent also himself, what kind of person he is, and this disclosure, which is involuntary, gains in validity to the degree that it has liberated itself from merely individual idiosyncrasies." This "who," we recall, is a public persona, as distinguished from "what one is" (that is, ascribed identities such as race, gender, sex, and class). Judging is the world-building practice by which we discover, not simply the personal preferences of other people (which help us understand them as individuals), but the extent and nature of what we have in common. "We all know very well how quickly people recognize each other, and how unequivocally they can feel that they belong to each other, when they discover a kinship in questions of what pleases and displeases."[89] In contrast with identity or experience, both of which have served—in deeply problematic ways—to ground feminist community, the kinship based in the practice of judgment is something one discovers—or fails to discover—in the practice itself.

Like aesthetic judgment, the practice of political judgment is a way of constructing or discovering community through the articulation of individuality rather than its suppression, for this articulation will always involve taking the perspectives of others into account. Whereas agreement in science or logic excludes or tries to exclude (for example, through certain procedures or method) subjectivity, political and aesthetic judgments entail mastering one's subjectivity in certain ways, learning to make claims that take others into account and to elicit criteria in an effort to persuade them of one's own view.[90] As we saw with the Milan women, feminism has always had a difficult relationship to claims to individuality, for they appear to be at odds with claims to community (and, in certain iterations of liberalism at least, they are). In a practice of judgment (discovered by the Italians in their own way), however, the articulation of individuality is the very condition of any idea of community that is political. This sort of community is not guaranteed by membership in a particular group, be it "natural" or "social" (that is, "what" someone is), but is only possible insofar as every such guarantee is relinquished. Insofar as we impute the agreement of others when we judge aesthetically or politically, we claim to speak for them. Thus far from the guarantee of agreement, such a community always involves the risk that we will be rebuffed or find ourselves isolated from others, that is, with no sense of community at all.

Judgment is a way of constructing and discovering (the limits of) community, but this does not mean that it would or ought to translate into a blueprint for political action. If Arendt's reading of Kant comes close to affirming the existence of something like a *Wiederstreit*, it is more like the conflict between action and judgment than between the faculties. Judgment need not provide a guide for action and, in fact, may even be at radical odds with action—as it was in Kant's enthusiasm for the French Revolution. That is why Arendt, like Kant, emphasized the position of the spectator, from which one is able to see the whole without the mediation of a concept based on the presence of an interest. Spectators do not produce judgments that ought to serve as *principles* for other judgments or for action; they create, rather, the *space* in which the objects of political judgment, the actors and actions themselves, can appear, and in this sense alter our sense of what belongs in the common world.

If the world, as Arendt argues, "is the space in which things become public," then judging is a practice that alters that world. In this space, created by judging, the objects of judgment appear. She writes, "[T]he judgment of the spectator creates the space without which no such objects could appear at all. The public realm is constituted by the critics and the spectators, not by the actors and the makers. And this critic and spectator sits in every actor" (*LKPP*, 63); "spectator" is not another person, but simply a different mode of relating to, or being in, the common world. This shift in emphasis amounts to a Copernican turn in the relationship of action to judgment: without the judging spectators and the artifacts of judgment (for example, narratives and stories), action would have no meaning, it would vanish without a trace—it would not be a world-building activity. Arendt attributes this turn to Kant, but it is Hannah Arendt herself who discovers, in her idiosyncratic reading of Kant, that it is the judging activity of the spectators, not the object they judge or its maker, that creates the public space.

Calling our attention to the activity of judging as formative of the public realm, of political community, Arendt emphasizes what aesthetic theory calls practices of reception. But she seems to discount the potentially transformative and generative contribution of the object of judgment itself, as well as the creative activity of the artist, actor, or maker. By contrast with Arendt, Kant emphasizes not only the spectators but the artist and the formative power of creative imagination, the ability to present objects in new, unfamiliar ways—what he calls "genius." In his discussion of "aesthetic ideas," Kant describes the imagination as "very mighty when it creates, as it were, another nature out of the material that actual nature gives it" (*CJ*, §49, p. 182). Indeed, "[w]e may even restructure experience," and "[i]n this process we feel our freedom from the law of association (which attaches to the empirical [that is, reproductive] use of the imagination); for although it is under that law that nature lends us material, yet we can process that material into something quite different, namely into something that surpasses nature" (ibid.). This faculty of presentation "prompts much thought, but to which no determinate thought whatsoever, i.e., no [determinate] *concept*, can be adequate, so that no language can express it completely and allow us to grasp it" (ibid.). Such aesthetic presentations "strive toward something that lies beyond the bounds of experience" (hence they are called aesthetic ideas and are the counterpart of rational ideas), but they are presentations nonetheless. The faculty of presentation at work in the exhibition of aesthetic ideas, Kant writes, "expands the concept itself in an unlimited way" (*CJ*, §49, pp. 182–83).

In contrast with the *determinate* concepts we have been discussing, what we might call *indeterminate* concepts, as Salim Kemal parses Kant here, "are singular in that they organize only the material they are used to inform, cannot always warrant any general inferences about the nature of their object, and have a poetic, metaphorical, or idiomatic order."[91] The imagination can work on or order material in such a way that we are able to create out of it noncausal associations and even a new nature. If concepts themselves are not so much excluded, which is what Arendt's reading of Kant assumes, as expanded in an indefinite way, this has important consequences for how we think about our own political or aesthetic activity.

We might ask whether this concept-transforming activity of the imagination is confined to the activity of genius. Although Kant inclines to cast taste as the faculty that "clips its [genius's] wings" (*CJ*, §50, p. 188), bringing it in line with what is communicable (what others can follow and assent to), he also argues that the spectator, too (including the spectator that exists in every actor or artist), is called upon to exert imagination in trying to comprehend a work. In this way, then, our sense of what is communicable is not static but dynamic. The imagination is, after all, "in free play" when we judge reflectively, not only when we create new objects of judgment. If Arendt associates the faculty of productive imagination exclusively with genius, applauding Kant's subordination of genius to taste, that may be because she was determined to emphasize the importance of plurality in judging. In contrast with the solitary genius, "[s]pectators exist only in the plural" (*LKPP*, 63), and the need to take account of plurality, of other views, is what distinguishes a political or aesthetic judgment from a logical or cognitive one. Arendt was concerned with the creation of the public, the space in which objects of judgment appear.

But of course a text like the 1848 Declaration of Sentiments puts forward at once a collective judgment, which has been reached individually by each of its signers, and an imaginative "object," which not only serves as the occasion for future judgments but also stimulates the imagination of judging spectators and expands their sense of what is communicable, what they will count as part of the common world. Like a work of art, such a document is potentially defamiliarizing: working with what is communicable (for example, the idea, put forward in the Declaration of Independence, that all men are created equal), it does not so much exclude the use of concepts as it expands our sense of what we can communicate. Positing the agreement of all ("We hold these truths to be self-evident"), such a document creatively (re)presents the concept of equality in a way that, to cite Kant on productive imagination again, "quicken[s] the mind by opening up for it a view" (*CJ*, §49, p. 183), which is excluded by every logical presentation of the concept of equality.

We miss this creative expansion of the concept whenever we talk about the logical extension of something like equality or rights. The original concept of political equality, after all, is a determinate concept, historically constituted in relation to white, propertied male citizens. The Declaration of Sentiments did not simply apply this concept like a rule to a new particular (women). Rather, it exhibited the idea of equality much like an aesthetic idea: "a presentation of the imagination which prompts much thought, but to which . . . no [determinate] *concept*, can be adequate," to cite Kant again. Thus the "thought" that such a presentation "prompts" always exceeds the terms of the concept; "it expands the concept itself in an unlimited way" (*CJ*, §49, pp. 182–83). This expansion is not logical—the concept of equality does not contain within itself the mechanism for its own extension to disenfranchised groups—but imaginative: we create new relations between things that have none (for example, between the concept of equality and the relations between the sexes, or between the rights of man and the sexual division of labor). Every extension of a political concept always involves an imaginative opening-up of the world that allows us to see and articulate relations between things that have none (in any necessary, logical sense), to create relations that are external to their terms. Political relations are always external to their terms: they involve not so much the ability to subsume particulars under concepts but an imaginative element, the ability to see or to forge new connections.

We can judge reflectively, then, because we are not limited to *disputieren* (that is, agreement on the basis of proofs from established premises); we are capable of creating new forms or figures with which to make sense of objects and events. And we can argue about the meaning of those objects and events, contra Lyotard, without declaring a *Wiederstreit*, the impossibility of any agreement whatsoever. In this process of making sense or judging reflectively, we refuse to limit ourselves to proofs based on concepts already given and instead alter our sense of what is common or shared: we alter what Arendt calls the world. With time the forms and figures given by the reflective judgment, too, become ossified as rules (that is, judgments that serve as principles of judgment) that themselves demand the response of imagination to break up the closure of rule-governed practices, unsettling their settled instantiation in a freedom-denying mode of common sense.

What we affirm in a political judgment is experienced not as a cognitive commitment to a set of rationally agreed-upon precepts as they are encoded in, say, a constitution—though it *can* be experienced as that too—but as pleasure, as shared sensibility. "We *feel* our freedom," as Kant put it (*CJ*, §49, p. 182; my emphasis), when we judge aesthetically or, as Arendt shows, politically. This feeling is not the gratification Kant associated with what is agreeable in perception, but is based on the process of reflection whose condition is imagination and outsideness. What pleases, as Arendt reminds us, is not the object we judge "but *that* we judge it to be pleasing" (*LKPP*, 69). We take pleasure in our judgment. If the pleasure that obtains in a judgment arises not out of the immediate apprehension of the object but out of reflection (that is, it arises in relation to the nothing other than the judgment itself), then we are thrown back on ourselves and our own practice: we take pleasure in what we hold (for example, "these truths are self-evident"). *What gives us pleasure is how we judge, that is to say, that we judge objects and events in their freedom.* We don't have to hold these truths to be self-evident any more than we *have* to hold the oppression of women abominable or the rose beautiful; nothing compels us. There is nothing necessary in what we hold. That we do so hold is an expression of our freedom. In the judgment, we affirm our freedom and discover what we have—and do not have—in common. This is the simple but crucial lesson that feminists can learn from Arendt's reflections on political judgment.

Reframing the Freedom Question in Feminism

IN THE PRECEDING chapters, we have explored the stakes of a freedom-centered feminism and examined the limitations associated with thinking about feminist politics through the frames of the subject and the social questions. We have seen, for example, how our desire to be protected from power, to affirm "women" as a politically recognized identity, or to secure certain social goods can lead us to confuse constitutionally guaranteed rights with the experience of claiming political freedom. We have seen how our desire to authorize feminist public discourse can lead us to confuse knowledge claims with political claims. But how would reclaiming freedom as the raison d'être of feminism allow us to rethink the political project of feminism itself, as well as the problems of inclusion and exclusion that have beset feminism throughout its three waves?

Any answer to this question must begin by recognizing that the project of a freedom-centered feminism cannot be thought apart from the project of democratic politics more generally. Inspired by Arendt's account of political freedom, Claude Lefort observes that democracy is characterized by *"the dissolution of the markers of certainty,"* which brings about "a fundamental indeterminacy as to the basis of power, law, and knowledge, and as to the basis of relations between *self* and *other*, at every level of social life."[1] With the democratic revolution, the loss of natural and theological foundations leads to a situation in which all social and political relations are in principle open to challenge. Writes Lefort,

> There is no law that can be fixed, whose articles cannot be contested, whose foundations are not susceptible of being called into question. . . . There is no representation of a center and of the counters of society; unity cannot now efface social division. Democracy inaugurates the

experience of an ungraspable, uncontrollable society in which people will be said to be sovereign, of course, but whose identity will constantly be open to question, whose identity will remain latent.[2]

Like Arendt, Lefort emphasizes the aporetic character of political freedom, the impossibility—but also the temptation—of locating a ground or absolute on which to base the radical act of democratic political founding and to justify claims made in the people's name. Also like Arendt, he holds that it is the "public space" (rather than God, the king, or any other absolute source of authority) that assumes paramount importance in a democracy. This is the space of freedom, created and sustained by action and speech, which is irreducible to any foundational maxims or norms.

Both Lefort and Arendt invite us to emphasize contingency, indeterminacy, and ongoing debate as the condition of democratic politics, including feminism. On this view, democracy and feminism are defined by a commitment to openness and critical questioning. This celebration of the fundamental uncertainty that defines and haunts democracy resonates with the third-wave feminist claim that feminism's fundamental principles are provisional and always open to contestation. As Judith Butler observes, "That such foundations exist only to be put into question is, as it were, the permanent risk of the process of democratization. To refuse the contest is to sacrifice the radical democratic impetus of feminist politics."[3] And just as Lefort refutes the notion that the people exist prior to the speaking and acting that constitutes the public space, so, too, do many third-wave critics reject the idea that "women," as the subject of feminism, has a ground other than itself. Such a political subject comes into being only through the practice of politics, that is, though collective action, contest, and debate. Writes Butler, "'women' . . . becomes a site of permanent openness and resignifiability."[4]

Important as it is to question all claims to speak politically in someone's name (for example, that of "the people" or "women"), the idea that "the radicality of democracy . . . lie[s] in the way that the people form not so much a clear ground as the open site and object of permanent debate and contestation," argues Alan Keenan, tells only one side of the democratic revolution.[5] For a society to be *democratic*, he explains, "we must also be able to make a plausible case that the community as a whole in fact manages its own affairs, both in the sense of actively caring about and participating in collective decision-making and in terms of the quality of the decisions made—that is, in their respecting the basic equality of all citizens and in their orientation toward the common needs and concerns of the people themselves."[6] There are, Keenan explains, two competing strands of the radical promise of democracy that we need to keep in view:

> The radical promise of democracy would lie, in one sense, in the possibility of a community of equals, bound together in the common project of ruling themselves and maintaining the equality and commonality necessary to that rule and to achieving shared ends. Yet the radical nature of democracy would simultaneously reside in the experience of the basic uncertainty and questioning that comes with this "being-together-as-equals" with no ground other than that which the community members themselves determine. Whereas the radical nature of democracy on the first vision aims, at least in part, at the achievement of something like a shared identity—if only in a set of rights that all would equally enjoy—the radicality of democratic politics would, from the other angle, amount to the impossibility of ever achieving a people who could be said or seen to rule clearly.[7]

Emphasizing both the striving for commonality and the condition of openness, Keenan rightly calls our attention to the constitutive paradoxes and tension-ridden nature of democratic politics and to the fact that such conflicts cannot be eradicated—that is, not without destroying such politics. We can and ought to affirm openness, but any such affirmation will always entangle us in collective attachments. Furthermore, these less than perfectly open attachments to certain traditions, institutions, and forms of identity are the basis for any questioning or contestation of them. Just as there is no external standpoint from which to contest our beliefs, neither is there a place outside the particular forms that our democratic practices take from which we could question those practices.

The two strands of democracy just described can also be understood as expressions of the aporetic character of political freedom. It is because there is no transcendent ground or absolute upon which to base our political arrangements that any given set of arrangements or sense of community will be at once necessary and subject to question. Feminism, when it seeks prepolitical or nonpolitical grounds (for example, the shared identity of women as a natural or social group) for its claims, embraces one strand of democracy, namely, the closure necessary for the people's identity and rule; but it risks occluding the other strand, namely, the openness of contestation and revisability. Losing sight of openness, feminism gets entangled in the impossible fantasy that women could constitute a unified political group, without exclusion or remainder. Conversely, when feminism criticizes such exclusion and insists that "women" must remain "a site of permanent openness and resignifiability" (Butler), it risks losing track of its own dependence on the shared sense of community or identity that allows it to speak in the name of "women" against those who, too, claim to speak in that name. To put the same point somewhat differently, when seen from the perspective of the radical openness of democratic politics, no particular version of "women," no claim to speak in women's name, can lay claim to standing for all women. When seen from the perspective of democratic closure, however, every such claim puts forward a particular version of "women" that asserts itself as hegemonic, as speaking for all.

Feminism's Paradox of Founding

There is, then, a constitutive and ineradicable tension between openness and closure in feminism, just as there is in any democratic politics. This tension is related to the free act that calls into existence "women" as a *political* collectivity, just as the free act of political founding described by Arendt calls into existence "the people." But how can a political collectivity that does not yet exist call itself into existence as a political collectivity? This is the so-called paradox of founding that haunts feminism as it haunts democracy. If feminists have not attended to this paradox, it may be because feminism has not founded a political society akin to those brought into existence by such world-historical events as the French and American Revolutions. But, leaving aside works of fiction that vividly represent the problem of feminist founding—think of Les guérillères—feminists have founded political societies in the form of voluntary associations—think of the Milan Collective—that raise the great democratic paradox. More generally, thinking about feminism as a practice of freedom and "women" as a political collectivity presses us to engage this fundamental dilemma of democratic theory. More specifically, our concern with a nonsovereign, freedom-centered feminism presses us to ask, if feminine subjects are constituted as subjected, as feminists of all three waves in their different ways have held, how are they to engage in the free act of founding something new?

The democratic paradox of founding could be seen to animate, albeit implicitly, those strands of feminism that seek epistemological grounds for politics, such as standpoint theory. Notwithstanding attempts to equate oppression with insight, standpoint theory could never really gain critical purchase on its assumption that a subjected population like women would be ready to claim and practice freedom. That may well be because standpoint theory, covering over the abyss of freedom that characterizes the act of founding, sought extrapolitical grounds for an irreducibly political problem. It never faced up to the aporetic character of freedom itself, but instead held tightly to the idea of truth as the privilege of the disenfranchised and their political claims. What about the strands of feminist theory that reject the very idea of seeking foundations for feminist politics? Do they open the space for considering, in a feminist vein, the paradox of founding that structures the politics of democracy and its commitment to the people's self-rule? And what would it mean to think about feminist political founding, the radical and free act of constituting community anew, as irreducibly political?

Within the frames of the subject question and the social question, the paradox of founding and the constitution of political freedom might appear to be a problem of altering either feminine subjectivity or society—but how? As Rousseau, the great thinker of the paradox of founding, once put it, "In order for an emerging people to appreciate the healthy maxims of politics . . . the effect would have to become the cause; the social spirit, which should be the result of the institution, would have to preside over the founding of the institution itself; and men would have to be prior to laws what they ought to become by means of laws."[8] In other words, as Bonnie Honig parses Rousseau, "You cannot have good laws without good people, and you cannot have good people without good laws."[9] Rousseau's well-known solution to the paradox, she writes, was to create "a *deus ex machina* . . . in the figure of the founder, a good person prior to good law," who conveniently leaves after he establishes the law that will create a good people.[10] But why would the people, not yet good, recognize, understand, and accept the laws handed down by the good legislator? Isn't it rather the case, as Keenan observes, that "to establish the commonality that is necessary to the people being a [democratic] people, some such commonality must already be in place?"[11] Wouldn't the "emerging people" Rousseau describes have already to exist in order to accept the founder's laws as their own? And let us not forget that the laws must be their own if the political society is to be called democratic.

"The paradoxical task of the legislator—or rather, of all democratic political actors—then, is to make an appeal that sets the conditions for its own proper reception: one must appeal to the political community in such a way that its members will accept the regulations that will make them into the kind of (general) people able to 'hear' such an appeal," writes Keenan.[12] Such an appeal would have to "persuade without convincing," as Rousseau puts it, for the democratic principles according to which the emerging people reason do not yet exist.[13] Although such an appeal might take the form of an absolute—like the divine authority that Rousseau recommends and Arendt shows was favored by some of the French and American founders—its most important feature is that it is rhetorical: the appeal draws on the particular attachments and values already present in an "emerging people" in order to foster forms of democratic identification that are not yet present. Furthermore, the paradox of founding may be negotiated by rhetorical means, but it nonetheless persists in the form of an abyss at the heart of a democracy: there is no absolute ground upon which the people can call itself into being, and there is no point at which we can say that the people as its own ground has been constituted once and for all. "The work of (re)founding the people is thus never ending," writes Keenan. "If 'the people' ever come into existence it can only be in the form of *claims* made about them, on their behalf, or *in their name.* The paradox at the heart of the people's identity is (temporarily) bridged, that is, only through the rhetorical or argumentative force of such claims."[14]

If there is only the name with which a political collectivity calls itself into existence, then we can never be certain that speaking in that name is correct. Contrary to the claims of feminist standpoint theory, there is no extrapolitical standpoint from which we could determine the correctness of speaking in someone's name. This means that every such speaking will be inescapably political and open to question. And yet the very fact that a political collectivity such as "women" must call itself into being from a place where it does not yet exist means that there must be some form of closure. Insofar as second- and third-wave feminist theory has not been wholly blind to this constitutive condition of democratic openness and closure, it has tended to see that condition as installing a crisis at the heart of feminism: posited as a unified category given in advance of politics, "women" generates exclusions; posited as "a site of permanent openness and resignifiability," "women" precludes the possibility of speaking collectively. Although the tension between openness and closure *can* be experienced as a crisis for political actors, we have seen that it is also the irreducible condition of feminist and democratic politics. Consequently, the task cannot be to eradicate this tension but to find resources within such politics that would attenuate its effects, especially the sense that politics is not worth pursuing if it cannot secure, once and for all, the grounds of its own existence.

One way in which some feminists have tried to resolve the tension that lies at the heart of democratic politics is by framing political questions in epistemological terms. As we saw in chapters 1 and 4, feminists have been inclined to think about speaking authoritatively in someone's name as a matter of being able to provide foundations or grounds for such speaking. Thinking about political claims as truth claims, feminists have sought to underwrite their action and speech in ways that would, more or less, be unassailable as better if not correct views of the world. Those feminists who have questioned the drive toward closure implicit in this epistemological framing of politics have insisted that every claim is contestable. Insofar as they have been inclined to underwrite the possibility of radical doubt, however, they have not really escaped the hold that epistemic conceptions of politics have on feminist theory and practice. Whether they have sought to ground or to question claims to speak authoritatively in the name of women, feminists have not adequately articulated the difference between speaking about women as a demographic or social group and speaking about women as a political collectivity. To take account of this difference, we need to understand better what it means to make a political claim.

What a Political Claim Is

In the last chapter I argued that we would be mistaken to interpret political claims as truth claims, for the problem of politics is not to discover new facts about society; the facts are there to be had. The problem is for each of us to discover our position with respect to these facts: with whom am I in community?[15] This question takes for granted that, in a democracy, political freedom means that "women" or "the people" have no ground prior to their own constitution, hence they can only come into political existence through some kind of closure. But it also takes for granted that any such closure will be open to contestation. With this tension between openness and closure in mind, we can now better appreciate why political claims have a fundamentally *anticipatory* structure: we posit the agreement of others, that is, we perform an act of closure. Whether others do agree, however, is another matter and part of the openness of democratic politics itself.

Tempted to deny the predicative moment of our speaking and acting by locating a standard of correctness outside them in some idea of objective truth conditions, feminists, I've argued, have treated political claims as knowledge claims. Such claims, which can be adjudicated on the basis of giving proofs, occlude just this predicative moment of politics: *we hold, we say.* As we saw in chapter 4, the predicative moment of politics involves not the exchange of proofs but the ability to *claim* commonality (understood as affinities, similarities, and resemblances). When one

speaks politically, one speaks not only for oneself but also for others—
and those others may well speak back, that is, say whether they find themselves spoken for. As Stanley Cavell explains,

> To speak for oneself politically is to speak for the others with whom you
> consent to association, and it is to consent to be spoken for by them—
> not as a parent speaks for you, i.e., instead of you, but as someone in
> mutuality speaks for you, i.e., speaks your mind. Who these others are,
> for whom you speak and by whom you are spoken for, is not known a
> priori, though it is in practice generally treated as given. To speak for
> yourself then means risking the rebuff—on some occasion, perhaps once
> for all—of those for whom you claimed to be speaking; and it means
> risking having to rebuff—on some occasion, perhaps once for all—those
> who claimed to be speaking for you.[16]

I take Cavell to mean more than the now familiar idea that commonalities are not given in advance of politics. He points to the rather different idea that the condition of democratic politics is at once the positing
of commonalities *and* the speaking back. Only then is positing commonality a form of world-building based on the exchange of opinions through
which we gauge our agreement in judgments. The idea that speaking for
others necessarily generates exclusions and refusals and therefore should
be avoided is to miss the whole point of democratic politics. Such politics
consists precisely in the making of universal claims (speaking for), hence
in closure, and in their acceptance or refusal (speaking back), hence also
in openness. Fundamentally anticipatory in character, speaking politically
is about testing the limits to every claim to community, about testing the
limits and nature of agreement, and about discovering what happens
when the agreement breaks down or never materializes in the way we
thought in the first place, that is, when we spoke politically (in other
words, claimed to be speaking for others).

Following Arendt's account of political judgment as a practice in
which we posit the agreement of others, we have seen that feminist community—rather than being given in shared experience or identity or being
impossible due to the lack of anything shared—can be created, and created anew, through such a practice. To assume, as some third-wave feminists have, that the collapse of women as a coherent category translates
into the collapse of feminism as a political movement is to neglect both
the predicative moment of politics and the community-constituting
moment of political judgment. It is as if the category itself secured, or
failed to secure, the ability to make political claims.

Indeed, these constitutive moments of our own political activity remain invisible to us when we think about politics as turning on the stability or instability of concepts like "women" under which to subsume particulars. Most feminist theorists of the second wave and some of the third assumed that women is a category to be applied like a rule to particulars (for example, differences). Some feminists of both waves objected, arguing that there is no such coherent category to be applied. If their protests led to a sense of crisis in the 1990s, I argued in chapter 1, it is because these critics did not develop an alternative to the idea of politics as a means-ends activity involving rule application.

What if we thought of "women"—that is, women as the collective political subject of feminism, rather than as a social or "natural" group— not as a category to be applied like a rule in a determinant judgment but as a claim to speak in someone's name and to be spoken for? If such a claim can only be anticipatory, then it is always in need of agreement and consent. This agreement is *posited* (for example, others, too, *ought* to agree with my judgment about who "women" are and what they demand), which means it is not "there" from the start, given, say, in the very logic of concept application. Rather, the agreement is what we at once take for granted and hope to achieve whenever we take the risk— and let us not forget that it is a risk—of speaking politically.

To recognize the fundamentally anticipatory structure of political claims is to understand why feminism cannot avoid the universal. There are, of course, ways of constituting the universal that are not at all anticipatory or world-opening but merely the filling or completion of a prior determination, where universal is that which unfolds logically or socially according to a pregiven logic (for example, the logic of rights). As Ernesto Laclau has powerfully shown, the idea of universality appropriate to democratic politics is not One, for it does not rely on the correct application of concepts but on the contingently based public practice of soliciting the agreement of others to what each of us claims to be universal.[17] The universal is not a process of subsuming particulars under rules but a practice of making political claims in a public space, a space that, as both Arendt and Lefort hold, is constituted through the very practice of making such claims.

If we consider the struggle for "women's human rights," we can see how speaking politically can forge associations not given in the logical relations of determinate concepts themselves. First incorporated into the United Nations legislation at the 1993 World Conference on Human Rights, the statement "Women's rights are human rights" signified a different way of thinking about feminist struggle in the context of shared practices. As Charlotte Bunch and Samantha Frost explain, "A woman's human rights framework equips women with a way to define, analyze, and articulate their experiences of violence, degradation, and marginality. Finally, and very importantly, the idea of women's human rights provides a common framework for developing a vast array of visions and concrete strategies for change."[18] The point here is not that the framework came before the practice (that is, was handed down by the few—the "theorists"—like a set of precepts to the many), nor that the framework defines in a unilateral way what kinds of problems can arise and be solved; rather, the framework arises and is sustained and transformed only through the shared practice of claiming "women's rights as human rights" in relation to the concrete but varied conditions of women's lives. Indeed, not only did the framework arise in response to perceived shortcomings in earlier paradigms for feminist struggle (for example, "Sisterhood is global"), it also went through numerous changes, which reflected the difficulties associated with building international political alliances around a Western concept of "women" and also with the androcentrism that attached to the classic UN formulation of "human rights."

In some sense, the claim "Women's rights are human rights" can be understood as an expression of common sense or what rhetorical theory calls "common places." Bunch and Frost write,

> On the one hand, the idea of women's human rights makes common sense. It declares, quite simply, that as human beings women have human rights. Anyone would find her- or himself hard-pressed to publicly make and defend the contrary argument that women are not human. So in many ways, the claim that women have human rights seems quite ordinary. ("Women's Human Rights")

That the claim both is and is not ordinary in the sense of commonly accepted is likewise obvious; otherwise there would be no need to make the political claim. To make the claim is not simply to say what is obvious because it is already given in the premises (as, say, a syllogistic logic would have it: human beings have rights, women are human beings, ergo women have human rights). Rather, it is to hold something that cannot be argued—not simply—in the manner of giving proof. Political artifacts such as rights don't expand by means of an intrinsic logic that every rational person would have to accept; they are claims made by some individuals or groups that seek to persuade others, too, to *hold* them valid.

It is important for feminists not to lose sight of the predicative moment of claim making and the common world in which political claims can be heard and realized. As Lefort argues in his discussion of the French Declaration of the Rights of Man and the American Declaration of Independence, "[T]he naturalistic conception of right masked an extraordinary event."[19] For each declaration "was in fact a self-declaration, that is, a declaration by which human beings . . . erected themselves into their own judges, their own witnesses."[20] Likewise, Arendt emphatically stresses the radical conventionality of rights, the artificiality of the political principle of equality, and political membership as the condition of "the right to have rights." She questions the idea that this "right to have rights, or the right of every individual to belong to humanity, should be guaranteed by [one's membership in] humanity itself."[21] It is only as members of political communities that human beings have rights; "a man who is nothing but a man has lost the very qualities which make it possible for other people to treat him as a fellow man," Arendt observes.[22]

The appeal to nature as the basis for women's human rights can blind us to the fundamental and radical act of claiming them and also to the existence of a common world in which those claims are more than mere abstractions, in which rights claims have political weight. If a self without a public persona, or what Arendt calls "the mask" that affixes to individuals as citizens with rights and duties, is unprotected, then the putatively natural basis of human rights may be an effective rhetorical device for extending rights to disenfranchised peoples and groups, but it is not without political costs.[23] To say, therefore, that women qua human beings are entitled to rights risks missing the deeply political character of all rights claims and the common world that is their condition. Once rights are seen as having to be claimed rather than discovered (in nature), moreover, they become radically uncertain. As Lefort writes, "[B]y reducing the source of right to the human utterance of right, they [the French and American revolutionaries] made an enigma of both humanity and right."[24] Rights are never established once and for all, because it is only in the act of claiming them that the so-called ground of those rights ("man" or "humanity") comes into existence.

Although the questioning of community that belongs to making new rights claims is an expression of the openness of democratic politics, Lefort also suggests that such claims have as their condition democratic closure. Every attempt to redefine who the people are through the making of new rights claims takes for granted a prior definition of "the people." Demands for new rights have to be articulated in a political language whose terms the disenfranchised do not set. "One of the preconditions for the success of any demand is the widespread conviction that the new right conforms to the demand for freedom enshrined in existing rights," observes Lefort.[25] It was only once a majority of workers and nonworkers recognized the rights to strike and to organize unions "as a legitimate extension of the right to freedom of expression or the right to resist oppression," says Lefort, that these new rights were won.[26] It was only once men and women recognized the right to abortion and birth control as a legitimate extension of the right to privacy and the right to bodily integrity, we might add, that these new rights too were won. Thus the act of persuading members of the community to accept a new right must appeal to the current sense of who the community is and thus its values. This means that the potentially radical character of new demands will be attenuated by the values that exist and, what is more, that some demands will never get heard at all, save as legitimate extensions of what exists. That is why the radical demand for sexual freedom, as we saw in chapter 4, is so easily neutralized by the demand for gay marriage and inscribed within the liberal logic of the right to privacy.

Understanding the real constraints under which political actors must operate in a democracy, we can better appreciate the difficulties faced by feminists who have tried to introduce the idea of sexual difference into the political declaration of equality. Like every political struggle within the history of feminism, the struggle for women's human rights involves both a demand for equality and a demand for difference. On the one hand, what Joan Scott called the "paradox" that constitutes modern feminism only arises within the frame of logic (and its principle of contradiction).[27] According to an understanding of politics as a logical discourse based on the application of determinate concepts, to claim at once equality and difference is to contradict oneself. In a discursive political universe of A and not-A, one must choose—and for women, as the Milan Collective protested, this amounts to an impossible choice. On the other hand, this paradox expresses the aforementioned constraints on introducing a radically different version of "the people" into public debate, for example, inscribing sexual difference into the people or political collectivity in a way that does not undercut women's claims to equality.

At any given moment, then, it can seem that there is a particular version of "the people" or the political community that is effectively invulnerable to challenge and that sets the terms of every questioning of its legitimacy. The same applies of course to the political collectivity called "women." The third-wave feminist demand that "women" remain permanently open and contestable is just that—a demand. It can never function as a theoretical principle that guarantees such openness. There is no such guarantee, neither in feminist theory nor practice. Whether we judge any particular feminist community or idea of "women" to be legitimate in democratic terms will turn on its availability for questioning. But there is no neutral place from which we could so judge. The idea that a formal procedure could provide the guarantee of equal access to any debate about who is included in the feminist community, as advocates of Habermas's discourse ethics suggest, does not adequately address the question of what such access can mean if a certain version of the community is more or less invulnerable to question, or if the kind of questioning that can occur must remain within the parameters of what constitutes a certain definition of "women."[28]

A commitment to open debate and questioning and to putting in place procedures that facilitate them clearly matters, only there will be no procedure that will guarantee the realization of—and no place outside the particular form of community we want to question from which to judge whether we are living up to—that commitment. There is not only no procedure but also no feminist theory of politics that could provide the criteria according to which such a judgment could be made. There is only the practice of freedom, of making political claims in particular contexts that question the reigning idea of "women," contexts that also set the terms of that questioning. This is cause for despair only on the view that feminism could find in its theories release from the difficult and unruly work of democratic politics. But isn't this temptation, understandable as it is, just one more attempt to cover over the abyss of freedom?

Feminism Is a World-Building Practice

If we think about feminism as a conflict-ridden, world-building practice of freedom which no theory can adjudicate, we can begin to move away from the debates over women as a coherent category that raged through the 1990s and that continue to define the agenda of many feminist theorists today. Those debates were concerned with challenging shared experience as the basis for feminism, but they tended to remain beholden to a notion of critique that is skeptical. In her critical interpretation of Judith Butler, for example, Joan Copjec holds that the so-called historicist claim that there can be no general category of women—because, historically speaking, the concept of women is continually changing—is presumptuous: "The truth of this assertion is simply not available to a historical subject."[29] Copjec does not defend "the collectibility of women into a whole," but, like Butler, challenges it and "all efforts at coalition politics" based on it.[30] But her approach, like the early work of Butler, is distinctly inflected by the problem of knowledge examined in chapter 1. Citing

Kant's response to both dogmatists and skeptics in the first *Critique* regarding claims about the existence of the world (that is, the world as an object of knowledge), Copjec concludes her critique of Butler, claiming that all that can be said of woman/women, like the world, must take the form of an "indefinite judgment."[31] We can neither affirm nor deny that women as a unified group or category exist any more than, according to Kant, we can affirm or deny the existence of the world.

The problem with this approach to the question of political community based on claims to commonality is that, caught within the problem of empirical knowledge that defines the project of Kant's first *Critique*, it remains tied to a strictly epistemological conception of what such world-constituting claims are. Kant's response to both skepticism and dogmatism in the *Critique of Pure Reason*, after all, merely contests their competing but related conclusions about whether the world as such can be known; it does not contest the more fundamental assumption, shared by skeptic and dogmatist alike, that our basic relation to the world is one of knowing. By contrast with the overwhelming concern to secure empirical knowledge that characterizes that work, the third *Critique* distinguished between a "theoretical judgment" (which has objective universality, contains an "is or is not," and pertains strictly to matters of cognition and truth), on one hand, and an "aesthetic judgment" (which has subjective universality, refers not to the object but the subject, and makes no cognitive claim whatsoever), on the other hand. Following Arendt, I suggested that feminists turn not to the first *Critique*, which is Copjec's main text, but to the third, for when it comes to politics, to cite Kant on aesthetics, "what we want to know is not whether we or anyone else cares, or so much as might care, in any way about a thing's existence, but rather how we judge it in our mere contemplation of it."[32] At issue in social relationships and bodies that do not conform to the concepts of sexual dimorphism, for example, is not simply the cognitive judgment of their existence—as if we did not know of it—but the reflective judgment of how they, in their singularity, will count for us. To speak with Cavell, it is not a matter of what we *know*, but what we will *acknowledge*, that is, count as part of our common world and in this way accord value.

More specifically, when it comes to feminism what we want to know is not whether women/woman exists (for example, in the form of a social group bound by shared experience), but what "women/woman" means for those who make a claim to speak politically in that name. Such speaking might result in further sedimentation of a norm, but it might also transform the norm, "expand the concept in an indefinite way," to cite Kant. Whether speaking in the name of "women" secures a prior definition of women or opens that definition to contest, debate, and imaginative refiguration is something that feminist political actors *simply cannot know* prior to that speaking. If we *should* choose to hold an "indefinite judgment" about women/woman, then, that is not because the category itself is secured as indefinable or precluded from public debate by virtue of what can count as a legitimate object of knowledge. Although Copjec does not rely on the notion of truth to adjudicate public debate, she uses the impossibility of declaring the truth of a political claim or judgment as an occasion to foreclose debate from the start. Rather than being a practice of making "indefinite judgments," as Copjec would have it, politics is about making claims and judgments—and having the courage to do so—in the absence of the objective criteria or rules that could provide certain knowledge and the guarantee that speaking in women's name will be accepted or taken up by others.

"The very urgency, the *a-scholia*, of human affairs demands provisional judgments, the reliance on custom and habit, that is, on prejudices."[33] Arendt's point here, of course, is not to endorse prejudices; it is to call our attention to the fact that the practice of judgment always makes reference to an agreement in judgments that is not available for empirical testing but, rather, is the very basis for anything that we count as empirical. Although this agreement, as Wittgenstein showed us, is by no means unrevisable, it is not something that we ordinarily put into doubt; rather, it serves as the ungrounded ground of our doubting practices. In Arendt's view, the idea that practices of freedom such as action or judgment must put such an agreement into doubt (that is, that a practice of freedom consists in just such an act of radical doubt) is not only philosophically wrongheaded but also politically so. If politics is the realm of the probable, not the certain; of opinion, not truth—hence politics can no more be a science for Arendt than aesthetics could be for Kant—then a politics like feminism that seeks to change social relations such as gender cannot be— not simply—a practice of doubt.

If it has been difficult to imagine a feminist political practice that did not begin with radical doubt, that is because our two-sex system—though we surely can and do raise questions about criteria—has an always-already-there quality that tempts us to see sexual difference itself as quasi-transcendental, the condition at once of human subjectivity and practice. To say, as a Lacanian thinker like Copjec does, that the symbolic law of sexual difference is an empty or merely formal rule of subject constitution without any particular social content risks not taking seriously enough the concern that what we call symbolic might well be what Butler calls "the sedimented ideality of the norm."[34] Butler is right, in my view, to say that we can concede that sexual difference is "radically conditioned without claiming that it is radically determined," and that we can insist on the possibility of transforming its structures without returning to "classical notions of freedom"—but how?[35] Clearly, the transformation of a norm like sexual difference requires that we do more than raise radical doubts about the norm, as if it, and the particular idea of "women" the norm expresses, were not always already the condition of whatever doubts we raise and alternative political community we constitute.

Recovering Feminism's "Lost Treasure"

A freedom-centered feminism would strive to bring about transformation in normative conceptions of gender without returning to the classical notion of freedom as sovereignty that all three waves of feminism have, in their different ways, at once accepted and rejected. Such feminism would be a world-building practice that changes political freedom from the "I-will" into the "I-can." This I-can is nothing other than the public persona described earlier, what Arendt called "the mask" of citizenship and the rights and duties that correspond to being a member of a political community. I-can belongs to women neither as a sex nor a gender, neither as a "natural" nor a social group. I-can belongs, rather, to "women" as a political collectivity, and it obtains in the practice of speaking in women's name (which involves speaking for others, being spoken for, and speaking back). I-can is the nonsovereign freedom of feminists as citizens engaged in word and deed, who are committed to the irreducibly non-natural basis of political membership.

Arendt teaches that it is only by respecting the artificiality or conventionality of the public sphere, its fundamentally non-natural character, and by wearing the mask that the self is able to disclose itself beyond categories of social membership, that is, in its uniqueness and distinction. Recall that such disclosure is not of "what" one is, but "who" one is. The mask facilitates the emergence of a (feminist) subject that is neither identical with the mask itself nor with the "what" that wears the mask, be it the social attributes of sex, race, and class or the singularity that pertains to being me and no other who shares those attributes. Without the mask, without "the tremendous equalizing of differences which comes from being citizens of some commonwealth," writes Arendt, people are "thrown back . . . on their natural givenness, on their mere differentiation." Although the political principle of equality always threatens to eradicate this differentiation, she recognizes, the paradox is that without equality and the rights of citizenship, natural and social differences, including sexual difference, have no place in the world. Once "deprived of expression within and action upon a common world," Arendt observes, difference "loses all significance."[36] It has, as it were, no political voice, no say in how this world of ours will look, what we see and hear in it, what will count for us and how.

Any attempt to alter norms of gender or take non-normative account of sexual difference, then, cannot avoid the political as the practice of freedom and the constitution of the in-between space of the common world. "It is the space between them that unites them, rather than some quality inside each of them," to cite again Margaret Canovan's account of the Arendtian difference between a community based in "what" someone is (that is, in identity) and one based in "who" someone is (that is, in world-building).[37] My point throughout this book has not been to rule out the "what," that is, the questions of subjectivity and identity that have preoccupied feminists. It has been to insist that the kind of transformation envisioned by thinkers who focus on these questions—if it is not to be restricted to individual cases that can then be written off as anomalies—requires the tangible and intangible political relations that Arendt calls a worldly in-between: that which at once relates us and separates us. It is in this space of the common world that differences become meaningful and the newly thinkable, other ways of constituting identities and configuring social arrangements such as gender, appears.

Something like the quest for the newly thinkable is visible in Arendt's account of the American founding. Faced with the abyss of freedom, the men of the American Revolution were prompted to search for an absolute to legitimate the novelty of their act, the founding of political freedom. If what those men sought was a figure for symbolizing their creation, what they found, it would appear, was nothing but what was there all along, namely the founding legends of the West, which they hoped would ground their free act in precedents, thereby concealing "the arbitrariness inherent in all beginnings."[38] What they could not see as they searched for a causal chain that would lead from liberation to freedom, from a no-longer to a not-yet, claims Arendt, was that beginning carries its own principle within itself: "beginning and principle, *principium* and principle, are not only related to each other, but are coeval," that is, what legitimates beginning is beginning itself.[39]

If the men of revolution, as "they ransacked the archives of antiquity," were looking for a rule to guide them or a principle to justify their actions, writes Arendt, what they found instead were "paradigms to guide their own intentions," models that could be imitated.[40] Their search yielded no absolute that could be applied in rule-like fashion, then, but examples of a universal rule that we cannot state, to invoke again Kant's account of a reflective judgment. Their search, after all, was for something that cannot be expressed in the form of a rule, but only figured in the form of an example and as part of a practice, namely freedom itself.

The same of course can be said of Wittig's global feminist revolution, the Milan Collective's new social contract, and the Seneca Falls Declaration of Sentiments. In each case we return to beginnings and legitimate the principle of political freedom through the claim to political freedom itself (for example, "*We hold* these truths to be self-evident"). In each case feminists demanded freedom and, in demanding it, offered figures of the newly thinkable as well as themselves in the form of examples that, if we would rightly attend to them, might well facilitate the shared practice of recovering our lost treasure of political freedom: that which cannot be proved like a truth or possessed like a substance, but only practiced or enacted by present and future generations of feminists.

INTRODUCTION

1. See Christina Hoff Sommers, *Who Stole Feminism?: How Women Have Betrayed Women* (New York: Simon & Schuster, 1995); Daphne Patai, *Heterophobia: Sexual Harassment and the Future of Feminism* (Boston: Rowman & Littlefield, 1998); Katie Roiphe, *The Morning After: Fear, Sex, and Feminism on Campus* (Boston: Little, Brown, & Co., 1993); Camille Paglia, *Sexual Personae: Art and Decadence from Nefertiti to Emily Dickinson* (New York: Vintage, 1991).

2. The first wave of American feminism, whose diversity and radicalism is domesticated by the term *suffrage movement,* is a case in point. Nancy Cott observes,

> Any attempt to sum up the meanings and accomplishments of the nineteenth-century woman movement inevitably betrays the several strands of interests and approaches and convictions, as well as conflicts, within it. Even within the groups most clearly identifiable and best documented—that is, the national and state associations formed to pursue the specific goal of woman suffrage—changing composition, shifting priorities, and fateful alliances can easily be pointed out. The issues of whether to ally—and if so with whom—perpetually recurred. The post–Civil War rift between Elizabeth Cady Stanton and Susan B. Anthony and their colleagues in abolition and women's rights, Lucy Stone and Henry Blackwell, over the relative priority of black male suffrage and woman suffrage, is well known. The change over time from Stanton's and Anthony's fiery leadership in the 1860s to the NAWSA [National American Woman Suffrage Association] leadership in 1900, indebted to temperance and social purity advocates, is now often stressed in histories of the woman suffrage movement. These represent only a fraction of the controversies and tensions, the different emphases in ideology, means, and alliances among constituents of the aggregate woman movement.

Nancy Cott, *The Grounding of Modern Feminism* (New Haven, CT: Yale University Press, 1987), 18.

3. To take just one example, the feminist movement in New York City is commonly traced to the emergence of two groups: New York Radical Women (NYRW)

and the National Organization for Women (NOW). In early 1969 members of NYRW (e.g., Ellen Willis, Shulamith Firestone, Carol Hanish, and Kathie Sarachild) split off to form Redstockings, while the president of the New York chapter of NOW, Ti-Grace Atkinson, split off to form The October 17th Movement together with former members of NYRW, such as Anne Koedt. By the end of 1969, the October 17th Movement was called The Feminists, and its members were deeply at odds with the fundamental tenets of Redstockings (to say nothing of NOW), including its refusal of sexual separatism. Toward the end of 1969, Firestone and Koedt (who had been members of these two opposing groups) split off from their respective groups to found a third group called New York Radical Feminists, which rejected in turn the major tenets of both Redstockings and The Feminists. For an account of the deep divisions in early second-wave American feminism, see Ellen Willis, "Radical Feminism and Feminist Radicalism," in *Social Text* 0, no. 9/10 (Spring–Summer 1984): 91–118; Alice Echols, *Daring to Be Bad: Radical Feminism in America, 1967–75* (Minneapolis: University of Minnesota Press, 1989).

4. For some feminists a public realm included no men, male children, and heterosexual or married women; for others it included all these groups, but on the condition of a strict egalitarianism in the division of tasks and public speaking that Jo Freeman, writing under the pen name Joreen, called "the tyranny of structurelessness." Joreen, "The Tyranny of Structurelessness," in *Radical Feminism*, ed. Anne Koedt, Ellen Levine, and Anita Rapone (New York: Quadrangle, 1973), 285–99.

5. Hannah Arendt, *The Human Condition* (Chicago: University of Chicago Press, 1989), 11. Hereafter cited in the text and notes as *HC* with page references.

6. "It is decisive that society . . . excludes the possibility of action, which formerly was excluded from the household. Instead, society expects from each of its members a certain kind of behavior, imposing innumerable and various rules, all of which tend to 'normalize' its members, to make them behave, to exclude spontaneous action or outstanding achievement" (Arendt, *HC*, 40).

7. For a good comparative reading of Arendt and Foucault, see Amy Allen, "Power, Subjectivity, and Agency: Between Arendt and Foucault," *International Journal of Philosophical Studies* 10, no. 2 (2002): 131–49.

8. Mary Dietz, *Turning Operations: Feminism, Arendt, and Politics* (New York: Routledge, 2002). Dietz's collection of essays creatively employs Arendt's concept of action to challenge the subject-centered (and highly philosophical) orientation of contemporary feminist theory. She also provides an informative summary of the various writers who have attempted to redeem Arendt's work for feminism (132–35). See also the essays by Dietz, Bonnie Honig, and Susan Bickford in *Feminist Interpretations of Hannah Arendt*, ed. Bonnie Honig (University Park: The Pennsylvania State Press, 1995); Kimberly Curtis, *Our Sense of the Real: Aesthetic Experience and Arendtian Politics* (Ithaca, NY: Cornell University Press, 1999); Lisa Disch, *Hannah Arendt and the Limits of Philosophy* (Ithaca, NY: Cornell University Press, 1994); Jennifer Nedelsky, "Embodied Diversity and the Challenges to Law," in *Judgment, Imagination, and Politics: Themes from Kant and Arendt*, ed. Ronald Beiner and Jennifer Nedelsky (New York: Rowman & Littlefield, 2001), 229–56.

9. Hanna Fenichel Pitkin, "Justice: On Relating Private and Public," *Political Theory* 9, no. 3 (August 1981): 327–52. Pitkin argues that Arendt's critical account of the social question can more generously be read as a critique of the instrumentalist spirit or attitude that we take when we address problems like poverty. For a

reading of "the social" in Arendt's thought, see Hanna Fenichel Pitkin, *The Attack* ⊛
of the Blob: Hannah Arendt's Concept of the Social (Chicago: University of Chicago
Press, 1998); Seyla Benhabib, *The Reluctant Modernism of Hannah Arendt*
(Thousand Oaks, CA: Sage, 1996), esp. 22–34.

10. Bonnie Honig, "Toward an Agonistic Feminism," in *Feminist Inter-* ⊛
pretations of Hannah Arendt, ed. Bonnie Honig, 135–66; quotation is from p. 143.

11. Mary Wollstonecraft, *A Vindication of the Rights of Woman*, ed. Charles
W. Hagelman Jr. (New York: Norton, 1967), 24. For an excellent account of
Wollstonecraft's challenge to the androcentric political theory canon, see Wendy
Gunther-Canada, *Rebel Writer: Mary Wollstonecraft and Enlightenment Politics*
(DeKalb: Northern Illinois University Press, 2001). Wollstonecraft's norm-defying
life became the model for the most radical elements of the nineteenth-century
women's movement, which rejected the idea, advanced by the National American
Woman Suffrage Association in the 1900s, that woman's responsibility for the
moral uplift of the race was the grounds for granting her the vote. See Cott, *The
Grounding of Modern Feminism*, 37.

12. John Stuart Mill, "The Subjection of Women," in *Essays on Sex Equality*,
ed. Alice Rossi (Chicago: University of Chicago Press, 1970). I examine Mill's
ambivalence on the question of women's freedom in Linda M. G. Zerilli, *Signifying
Woman: Culture and Chaos in Rousseau, Burke, and Mill* (Ithaca, NY: Cornell
University Press, 1994), chap. 3.

13. Cott, *The Grounding of Modern Feminism*, 30.

14. Ibid.

15. Joan Scott, *Only Paradoxes to Offer: French Feminists and the Rights of
Man* (Cambridge: Harvard University Press, 1996).

16. Denise Riley, *"Am I That Name?": Feminism and the Category of 'Women'* ⊛
in History (Minneapolis: University of Minnesota Press, 1988), 66.

17. This is a crucial point overlooked by Arendt. Had she considered it, she
might have addressed the gender issues that are so starkly absent from her political
theory.

18. Riley, *"Am I That Name?,"* 66.

19. Ibid., 48. "'Women' are overwhelmingly sociological and therefore, given
these new definitions, not political entities," writes Riley (ibid., 51). Like Arendt,
Riley sees an erosion of the private and public distinction in the rise of the social.
Arendt argues that previously private or protosocial issues get—falsely, in her
view—defined as political. Riley, by contrast, holds that political issues such as
poverty get defined as social. Thus the dislocation of the political, in Riley's view,
concerns the shrinkage of the political realm as more and more issues get redefined
as social. Riley takes for granted that the issues Arendt calls social are really political, such as poverty, housing, and wages. See ibid., 50.

20. Ibid., 51. The sexualization of delinquent groups, and the positioning of
women as both agents and objects of reform, is vividly displayed in the ambivalent
feminism of John Stuart Mill. A strong advocate of women's rights and critic of the
sexual double standard, Mill nonetheless remained hostage to the Victorian ideal of
woman as the virtuous sex responsible for the moral uplift of the race. He also
expressed a deep fear of female sexuality, which he associated literally with the thou-
sands of unemployed and underemployed women who worked as prostitutes and fig-
uratively with the entire class of the unemployed poor. Mill's anxiety about sexuality

led him to take an ambivalent position on the Contagious Diseases Acts and Poor Law Reform. It also strongly influenced his view of the sexual division of labor, which, despite his critical account of private male despotism, he never questioned. See Zerilli, *Signifying Woman*, chap. 3.

21. William L. O'Neill, *Everyone Was Brave: The Rise and Fall of Feminism in America* (Chicago: Quadrangle Books, 1971 [1969]). For a good critique of the concept "social feminism," see Nancy Cott, "What's in a Name? The Limits of 'Social Feminism'; or, Expanding the Vocabulary of Women's History," *The Journal of American History* 76, no. 3 (December 1989): 809–29.

22. Whether this included improvements in the social and economic status of women is not in question here. Claims to the political status of citizen had to be made as claims to participate in an enlarged "social housekeeping." This housekeeping keeps politics bound to a means-ends economy and women bound to traditional conceptions of femininity. Within this economy, it was only natural that women should have political rights not *despite* their difference from men, as Stanton and Anthony had argued, but *because* of it. Thus gender difference came, by the 1910s, to be an argument *for* women's rights. This change, vividly described by Cott, Scott, and Riley, is unintelligible in the absence of a broader understanding of the framing of democratic politics in terms of the social question.

23. Cited in Elisabeth Young-Bruehl, *Hannah Arendt: For Love of the World* (New Haven, CT: Yale University Press, 1982), 513n54.

24. In her feminist critique of the political theory canon, Susan Okin observed that theorists ask, what can men *do*, but what is a woman *for*? "The tendency to regard men as complete persons with potentials and rights, but to define women by the functions they serve in relation to men," argues Okin, is pervasive in the tradition of political thought, including democratic theory. Susan Okin, *Women in Western Political Thought* (Princeton, NJ: Princeton University Press, 1979), 304. The reduction of women to their social function (e.g., motherhood) is also at the heart of the early second-wave feminist critique. In *Amazon Odyssey*, for example, Ti-Grace Atkinson famously argued that patriarchal culture fails to distinguish between women's "function" and "capacity" to reproduce. The strictly functionalist view of women occludes the crucial role of power, which turns a biological capacity into a social function. Ti-Grace Atkinson, *Amazon Odyssey* (New York: Links Books, 1974), xxii.

25. Arendt, "What Is Freedom?," in *Between Past and Future: Eight Exercises in Political Thought* (New York: Penguin Books, 1993), 143–71; quotation is from p. 165.

26. Free will versus determinism is probably the most extensive debate in the history of Western philosophy. It is a debate that has strongly influenced political conceptions of freedom. The free will issue in philosophy, as Robert Kane observes, is related to a cluster of issues, including (1) moral agency and responsibility; (2) the nature and limits of human freedom, autonomy, coercion, and control in social and political theory; (3) compulsion, addiction, self-control, self-deception; (4) criminal liability, responsibility, and punishment in legal theory; (5) the relation of mind to body, consciousness, and the nature of action; (6) questions about divine foreknowledge, predestination, and evil. Robert Kane, *The Oxford Handbook of Free Will* (New York: Oxford University Press, 2002), 4. As Kane's list of related issues suggests, the social question is implicit in articulations of the problem of free will within legal theory and social and political theory. Arendt, by contrast, wants to

think of freedom apart from the social question and as a predicate of action, not will. Although I discuss the problem of the will as the faculty of freedom in the following chapters (especially chapter 2), this book does not even begin to address the voluminous literature on the problem of free will. Rather, I take up Arendt's claim that freedom is not exhausted by the idea of the *liberum arbitrium*, that is, a freedom of choice that arbitrates and decides between two given things. Such freedom is not inaugural but by definition restricted to what exists.

27. Arendt, "What Is Freedom?," 155. "Politically, this identification of freedom with sovereignty is perhaps the most pernicious and dangerous consequence of the philosophical equation of freedom and free will. For it leads either to a denial of human freedom—namely, if it is realized that whatever men may be, they are never sovereign—or to the insight that the freedom of one man, or a group, or a body politic can be purchased only at the price of the freedom, i.e., sovereignty, of all others" (ibid., 164). For an excellent account of a nonsovereign freedom from within the liberal tradition, see Richard E. Flathman, *Freedom and Its Conditions: Discipline, Autonomy, and Resistance* (New York: Routledge, 2003).

28. Two separate bodies of literature have developed around the question of freedom. The first centers on free will, the second focuses on political liberty. Philip Pettit observes that classical authors like Hobbes, Kant, and Mill did not see these issues as separate. Philip Pettit, *A Theory of Freedom: From the Psychology to the Politics of Agency* (New York: Oxford University Press, 2001).

29. Nancy Hirschmann shows that presuppositions of individual sovereignty underwrite accounts of freedom that disadvantage women. Hirschmann's topic is not freedom as action but freedom as liberty and thus "the ability of the self to make choices and act on them." Occluded in the debate on this topic is "the question of what or who the 'self' is that makes these choices," she writes. The self is taken to be rational and undivided, which, in her view, is hard to square with the lived reality of the subject's internal conflict over what choices to make. This view of "the subject of liberty" fails to consider the ways in which the rules and norms of a patriarchal society get internalized as constraints on women's very sense of choice. Hirschmann's feminist theory of freedom usefully shows the limits of theories based on concepts of sovereignty, autonomy, and individualism. It is less successful in escaping the subject-centered frame that generated *the* subject of liberty in the first place. Nancy Hirschmann, *The Subject of Liberty: Toward a Feminist Theory of Freedom* (Princeton, NJ: Princeton University Press, 2003), 4, 39, 29.

30. The tendency to model political relations on kinship relations, argues Arendt, is "the ruin of politics." Politics involves the coming together of people who are different from one another and who therefore hold different points of view on the world. Hannah Arendt, *Was ist Politik?*, ed. Ursula Ludz (Munich: Piper Verlag, 1993), 10. The idea of a sisterhood merely extends the would-be sovereign "I and myself" into an equally would-be sovereign "we."

31. Nancy Fraser, "From Redistribution to Recognition?: Dilemmas of Justice in a 'Postsocialist' Age," in *Justice Interruptus: Critical Reflections on the "Postsocialist" Condition* (New York: Routledge, 1997), 11–40. According to Fraser,

> Insofar as women suffer at least two analytically distinct kinds of injustice, they necessarily require at least two analytically distinct kinds of remedy: both redistribution and recognition. The two remedies pull in opposite directions, however, and are not easily pursued simultaneously. Whereas the logic of

redistribution is to put gender out of business as such, the logic of recognition is to valorize gender specificity. Here, then, is the feminist version of the redistribution-recognition dilemma: How can feminists fight simultaneously to abolish gender differentiation and to valorize gender specificity? (ibid., 21)

Fraser's attempt to answer this question never doubts the idea that politics is both a social question and a subject question. The point of politics in her view is to procure a good, be it the recognition of an identity or the redistribution of wealth.

32. Simone de Beauvoir, *The Second Sex*, trans. H. M. Parshley (New York: Vintage, 1989). Beauvoir accepts the philosophical (Hegelian) and anthropological (Levi-Straussian) frameworks in which the Subject is constituted in relation to an Other. What she contests is woman's permanent status as Other, her inability to transform the *en-soi* into the *pour-soi*. See ibid., xxvii–xxx.

33. In her autobiography, Beauvoir writes,

I maintained that, from the point of view of freedom, as Sartre defined it—not as a stoical resignation but as an active transcendence of the given—not every situation is equal: what transcendence is possible for a woman locked up in a harem? Even such a cloistered existence could be lived in several ways, Sartre said. I clung to my opinion for a long time and then made only a token submission. Basically [she comments in 1960] I was right. But to have been able to defend my position, I would have had to abandon the terrain of individualist, thus idealist morality, which is where we [she and Sartre] stood.

Quoted in Sonia Kruks, "Simone de Beauvoir and the Limits of Freedom," *Social Text: Theory, Culture, Ideology* 17 (Fall 1987): 111–22; quotation is from p. 111. The problem of a woman in a harem is more than a problem of subjective desire. The woman in the harem, who does not choose to leave, is not free because choosing to stay in the harem is itself contingent on the objective social circumstances of male power. Beauvoir's account of freedom here seems consistent with thinkers who emphasize objective conditions, that is, the concrete reality of actual choices. But Beauvoir also emphasizes the importance of creating options that do not exist, not simply choosing among those that are already given. For a good discussion of freedom as a problem of objective conditions, see Hirschmann, *The Subject of Liberty*, 6.

34. Beauvoir, *The Second Sex*, xxxi–xxxii.

35. Judith Butler, *Gender Trouble: Feminism and the Subversion of Identity* (New York: Routledge, 1990), 8.

36. Ibid.

37. Judith Butler, *The Psychic Life of Power: Theories in Subjection* (Stanford, CA: Stanford University Press, 1997), 29–30. "The double aspect of subjection appears to lead to a vicious circle: the agency of the subject appears to be an effect of its subordination. Any effort to oppose that subordination will necessarily presuppose and reinvoke it," writes Butler. "Luckily, the story survives this impasse." Survival is based on the possibility of "resistance within the terms of reiteration" (ibid., 12).

38. Butler rightly contests both the idea that "assuming and stating a 'subject-position' is the consummate moment of politics" and the "dismissal of the subject as a philosophical trope," but she never doubts the idea that politics is centrally concerned with the subject question (ibid., 29). On the contrary, she emphasizes the importance of this question in a critical feminism. "The question of 'the subject' is

crucial for politics, and for feminist politics in particular, because juridical subjects are invariably produced through certain exclusionary practices that do not 'show' once the juridical structure of politics has been established" (Butler, *Gender Trouble*, 2).

39. Deeply aware of this problem, theorists of subject formation such as Butler try to balance the subject-centered politics of liberal democracies with a call for disidentification, that is, "risking the *incoherence* of identity" (Butler, *The Psychic Life of Power*, 149; emphasis in the original). Leaving aside the question of what it would mean to refuse an identification that, on Butler's own account, is the very condition of the subject's social existence, she never really explains how to square such disidentification with the critical insight that politics requires a subject (i.e., it is a practice undertaken in someone's name).

40. Mary Dietz provides a useful summary of the politics of identity. She schematically divides the debates over identity into three moments: (1) ideas regarding women's distinctive difference as a group; (2) the hybridization of the group "in terms of an identity complex of race, class, ethnicity, culture, sexual identity and/or sexuality"; (3) the "designat[ion] of 'women' as an 'undesignatable field of differences, one that cannot be totalized or summarized by a descriptive identity category [Butler].'" Dietz, *Turning Operations*, 132–33. Notwithstanding these crucial differences, the movement from the first to the third moment remains characterized by a focus on questions of subjectivity. The movement is not outside the problematic of identity but rather into its negative space.

41. If we cast politics in terms of the subject question, we will tend to be drawn into the difficulties associated with the politics of recognition. Briefly summarized, says Patchen Markell, these difficulties include a "fundamental *ontological* misrecognition, a failure to acknowledge the nature and circumstances of our own [political] activity." The quest for recognition, he argues, entangles us in "a failure to recognize one's own finitude, rooted in the condition of human plurality"—it entangles us, in other words, in a fantasy of sovereignty. This fantasy need not take the classic form criticized by Arendt. Indeed, as Markell deftly shows, it may take the form of demanding political recognition of one's identity as an oppressed person or group. What persists, however, is the myopic focus on the existence or attainment of a certain form of subjectivity. Patchen Markell, *Bound by Recognition* (Princeton, NJ: Princeton University Press, 2003), 59.

42. Arendt writes, "The manifestation of who the speaker and doer unexchangeably is, though it is plainly visible, retains a curious intangibility that confounds all efforts toward unequivocal verbal expression. The moment we want to say *who* somebody is, our very vocabulary leads us astray into saying *what* he is; we get entangled in a description of qualities he necessarily shares with others . . . with the result that his specific uniqueness escapes us" (*HC*, 181).

43. "[T]he political realm rises directly out of acting together, the 'sharing of words and deeds.' This action not only has the most intimate relationship to the public part of the world common to us all, but is the one activity which constitutes it" (ibid., 198).

44. "The challenge for rethinking gender categories outside of the metaphysics of substance will have to consider the relevance of Nietzsche's claim in *On the Genealogy of Morals* that 'there is no "being" behind doing, effecting, becoming; "the doer" is merely a fiction added to the deed—the deed is everything'" (Butler, *Gender Trouble*, 25). A critique of gender identity as a substance, Butler's invocation

of Nietzsche is something that Arendt herself might accept. Arendt, too, was deeply concerned to dispute any notion of human nature. But whereas Butler's critique focuses on the subject, Arendt's focuses on the world in which the subject acts. For a good account of Arendt's challenge to traditional conceptions of identity, see Honig, "Toward an Agonistic Feminism."

45. Hannah Arendt, "The Concept of History," in *Between Past and Future*, 41–90; quotation is from p. 84. "The reason why we are never able to foretell with certainty the outcome and end of any action is simply that action has no end. The process of a single deed can quite literally endure throughout time until mankind itself has come to an end" (Arendt, *HC*, 233).

46. Most critiques of the "subject" take for granted the contingency of the world that is at issue here. My point, however, is that they tend to lose sight of the world, and contingency starts to look like it is wholly internal to the subject, be it in the form of an unconscious that undercuts the illusion of a masterful cogito or the multiplicity of subject-positions that are at play in the subject-constituting process of identification.

47. Hannah Arendt, "'What Remains? The Language Remains': An Interview with Gunther Gauss," in Hannah Arendt, *Essays in Understanding, 1930–1954*, ed. Jerome Kohn (New York: Harcourt Brace & Co., 1994), 1–23; quotation is from p. 20; my emphasis.

48. Atkinson, *Amazon Odyssey*, 49; Wendy Brown, *States of Injury: Power and Freedom in Late Modernity* (Princeton, NJ: Princeton University Press, 1995). Atkinson defined the problem of feminine subjectivity primarily in terms of the external power of patriarchal institutions like the family. Brown finds in this definition an evasion of the very thing that makes such power so destructive and tenacious, namely, the subject's deep investment in its own injury or subjection. The "tendency to externalize political disappointment by blaming failures on the character of power 'out there,'" she writes, displaces "the more sober practice of searching for political disappointment's 'cause' in our own psychic and social ranks" (ibid., xii). As I discuss in chapter 3, Brown (like other third-wave theorists of subjectification) does not dispute the idea that institutions are crucially important in understanding the effects of power, but she wants to shift the focus of the debate over freedom to an analysis of the "install[ation] of injury as identity." For such identity, in her view, keeps subjects caught in "a melancholic logic" of repeating the past, especially when they turn to the state to demand reparation (xi, 8). The subject's self-hindering, or "attachments to unfreedom," sets the terms for rethinking the possibility of freedom in late modernity, according to Brown (xii).

49. Arendt, *Was ist Politik?*, 24.

50. Two sides of the same coin, focus on the self and world-alienation are expressions of the radical doubt associated with skepticism, Arendt holds. But the subjectivism that characterizes modernity cannot be traced back in any causal fashion to the doubting practices of modern philosophy. Such a view treats ideas as if they were autonomous. "[N]ot ideas but events change the world," she asserts. The heliocentric system, for example, "is as old as Pythagorean speculation," but it is only with the invention of the telescope that this idea had the force of an event. Indeed, she declares, "the author of the decisive event of the modern age is Galileo rather than Descartes" (Arendt, *HC*, 273).

51. Michel Foucault, "The Ethics of the Concern of the Self as a Practice of Freedom," in *Essential Works of Foucault*, vol. 1, ed. Paul Rabinow (New York:

The New Press, 1997), 281–301; quotation is from p. 282. The later Foucault turns to the ancient conception of "*epimeleia heautou*, which means taking care of one's self," in order to elaborate freedom in relation to the paradoxical character of subject formation described, in his earlier writings, in terms of the disciplinary institutions of modern society. Michel Foucault, "On the Genealogy of Ethics," in *Essential Works of Foucault*, 1:253–80; quotation is from p. 269. Distinguishing such care from "simply being interested in oneself" (i.e., self-absorption or self-attachment), Foucault associates the practice of freedom with the ethical practice he calls "the relationship of the self to itself" (*rapport à soi*) or the formation of the self "as a work of art" ("The Ethics of the Concern of the Self . . . ," 284; "On the Genealogy of Ethics," 263, 262). In contrast with morality, ethics as a "practice of freedom" is not driven by social questions of utility or expediency ("The Ethics of the Concern of the Self . . . ," 284). "For centuries we have been convinced that between our ethics, our personal ethics, our everyday life, and the great political and social and economic structures, there were analytical relations, and that we couldn't change anything, for instance, in our sex life or our family life, without ruining our economy, our democracy, and so on. I think we have to get rid of this idea of an analytical or necessary link between ethics and other social or economic or political structures," observes Foucault ("On the Genealogy of Ethics," 261). Ethics based on expediency leads to ethical failure, that is, as William Connolly explains, a failure of "critical responsiveness to constituencies who have been degraded unnecessarily by the *very codifications of normality and justice currently in vogue*. . . . The ethical point is to struggle against the temptation to allow an existing code of authority or justice to dominate the field of ethics entirely." William Connolly, *The Ethos of Pluralization* (Minneapolis: University of Minnesota Press, 1995), 127; emphasis in the original. The point, then, is not to have no ethics—as Foucault's critics like to accuse—but to have a vigilantly critical relation to existing ethical codes. Furthermore, freedom requires not only that we liberate ourselves from the tyranny of whatever codes may exist but also develop alternative practices of ethical conduct, without allowing them to ossify into yet other codes that are beyond question.

52. Foucault agrees with the interviewer's comment that his understanding of ethics resonates with "Nietzsche's observation in *The Gay Science* that one should create one's life by giving style to it through long practice and daily work" (Foucault, "On the Genealogy of Ethics," 262). "What makes it [care for the self] ethical for the Greeks," observes Foucault approvingly, "is not that it is care for others. The care of the self is ethical in itself; but it implies complex relations with others insofar as this *ethos* of freedom is also a way of caring for others." Nevertheless, "Care for others should not be put before the care of oneself. The care of the self is ethically prior in that the relationship with oneself is ontologically prior" (Foucault, "The Ethics of the Concern for the Self . . . ," 287). Foucault's return to the Greeks is not a wholesale adoption of their conception of care for the self, but he clearly sees them as offering the most productive basis from which to elaborate a new ethics.

53. Notwithstanding significant affinities with Arendt (e.g., her critical view of utilitarian thinking and our tendency to follow rules of all kinds), the political dimension of care of the self or how it relates to care for the world is not immediately obvious—unless one assumes that to talk about questions of subjectivity and ethics is ipso facto to talk about politics. Asked whether care for the self could offer insights into politics, Foucault responds,

> I admit I have not got very far in this direction, and I would very much like to come back to more contemporary questions to try to see what can be made of all this in the context of the current political problematic. But I have the impression that in the political thought of the nineteenth century—and perhaps one should go back even farther, to Rousseau and Hobbes—the political subject was conceived of essentially as a subject of law, whether natural or positive. On the other hand, it seems to me that contemporary political thought allows very little room for the question of the ethical subject.

Foucault, "On the Genealogy of Ethics," 294. The connection to politics would be elaborated around the complex Foucault called "governmentality" (ibid., 300), rather than the citizen as the subject of law. Critical disseminators of Foucault's later work who want to extend his comments on ethics as a practice of freedom to the political domain include Connolly, *The Ethos of Pluralization*; Thomas Dumm, *Michel Foucault and the Politics of Freedom* (Thousand Oaks, CA: Sage, 1996); Wendy Brown, *States of Injury*; James Tully, "The Agonic Freedom of Citizens," in *Economy and Society* 28, no. 2 (May 1999): 161–82.

54. Whenever we discuss the problem of self-hindering, or what Brown, following Foucault, calls "attachments to unfreedom," it is worth recalling with Arendt that an almost exclusive concern with the relation of the self to itself was characteristic of the centuries-long debate about the internal forces of causality that hinder a subject in its freedom. "One of the most persistent trends in modern philosophy since Descartes . . . has been an exclusive concern with the self, as distinguished from the soul or person or man in general, an attempt to reduce all experiences, with the world as well as with other human beings, to experiences between man and himself" (Arendt, *HC*, 254). Foucault criticizes the philosophy of consciousness associated with Descartes, but he does not adequately criticize the focus on the self as the primary element of all social and political transformation. Foucault's reference point in these matters is of course not Descartes but Nietzsche.

55. Foucault writes, "Liberty is a practice . . . [and] the liberty of men is never assured by the institutions and laws that are intended to guarantee them. This is why almost all of these laws and institutions are quite capable of being turned around. Not because they are ambiguous, but simply because 'liberty' is what must be exercised. . . I think that it can never be inherent in the structure of things to guarantee the exercise of freedom. The guarantee of freedom is freedom" Michel Foucault, "Space, Knowledge, and Power," in *The Foucault Reader* (New York: Pantheon Books, 1984), 239–56; quotation is from p. 245.

56. Arendt, "What Is Freedom?," 153.

57. Ibid., 148. Both Arendt and Foucault return to the ancients to recover a conception of freedom as a practice, as something we must exercise in deeply quotidian ways, but they reach very different conclusions. For Arendt, the ancients had a political understanding of freedom as the I-can. For Foucault, the ancients understood freedom as the ethical relation of the self to itself.

58. Ibid., 160. Whereas philosophy, focused on the self's relation to itself, requires no more than an I-will, "independent of circumstances and of attainment of the goals the will has set," writes Arendt (citing Montesquieu), "political freedom . . . consists in being able to do what one ought to will." For the ancients as well as later political thinkers like Montesquieu, "it was obvious that an agent could no longer be called free when he lacked the capacity to do—whereby it is irrelevant whether this failure is caused by exterior or interior circumstances" (ibid., 161).

59. Ibid., 165.

60. Margaret Canovan, "Politics as Culture: Hannah Arendt and the Public Realm," *History of Political Thought* 6, no. 3 (1985): 617–42; quotation is from p. 634.

61. "[T]he term 'public' signifies the world itself, in so far as it is common to all of us and distinguished from our privately owned place in it" (Arendt, *HC*, 52).

62. This relation of rule, argues Arendt, was first introduced by Plato as an escape from action.

> The problem, as Plato saw it, was to make sure that the beginner would remain the complete master of what he had begun, not needing the help of others to carry it through [and not encountering them as obstacles either. Plato distinguishes between beginning and acting.]. . . . [A]nd the beginner has become a ruler . . . who "does not have to act at all (*prattein*), but rules (*archein*) over those who are capable of execution." Under these circumstances, the essence of politics is "to know how to begin and to rule" . . .; action as such is entirely eliminated and has become the mere "execution of orders" [which foreshadows the eventual and complete instrumentalization of politics]. Plato was the first to introduce the division between those who know and do not act and those who act and do not know, instead of the old [pre-Socratic] articulation of action into beginning and achieving, so that knowing what to do and doing it became two altogether different performances.

Arendt, *HC*, 222–23.

63. Jacques Rancière, *Dis-agreement: Politics and Philosophy*, trans. Julie Rose (Minneapolis: University of Minnesota Press, 1999), 40.

64. Ibid., 41.

65. Arendt, "What Is Freedom?," 151.

66. Ibid., 169.

67. Arendt, "The Concept of History," 88; Hannah Arendt, "Truth and Politics," in *Between Past and Future*, 227–64; quotation is from p. 243.

68. Hannah Arendt, *The Life of the Mind*, 1-vol. ed. (New York: Harcourt Brace & Co., 1978), vol. 2, "Willing," 207.

69. Hannah Arendt, *On Revolution* (New York: Viking, 1971), 225.

70. Alice Echols, *Daring to Be Bad*; Susan Brownmiller, *In Our Time: Memoir of a Revolution* (New York: The Dial Press, 1999); Susan Faludi, *Backlash: The Undeclared War against American Women* (New York: Crown, 1991).

CHAPTER ONE

1. Readers will recognize in this anecdote the pathos of third-wave debates about the category of women. As I argue below, these debates took for granted the idea that one can doubt the existence of women as the skeptic doubts the existence of empirical objects such as tables and chairs.

2. Once heralded as the successor to Woman (the masculinist monolith) and as the mark of a political constituency bound by a shared identity and common experience, women has lost its appeal as a category of feminist theory and as the subject of feminist praxis. Third-wave debates over the category of women more or less focused on the problem of exclusion: every theoretical and political claim to the category brings with it a normative conception of women that excludes those who do

not conform. Rejected by many feminists was the idea that gender identity is the basis for a political movement of women, regardless of other social differences such as race, class, or sexuality. Likewise rejected was the idea that gender is a cultural interpretation of a biological given (sex).

3. Arthur Danto, *The Transfiguration of the Commonplace: A Philosophy of Art* (Cambridge: Harvard University Press, 1981).

4. Ludwig Wittgenstein, *The Blue and Brown Books* (Oxford: Basil Blackwell, 1964), 17, 18. These uses and abuses include the production of such figures as "The Third World Woman." See Chandra Talpade Mohanty, "Under Western Eyes: Feminist Scholarship and Colonial Discourses," in *Third World Women and the Politics of Feminism*, ed. Chandra T. Mohanty, Ann Russo, and Lourdes Torres (Bloomington: Indiana University Press, 1991), 51–80.

5. The phrase is from David Pears, *The False Prison: A Study of the Development of Wittgenstein's Philosophy* (Oxford: Clarendon Press, 1988), 2:488.

6. Judith Butler, *Gender Trouble: Feminism and the Subversion of Identity* (New York: Routledge, 1990).

7. Cornelius Castoriadis, *The Imaginary Institution of Society*, trans. Kathleen Blamey (Cambridge: MIT Press, 1987), 69. Hereafter cited in the text and notes as *IIS* with page references. Castoriadis argues that Marxism sought to reformulate the relationship between theory and praxis. The task of theory was not to establish eternal truths but to think the product of human activity so as to alter our social arrangements. Marx's attempt to recast the relationship of theory to praxis never bore fruit, says Castoriadis, for what began as an attempt to critique capitalism "rapidly becomes an attempt to explain this economy in terms of the operation of laws independent of the action of men, groups or classes." With praxis reduced to the mere realization of predictive theoretical laws, "It is no longer a matter of transforming the world instead of interpreting it. It is a matter of thrusting to the fore the one and only true interpretation of the world, which assures that it must and will be transformed in the sense deduced by the theory" (Castoriadis, *IIS*, 66). Theory became restricted to knowing, while praxis came to be associated with doing as the application of rules. This view of theory is especially evident in second-wave socialist feminist texts like Alison Jaggar's *Feminist Politics and Human Nature* (Totowa: Rowman & Allanheld, 1983). For an insightful critique of Jaggar and the idea of a total theory, see Kirstie McClure, "The Issue of Foundations: Scientized Politics, Politicized Science, and Feminist Critical Practice," in *Feminists Theorize the Political*, ed. Judith Butler and Joan Scott (New York: Routledge, 1992), 341–68.

8. Hannah Arendt, *The Human Condition* (Chicago: University of Chicago Press, 1989), 227.

9. Hannah Arendt, "'What Remains? The Language Remains': A Conversation with Gunther Gauss," in *Essays in Understanding, 1930–1954*, ed. Jerome Kohn (New York: Harcourt Brace & Co., 1994), 1–23; quotation is from p. 23.

10. "Plato was the first to introduce the division between those who know and do not act and those who act and do not know, instead of the old articulation of action into beginning and achieving, so that knowing what to do and doing it became two altogether different performances" (Arendt, *The Human Condition*, 223). Ideally the philosopher is the one who knows and rules on the basis of that knowledge. Arendt sees this distinction between knowing and doing, rulers and ruled, as an attempt to

NOTES TO PAGES 38-39 | 195

"[e]scape from the frailty of human affairs into the solidity of quiet and order," which has defined the Western tradition of political philosophy (ibid., 222).

11. The list of feminist works that foreground the centrality of epistemic issues to feminist politics would be too long to cite here. The so-called foundations debate of the 1990s was just one example of how central the idea of justification has been to feminism. As I argue in chapter 4, Susan Hekman's claim that "feminist politics are necessarily epistemological" represents not only a contemporary attempt to resurrect standpoint theory but a more general claim about feminism's need for an epistemology, without which it is assumed that feminists cannot make persuasive political claims and would have no discursive authority whatsoever. Susan Hekman, "Truth and Method: Feminist Standpoint Revisited," *Signs: Journal of Women in Culture and Society* 22, no. 2 (1997): 341–65; quotation is from p. 342. Seyla Benhabib likewise sees the problem of feminist politics as primarily epistemological, i.e., as involving broad questions of knowledge and justification. The project to reconstruct a postmetaphysical universalism must begin with its "epistemological deficits." Seyla Benhabib, *Situating the Self: Gender, Community and Postmodernism in Contemporary Ethics* (New York: Routledge, 1992), 13. Well-known works from the 1980s that set out the epistemological premises of feminism include Nancy C. M. Hartsock, *Money, Sex and Power: Toward a Feminist Historical Materialism* (New York: Longman, 1983); Sandra Harding and Merrill B. Hintikka, *Discovering Reality: Feminist Perspectives on Epistemology, Metaphysics, Methodology, and Philosophy of Science* (Dordrecht: D. Reidel, 1983); Catherine A. MacKinnon, *Feminism Unmodified: Discourses on Life and Law* (Cambridge: Harvard University Press, 1987). Works of the 1990s, such as those discussed here and in the following chapters, question the idea that foundations are central to feminist politics. But these works, many of which put the need for foundations into doubt, rarely interrogate the conception of politics that lies behind the quest for a grounded feminist theory, i.e., a theory that could provide foundations for action.

12. For a glimpse of the stakes in this debate, see Seyla Benhabib, Judith Butler, Drucilla Cornell, and Nancy Fraser, *Feminist Contentions: A Philosophical Exchange* (New York: Routledge, 1995).

13. James Tully, "Wittgenstein and Political Philosophy: Understanding Practices of Critical Reflection," in *The Grammar of Politics: Wittgenstein and Political Philosophy*, ed. Cressida Heyes (Ithaca, NY: Cornell University Press, 2003), 17–42.

14. Ibid.; see especially 18–35. Wittgenstein focuses our attention on the series of assumptions that do not enter our frame of reference as objects that are contemplated, defended, or contested (such as a foundation), objects that are instead the invisible "scaffolding of our thoughts," the ungrounded ground that does not get questioned—and need not get questioned for us to act reasonably—and that keeps our various language games going (Ludwig Wittgenstein, *On Certainty*, ed. G. E. M. Anscombe and G. H. von Wright, trans. Denis Paul and G. E. M. Anscombe [New York: Harper & Row, 1969], §211. Hereafter cited in the text and notes as *OC* with section references). Our concepts are held in place not only by a series of propositions that can at any moment be doubted, refuted, verified, or confirmed—in a word, known—but also by a whole series of "hinge propositions" (e.g., "I have two hands"; "The world has existed for a long time"; "Every

human being has parents") that are not indubitable in the strong epistemic sense
that the foundationalist demands and the skeptic contests, but which are unlikely
candidates for doubt under ordinary conditions. These propositions form the
groundless framework (constituted through actions) rather than a foundation
(constituted by reasons) within which we play the language games of doubting, and
distinguish true and false. What stands fast for us is not a foundation, a piece of
noninferential knowledge, as the skeptical problematic would have it, but a series
of acts or trainings (*Abrichtungen*) in which the meanings of words are intimately
connected to human practices. As Wittgenstein writes, "Children do not learn that
books exist, that armchairs exist, etc. etc.—they learn to fetch books, sit in armchairs, etc. etc." (Wittgenstein, *OC* §476). I discuss these point in Linda M. G.
Zerilli, "Doing without Knowing: Feminism's Politics of the Ordinary," *Political
Theory* 26, no. 4 (August 1998): 435–58.

15. Anne Fausto-Sterling, "The Five Sexes: Why Male and Female Are Not
Enough," in *The Sciences* (March/April 1993): 20–25. At least 4 percent of the population is born intersexed, i.e., with some mixture of male and female characteristics. Depending on how one classifies them, there are five sexes, maybe more. Our
culture's surgical enforcement of heteronormativity on the intersexed infant is
symptomatic of its deep investment in the idea of sexual dimorphism. Proponents
of that idea say it reflects the facts of biology, but Fausto-Sterling says it is a social
norm posing as a fact of nature.

16. For a similar line of argument, see Martine Aliana Rothblatt, *The Apartheid
of Sex: A Manifesto on the Freedom of Gender* (New York: Crown Publishers,
1995). Like Anne Fausto-Sterling, Rothblatt (vice-chair of the Bioethics Sub-
committee of the International Bar Association and herself a transsexual) argues
that our two-sex system cannot accommodate the plurality of sexes and genders.
She contests standard criteria for sex difference, such as chromosomal differentiation and genitals, which she finds as irrelevant to one's place in society as skin tone.
The book argues for fundamental changes in our language and concludes with an
International Gender Bill of Rights.

17. Wittgenstein, *OC* §110, §§124–31.

18. Ludwig Wittgenstein, *Philosophical Investigations*, 3rd ed., trans. G. E. M.
Anscombe (New York: MacMillan, 1968), §§242, 241. Hereafter cited in the text
and notes as *PI* with section references. "If language is to be a means of communication there must be agreement not only in definitions but also (queer as this may
sound) in judgments. This seems to abolish logic, but does not do so.—It is one thing
to describe methods of measurement, and another to obtain and state results of
measurement. But what we call 'measuring' is partly determined by a certain con-
stancy in results of measurement" (*PI* §242). Wittgenstein's point here is that definitions are useless unless one knows how to apply words in certain contexts. The
facts obtained through the practice of measurement do not account for the practice
itself (though if we did not have agreement in those facts, we would not have what
we call measurement). "'So you are saying that human agreement decides what is
true and what is false?'—It is what human beings *say* that is true and false; and they
agree in the *language* they use. This is no agreement in opinions but in form of life"
(*PI* §241).

19. Second-wave feminist theory staked itself on the universality of the meaning
of concepts like "female" and "woman." The price was the inability to talk about
particulars or differences. Such theory exemplifies the tendency to think about words

as definitions that have meaning quite apart from any practice or context in which they are applied. It is in this sense perhaps that Wittgenstein writes, "to imagine a language means to imagine a form of life" (*PI* §19). It is not that language and form of life are identical, but that unless we understand how words are applied in (the) daily practice (of our own or other cultures), we cannot know what they mean. If Wittgenstein is right, concepts such as "female" mean something to us only in and through a particular practice in which the concept is applied in a specific context. What we call the general meaning of the word is an indication of the similarity it has for us in and across related practices of use. This discerned similarity—what he calls a "family resemblance"—is no more given in the rule for the application of the word than it is in something "objective," i.e., outside our practices of use. The rules themselves do not constrain their own implementation—this will always depend on the application itself. Though shared ways of applying concepts will be related to a certain consistency in results, form of life indicates something more than agreement in matters of fact; it is not reducible to, let alone guaranteed by, an accumulation of agreements in particular cases. Likewise, however, that we agree in form of life does not guarantee that we will agree in matters of fact, only that we will *recognize* cases of disagreement as just that, cases in which we disagree. Should these cases of disagreement (or uncertainty) far outnumber those of agreement, we may well revise (as did the Olympic Committee) the criteria for judgment.

20. As Cavell observes, "The idea of agreement here is not that of coming to or arriving at an agreement on a given occasion, but of being in agreement throughout, being in harmony, like pitches or tones, or clocks, or weighing scales, or columns of figures. That a group of human beings *stimmen* in their language *überein* says, so to speak, that they are mutually voiced with respect to it, mutually *attuned* top to bottom" (Cavell, *The Claim of Reason* [Oxford: Oxford University Press, 1979], 32).

21. Hilary Putnam, "Is Semantics Possible?," in *Philosophical Papers*, vol. 2, *Mind, Language and Reality* (Cambridge: Cambridge University Press, 1975), 139–52; quotation is from pp. 140–41. Putnam's concern is to show that terms are used referentially rather than attributively: we can refer to things in the world without predicating of them certain characteristics that they *must* share to count as members of a class. What interests me here is less the theory of direct reference than the implications his account has for our understanding of concepts as fixed.

22. Cavell writes,

In ordinary or official cases of criteria, while *judges* are not to alter the criteria they appeal to, there *is* an authority that has authority to change criteria [e.g., the Olympic Committee], set up new ones if the old, for some purposes, are inconvenient or unreliable . . .; that is, if the old do not allow one to make judgments for which the criteria are set up in the first place. Whereas in Wittgenstein's cases it is not clear what it would mean to alter our criteria. The "agreement" we act upon he calls [in *Philosophical Investigations*] "agreement in judgments" (*PI* §242), and he speaks of our ability to use language as depending upon agreements in "forms of life" (*PI* §241). But forms of life, he says, are exactly what have to be "accepted"; they are "given." Now the whole thing looks backwards. Criteria were to be the bases (features, marks, specifications) on the basis of which certain judgments could be made (non-arbitrarily); agreement over criteria was to make possible agreement about judgments. But in

Wittgenstein it looks as if our ability to establish criteria depended upon a prior agreement in judgments. [In fact,] [t]o say that in ordinary cases the authority can change their criteria is to say that they have some shared prior judgment about what the general results should be.

Cavell, *The Claim of Reason*, 30–31.

23. Ibid., 46.

24. Cavell, *Must We Mean What We Say?* (Cambridge: Cambridge University Press, 1976), 52. "We begin to feel, or ought to, terrified that maybe language (and understanding, and knowledge) rests upon very shaky foundations—a thin net over an abyss" (Cavell, *The Claim of Reason*, 178). This sense of vertigo leads us to search for a guarantee for meaning, such as the realist conception of rules.

25. Saul Kripke, *Wittgenstein on Rules and Private Language* (Cambridge: Harvard University Press, 1982).

26. Ibid., 97.

27. Ludwig Wittgenstein, *Bemerkungen über die Grundlagen der Mathematik*, collected work in 8 vols. (Frankfurt am Main, 1984), 6:§32, p. 334.

28. Donald K. Barry, *Forms of Life and Following Rules: A Wittgensteinean Defense of Relativism* (Leiden: E. J. Brill, 1996), 19. Barry emphasizes this point because it was the charge of idealism that Kripke's solution to the skeptical paradox was meant to answer.

29. Wittgenstein makes only five references to "form of life" in *Philosophical Investigations*. See Barry, *Forms of Life and Following Rules*, 87.

30. Recall the travails of the Olympic Committee, which suggest in what the difference between form of life and matters of opinion might consist. The debate over the criteria for femaleness arose in response to disagreement about particular cases. At a certain point it seemed that the criteria were not serving their function, which was to provide the standard according to which agreement in particular cases could be reached. Agreement and disagreement about such cases can only take place within language, i.e., against the background of agreement over the application of concepts or uses of terms, which Wittgenstein calls "agreement in judgments" or "form of life." Were that not the case, the Olympic Committee would have thrown in the towel on deciding who counts as female rather than opting for a new test (even if it was the old test).

31. According to Rorty, when Wittgenstein writes, "What has to be accepted, the given, is—so one could say—*forms of life*" (*PI*, II, 11, p. 226), he teaches that "ethnocentrism," understood as an epistemological position, is "an inescapable condition—roughly synonymous with 'human finitude.'" Liberal projects that seek to justify our moral standards to people who do not share our form of life, says Rorty, are doomed from the start. The liberal's justifications will inevitably run out, and reaching bedrock, he will be forced to conclude with Wittgenstein: "This is simply what I do" (*PI* §217). Richard Rorty, *Philosophical Papers*, vol. 1, *Objectivity, Relativism, and Truth* (Cambridge: Cambridge University Press, 1991), 15. Rorty distinguishes between two uses of the term *ethnocentrism*. In response to the hostility that his use of the term aroused in leftists, he seeks to clarify that ethnocentrism is an epistemological position, not simply a political statement of loyalty to bourgeois democracy.

32. Responding to the imaginary interlocutor who asks how we can instruct someone to follow a rule, Wittgenstein writes, "If that means 'Have I reasons?' the

answer is: my reasons will soon give out. And then I shall act, without reasons" (*PI* §211).

33. The idea that our actions are rational only if we can give reasons for them, or that they are rational in the absence of such reasons, sets us in search of a theory that would account for all future contingencies. Such a theory would function like a rule, like those rails to infinity, telling us what to expect from any practice. If I know that my practices must be and can be justified, then I know in advance of any actual application of a rule that my words and actions can have no meaning whatsoever unless I can give reasons for them. That is the position advanced by thinkers like Jürgen Habermas. Alternatively, if I know that my practices cannot be justified (at bedrock), then I know, also in advance, that I cannot speak meaningfully to someone who does not already share them. That is the position advanced by Rorty. However different, both positions remain caught within the justification problematic that Wittgenstein questions.

34. Judith Butler, "Contingent Foundations," in *Feminists Theorize the Political*, ed. Judith Butler and Joan Scott, 3–21; quotation is from p. 7.

35. Ibid., 7.

36. Butler's concern is with the philosophical notion of an "I" that stands over and against a world of objects and is master of its own discourse. See Butler, *Gender Trouble*, 144.

37. Ibid., 136. Gender is a convention that is constituted through the stylized repetition of acts and secured by community agreement: "Gender is, thus, a construction that regularly conceals its genesis; the tacit collective agreement to perform, produce, and sustain discrete polar genders as cultural fictions is obscured by the credibility of those productions—and the punishments that attend not agreeing to believe in them; the construction 'compels' our belief in its necessity and naturalness" (ibid., 140). Drag reveals the compulsory performance of gender we never see as such.

38. Like "the substantive I" on which it is based, gender identity "only appears as such through a signifying practice that seeks to conceal its own workings and to naturalize its effects" (ibid., 144). The central issue for Butler here is not so much the refutation of foundationalist thinking but the exposure of the constitutive effects of this signifying practice and the logic of exclusion that it supports.

39. Ibid., 149.

40. Ibid., 110; emphasis added.

41. Ibid., 137; emphasis in the original. Contesting feminist critiques that find drag degrading to women, Butler writes, "As much as drag creates a unified picture of 'woman' (what its critics often oppose), it also reveals the distinctness of those aspects of gendered experience which are falsely naturalized as a unity through the regulatory fiction of heterosexual coherence" (ibid.).

42. Ibid., 140; emphasis in the original.

43. Judith Butler, *Bodies That Matter: On the Discursive Limits of Sex* (New York: Routledge, 1993), 232. Butler's critics focus on three problems in her account of drag: first, the idea of gender as performance smacks of voluntarism; second, the idea of gender qua drag deprives gender of any sense of realness; and third, drag is hardly a political answer to the tenacious and ubiquitous heteronormativity Butler describes. Responding to these criticisms in *Bodies That Matter*, Butler acknowledges that gender cannot be like drag. Gender is a series of repeated and largely

unreflective acts, whereas drag is not. To equate gender with drag, moreover, would be to efface the distinction between the parodic citation of a norm and the forcible citation of a norm, thus inviting the charge of voluntarism. Whereas *Gender Trouble* seemed to suggest that performativity is the same as performance, *Bodies That Matter* insists on their difference: "performance as bounded 'act' is distinguished from performativity insofar as the latter consists in a reiteration of norms which precede, constrain, and exceed the performer and in that sense cannot be taken as the fabrication of the performer's 'will' or 'choice'; further, what is 'performed' works to conceal, if not to disavow, what remains opaque, unconscious, unperformable. The reduction of performativity to performance would be a mistake" (ibid., 234).

44. Butler, *Gender Trouble*, 138.

45. Ibid., 140.

46. Butler, *Bodies That Matter*, x.

47. Ibid.

48. Ibid., 10.

49. Jacques Derrida, *Limited INC*, trans. Samuel Weber (Evanston, IL: Northwestern University Press, 1988), 126. "Austin does not ponder the consequences issuing from the fact that a possibility—a possible risk—is *always* possible, and is in some sense a necessary possibility. Nor whether—once such a necessary possibility of infelicity is recognized—infelicity still constitutes an accident. What is a success when the possibility of infelicity [*échec*] continues to constitute its structure?" (ibid., 15) For a good comparative reading of the similarities and differences between Derrida and Wittgenstein, see Martin Stone, "Wittgenstein on Deconstruction," in *The New Wittgenstein*, ed. Alice Crary and Rupert Read (London: Routledge, 2000), 83–117.

50. Judith Butler, *Excitable Speech: A Politics of the Performative* (New York: Routledge, 1997), 151.

51. This temptation is parasitic on the temptation to think about a rule as something that, to have meaning, compels us. As the figuration of rules as rails suggests, "all the steps are really already taken"—"I have no choice." But "my description," Wittgenstein adds, "only made sense if it was to be understood symbolically.—

> I should have said: *This is how it strikes me*.
> When I obey a rule, I do not choose.
> I obey the rule *blindly*. (*PI* §219)

The point here is not to affirm the lack of choice when we follow a rule, as if that lack indicated the compulsory nature of rule-following. Rather, it is to highlight the temptation to think about rule-following as something characterized by necessity, where it is the rule that determines how we are to follow it quite apart from our actual practice of following it in specific contexts. The idea of choice is only the other face of such necessity.

52. Butler, *Excitable Speech*, 151.

53. Ibid.

54. The idea of interpretation goes hand in hand with the idea of failure, so necessary to the deconstruction of the normative in Derrida's (and Butler's) account. As Martine Stone observes, "To say that an interpretation is required in order to determine the normative reach, and hence the meaning, of a sign, is to say that there could

have been, and may be in the future, some other interpretation. Interpretations function as the space of other *possible* interpretations. So if we manage to embrace the thesis that to understand is to interpret, then, in such an account of what understanding is, we shall be exhibiting the possibility of 'misunderstanding' as essential" (Stone, "Wittgenstein on Deconstruction," 87–88). Once interpretation is in play, we are on skeptical territory, for the rule-following paradox described above is premised on the idea that every rule requires another rule to interpret it, and so on in an infinite regress.

55. Butler, *Excitable Speech*, 148.

56. Ibid., 145.

57. "Rather than clarify understanding, the interpretational explanation just displaces the problem of understanding one step back, to the proffered interpretation. How is it to be understood, and so on?" (Tully, "Wittgenstein and Political Philosophy," 37) Any way a person follows a rule could be made out to accord with the rule on this account of understanding as interpretation. Wittgenstein's answer to the paradox is to say that there is a way of following a rule that is not an interpretation (*PI* §198).

58. "An interpretation is a reflection on a sign; an opinion or belief about how it should be taken. To interpret a sign is to take it *as* one expression rather than another. In contrast, to understand a sign is not to possesses a sedimented opinion about it or to take it *as* something, but to be able to grasp it; that is, to act with it, using it in agreement and disagreement with customary ways" (Tully, "Wittgenstein and Political Philosophy," 40).

59. Wittgenstein, *PI*, II, 11, pp. 193e, 194e.

60. Tracy Strong explains, "We do not feel that we are testing the form of the rabbit; there is no real possibility of calling the rabbit into question, hence there is nothing to falsify or prove" (*The Idea of Political Theory* [Notre Dame, IN: University of Notre Dame Press, 1990], 96). The point is not to exclude the possibility that we could call the rabbit into question or that no context could arise in which we would feel the need to do so (e.g., it is a dimly lit room and I can barely see the figure: "Is that a rabbit?"). Assuming we can see clearly, the figure is clearly drawn, and we have the concept of a rabbit, we will not sense the need to test what we see.

61. Wittgenstein, *PI*, II, 11, p. 195; emphasis in the original (translation altered). The English translation of the passage, "Man '*hält*' auch nicht, was man bei Tisch als Essbesteck erkennt, *für* ein Essbesteck," is "One doesn't *take* what one knows as the cutlery." The German verb, translated by the English "knows," is *erkennen*. However, the primary meaning of *erkennen* is not "to know" but "to recognize." The entire discussion is about seeing and immediately grasping something as part of an unreflective practice. Indeed, the importance of the passage turns on understanding the difference between seeing as a form of knowing and seeing as a form of acting. One sees the cutlery at a meal as one moves one's mouth while eating.

62. Tully, "Wittgenstein and Political Philosophy," 39. See also Wittgenstein, *OC* §204; Ludwig Wittgenstein, *Zettel*, ed. G. E. M. Anscombe and G. H. Wright, trans. G. E. M. Anscombe (Oxford: Basil Blackwell, 1967), §§234–35.

63. Ludwig Wittgenstein, *Remarks on the Philosophy of Psychology*, vol. I, ed. G. E. M. Anscombe and G. H. Wright, trans. G. E. M. Anscombe (Oxford: Basil Blackwell, 1980), §427.

64. Wittgenstein, *PI*, II, 9, p. 212.

65. If I see the rabbit (after seeing the duck), that is because I have the concept "rabbit." If I see drag, that is because I have the concept "drag." If I see a woman, that is because I have the concept "woman." Under normal conditions, it makes as little sense to say "I am seeing this woman as a woman" as "I am seeing this fork as a fork." It *can* make sense to say that, but the sense comes from a certain language game in which seeing something as something is in play.

66. Butler, *Bodies that Matter*, 237.

67. Butler, *Gender Trouble*, 136.

68. The conditions of doubt are not universalizable in large part because neither are those of certainty. Certainty, on Wittgenstein's account, is not of a piece but a highly differentiated practice, and a doubt is not without an end but has its conditions. There is the kind of analytic certainty that we express in propositions such as 2 + 2 = 4. There is the certainty that we have about propositions that we have never so much as articulated, such as "The front door to my house does not open onto an abyss." Then there is the even deeper certainty, as Jules David Law explains, that "regards matters we wouldn't know *how* to doubt—certainties for which we couldn't even imagine or construct a recognizable counterbelief." Wittgenstein gives an example of this sort of certainty when he "asserts the impossibility of clearly and genuinely doubting that he has a hand." Jules David Law, "Uncertain Grounds: Wittgenstein's *On Certainty* and the New Literary Pragmatism," *New Literary History* 19, no. 2 (Winter 1988): 319–36; quotation is from p. 321. For the passages on doubting one's hand, see Wittgenstein, *OC* §§24, 54, 125, 247.

69. The certainty expressed in statements like "I have two hands" is fundamental to Wittgenstein's account of rule-following. There is a way of applying basic concepts that is subject neither to doubt nor justification, as it would be on a truth-conditional account. When I say "I have two hands," this judgment can be neither justified nor questioned for there is nothing more certain than my having two hands on the basis of which I could judge. One can imagine a language game in which doubting one's hands played a role, but that would always be in relation to a practice and thus to a context.

70. On this point, see Law, "Uncertain Grounds," 322. As the following passage indicates, the taken-for-granted background of our language games is on Wittgenstein's account by no means frozen or fixed:

> It might be imagined that some propositions, of the form of empirical propositions, were hardened and functioned as channels for such empirical propositions as were not hardened but fluid; and that this relation altered with time, in that fluid propositions hardened, and hard ones became fluid. The mythology may change back into a state of flux, the river-bed of thoughts may shift. But I distinguish between the movement of the waters on the river-bed and the shift of the bed itself; though there is not a sharp division of the one from the other. . . . And the bank of that river consists partly of hard rock, subject to no alteration or only to an imperceptible one, partly of sand, which now in one place now in another gets washed away, or deposited. (Wittgenstein, *OC* §§96–97, 99)

New candidates for doubt are always possible, just as present candidates may no longer be. The mistake is to confuse our ability to give reasons with our ability to play a language game, to follow a rule in ways that others would recognize as following it.

71. Law, "Uncertain Grounds," 322.

72. On these doubts, see Zerilli, "Doing without Knowing," 444–46. In each case Wittgenstein explores the various ways in which he might respond to his doubt: "What if it *seemed* to turn out that what until now had seemed immune to doubt was a false assumption? Would I react as I do when a belief has proved to be false? Or would it seem to knock from under my feet the ground on which I stand in making judgments at all? . . . Would I say 'I should never have thought it!' or would I (have to) refuse to revise my judgment because such a 'revision' would amount to annihilation of all yardsticks" (Wittgenstein, OC §92). One way of responding to this threat to his world-picture, says Wittgenstein, would be to doubt his doubt: "If something happened (such as someone telling me something) calculated to make me doubtful of my own name, there would certainly also be something that made the grounds of these doubts themselves seem doubtful, and I could therefore decide to retain my old belief." Another way would be to experience a conversion (OC §§516, 578). And so on. Certainty is not of one kind, neither is doubt.

73. As Wittgenstein puts this point, "If the true is what is grounded, then the ground is not *true*, nor yet false" (Wittgenstein, OC §205).

74. Cornelius Castoriadis, "Logic, Imagination, Reflection," in *World in Fragments: Writings on Politics, Society, Psychoanalysis, and Imagination*, ed. and trans. David Ames Curtis (Stanford, CA: Stanford University Press, 1997), 246–72; quotation is from p. 258.

75. Cornelius Castoriadis, "The Discovery of the Imagination," in *World in Fragments*, 213–45; quotation is from p. 242.

76. Ibid.

77. Cornelius Castoriadis, "The Imaginary: Creation in the Social-Historical Domain," in *World in Fragments*, 3–18; quotation is from p. 6.

78. Ibid., 7.

79. Castoriadis, "Logic, Imagination, Reflection," 269. "Reflection appears when thought turns back upon itself and interrogates itself not only about its particular contents but also about its presuppositions and its foundations. . . . Genuine reflection is therefore, ipso facto, a challenging of the given institution of society, the putting into question of socially instituted representations" (ibid, 267).

80. Ibid., 271; Castoriadis, "The Imaginary," 8.

81. These are different concepts, and to see the relationship of the one to the other is like, as Wittgenstein suggests, seeing a "bare triangular figure for the picture of an object that has fallen over." And "To see this aspect of the triangle requires *imagination*" (PI, II, 11, p. 207).

82. Ibid., p. 204.

83. See Castoriadis, "Logic, Imagination, Reflection," 262–64; Butler, *Gender Trouble*, 5.

84. Castoriadis defines *theory* in this way: "More generally, we may say that an important new theory—that of Newton, Einstein, Darwin, or Freud himself. . . .— is never a simple 'induction,' any more than it is the mere product, 'by subtraction,' of the 'falsification' of previously existing theories. It is, *under constraint of the data* (this is what in fact empirical knowledge as well as 'falsification' amount to), the positing of a new imaginary figure/model of intelligibility" (Castoriadis, "Logic, Imagination, Reflection," 270–71).

85. Ibid., 271.

86. Stanley Cavell, "Knowing and Acknowledging," in *Must We Mean What We Say?*, 238–66; quotation is from p. 257.

1. Immanuel Kant, *Critique of Pure Reason*, trans. Paul Guyer and Alan Wood (Cambridge: Cambridge University Press, 1977), B478. Quoted in Hannah Arendt, *The Life of the Mind*, 1-vol. edition, vol. 2, *Willing* (New York: Harcourt Brace & Co., 1978), 205. Hereafter cited in the text and notes as *LMW* with page references.

2. See, for example, Hélèn Vivienne Wenzel, "The Text as Body/Politics: An Appreciation of Monique Wittig's Writings in Context," *Feminist Studies* 7, no. 2 (Summer 1981): 264–87; Nina Auerbach, *Communities of Women: An Idea in Fiction* (Cambridge: Harvard University Press, 1978); Namascar Shaktini, "Displacing the Phallic Subject: Wittig's Lesbian Writing," in *The Thinking Muse*, ed. Jeffner Allen and Iris Marion Young (Bloomington: Indiana University Press, 1989), 195–210. Wenzel observes that Wittig's novels "take the reader on a journey through time and space, self and other, language and culture, to arrive ultimately at a genesis of a new language, and its redefinition of woman" (Wenzel, "The Text as Body/Politics," 275). An appreciative reader of Wittig, Wenzel is not wrong to see in this redefinition the creation of all "female worlds," but her analysis tends to reproduce the very category of lesbian fiction that Wittig herself contests. As I discuss below, Nina Auerbach expresses her distress at the loss of the "female subject" in those all-female worlds. Namascar Shaktini, in contrast, recognizes that Wittig's project goes way beyond the politics of inversion and the typical idea of "lesbian fiction." I have addressed some of the problems with the reception of Wittig in "The Trojan Horse of Universalism: Language as a 'War Machine' in the Writings of Monique Wittig," *Social Text: Theory/Culture/Ideology* 25–26 (1990): 146–70; "Rememoration or War? French Feminist Narratives and the Politics of Self-Representation," *differences: A Journal of Feminist Cultural Studies* 3, no. 1 (1991): 1–19.

3. According to Kant, phenomena must be reproducible in successive moments, for a representation takes time to be completed in my consciousness. But "if I were always to drop out of the thought the preceding representations (the first part of a line, the antecedent parts of the time period, or the units in the order represented), and did not reproduce them while advancing to those that follow, a complete representation would never be obtained" (Immanuel Kant, *Critique of Pure Reason*, A102). Furthermore, the reproduced representation must belong to the same whole as the present representations to which it is added. "If we were not conscious that what we think is the same as what we thought a moment before, all reproduction in the series of representations would be useless. For it would in its present state be a new representation which would not in any way belong *to the act whereby it was to be gradually generated*. The manifold of the representation would never, therefore, form a whole since it would lack that unity which only consciousness can impart to it" (B134; emphasis added). I discuss this problem of the time sequence as it relates to freedom in chapter 4.

4. Critically discussing the relationship of the possible to the real, Bergson writes,

> The fault of those doctrines—rare indeed in the history of philosophy—which have succeeded in leaving room for indetermination and freedom in the world, is to have failed to see what their affirmation implied. When they spoke of indetermination, of freedom, they meant by indetermination a competition between possibles, by freedom a choice between possibles—as if possibility was not created by freedom itself! As if any other hypothesis, by affirming an ideal pre-

existence of the possible to the real, did not reduce the new to a mere rearrangement of former elements! As if it were not thus to be led sooner or later to regard that rearrangement as calculable and foreseeable! By accepting the premiss [sic] of the contrary theory one was letting the enemy in. We must resign ourselves to the inevitable: it is the real which makes itself possible, and not the possible which becomes real.

Henri Bergson, *The Creative Mind: An Introduction to Metaphysics*, trans. Mabelle L. Andison (New York: Citadel Press, 1992), 104.

5. As Arendt explains, philosophers like Kant, among other thinkers, saw "proof" of spontaneity in artistic creation (*LMW*, 183).

6. Cornelius Castoriadis, "The Discovery of the Imagination," in *World in Fragments: Writings on Politics, Society, Psychoanalysis, and the Imagination*, ed. and trans. David Ames Curtis (Stanford, CA: Stanford University Press, 1997), 213–45; quotations are from pp. 223, 245. Castoriadis develops his idea of the first imagination by following a line of thought in book 3 of Aristotle's *De Anima*.

7. Monique Wittig, "The Site of Action," in *The Straight Mind and Other Essays* (Boston: Beacon Press, 1992), 90–107; quotation is from p. 91.

8. Ernesto Grassi, "The Roots of the Italian Humanistic Tradition" and "Rhetoric as the Ground of Society," in *Rhetoric as Philosophy: The Humanist Tradition*, trans. John Michael Krois and Azizeh Azodi (Carbondale: Southern Illinois University Press, 2001), 1–17, 68–101; quotations are from pp. 8 and 97.

9. Grassi, "Rhetoric as the Ground of Society," 98.

10. Ibid., 97. Castoriadis calls upon Aristotle to make a similar point: "The imagination in general, and the first imagination in particular, can be defined as one of the potentialities (or powers) of the soul that permits the latter to know, to judge, and to think" (Castoriadis, "The Discovery of the Imagination," 243).

11. Ernesto Grassi, "Language as the Presupposition of Religion: A Problem of Rhetoric as Philosophy?" and "Rhetoric as Philosophy," in *Rhetoric as Philosophy*, 102–14, 18–34; quotations are from pp. 105 and 20. The reduction of fantasy and of *ingenium* to conventional understandings of artistic practices such as literature confirms the privilege accorded rational language in the Western tradition. Within this tradition, as Grassi argues, fantasy, metaphor, and every form of figurative language are ascribed to the areas of rhetoric and literature. Ernesto Grassi, *Die Macht der Phantasie: Zur Geschichte abendländlischen Denkens* (Königstein: Athenäum Verlag, 1979), xvii; on fantasy as the activity of "letting appear," see 184–87.

12. Monique Wittig, "On the Social Contract," in *The Straight Mind and Other Essays*, 33–45; quotations are from pp. 41, 40, 41.

13. Like Arendt, I do not want to limit the notion of spontaneity to artistic creativity. Ontologically I want to locate it in the faculty of *ingenium*, the ability to see associations in otherwise discrete phenomena (Grassi and Castoriadis). Politically I want to locate it in the practice of freedom, associating with others in public (Arendt). Both of these conceptions are at odds with the philosophical tradition of Kant and most of his critics. Heidegger, for example, who was critical of Kant's "recoil" from the transcendental imagination in the B edition of the first *Critique*, was also hostile to the Italian humanist tradition, from which we have the idea of *ingenium*. Ernesto Grassi, *Einführung in die humanistische Philosophie: Vorrang des Wortes* (Darmstadt: Wissenschaftliche Buchgesellschaft, 1986), 17.

14. Wittig, "On the Social Contract," 45.

15. According to Arendt, "Every attempt to derive the concept of freedom from experiences in the political realm sounds strange and startling because all our theories in these matters are dominated by the notion that freedom is an attribute of will and thought rather than of action. And this priority is . . . derived from the notion that . . . 'perfect liberty is incompatible with the existence of society,' that it can be tolerated in its perfection only outside the realm of human affairs." Unmoored from its origins in the political sphere of doing and acting, modern freedom "ceased to be virtuosity . . . and became sovereignty, the ideal of a free will, independent from others and eventually prevailing against them." Contesting this antipolitical conception of freedom, Arendt protests: "If men wish to be free, it is precisely sovereignty they must renounce." Hannah Arendt, "What Is Freedom?," in *Between Past and Future: Eight Exercises in Political Thought* (New York: Penguin Books, 1993), 143–72; quotations are from pp. 155, 163, 165.

16. Wittig, "On the Social Contract," 45. This attempt to found the new order in oneself is part of the practice of literature and gives rise to a text like *Les guérillères*. That text, however, makes visible a space that is public, not private, in character and based on voluntary association with others.

17. Wittig sometimes refers to the universal subject of her writings as a "sovereign subject." Nevertheless, what she understands under sovereignty has nothing in common with the subject that Arendt criticizes. On the contrary, her sovereign subject is only possible in the sphere of human plurality. Wittig articulates a distinction between the freedom of the I-will and that of the I-can when she proclaims, first, that feminists "can form 'voluntary associations' here and now, and here and now reformulate the social contract as a new one," only to conclude that "if ultimately we are denied a new social order, which therefore can exist only in words, I will find it in myself." Although Wittig seems to settle here for the nonworldly freedom of an Epictetus, the bulk of her political essays as well as her fiction opposes the sovereign freedom of the I-will and insists, like Arendt, on the worldly, political freedom of the I-can. Wittig, "On the Social Contract," 45.

18. According to Butler, Wittig's work is situated

> within the traditional discourse of the philosophical pursuit of presence, Being, radical and uninterrupted plenitude. In distinction from a Derridean position that would understand all signification to rely upon an operational *différance*, Wittig argues that speaking requires and invokes a seamless identity of all things. This foundationalist fiction gives her a point of departure by which to criticize existing social institutions. The critical question remains, however, what contingent social relations does that presumption of being, authority, and universal subjecthood serve? Why value the usurpation of that authoritarian notion of the subject? Why not pursue the decentering of the subject and its universalizing epistemic strategies?

Judith Butler, *Gender Trouble: Feminism and the Subversion of Identity* (New York: Routledge, 1989), 118. The charge of humanism misses the political project of Wittig's work, which is not to decenter the subject—although, contra Butler, that too can be found in her texts—but to create the political conditions for freedom.

19. I owe this point to conversations with Teresa de Lauretis and Namascar Shaktini. An examination of the recently published bibliography of Monique Wittig criticism, for example, shows that only a handful of its 301 entries were written after

1990. Diane Crowder and Namascar Shaktini, "Selected Bibliography of Monique Wittig Criticism," in *On Monique Wittig: Theoretical, Political, and Literary Essays*, ed. Namascar Shaktini (Urbana: University of Illinois Press, 2005).

20. Wittig, "On the Social Contract," 43, 42, 40.

21. I disagree with Judith Butler's assessment of Wittig's essays as somehow less sophisticated than, and noncontiguous with, her literary texts. The political essays set out precisely the nature of the problem that the literary texts engage: the tenacity of the two-sex system, a system that cannot be undone through the feminist practice of doubting.

22. Monique Wittig, "The Category of Sex," in *The Straight Mind and Other Essays*, 1–8; quotation is from p. 5.

23. Anne Fausto-Sterling, "The Five Sexes: Why Male and Female Are Not Enough," *The Sciences* (March–April): 20–24; Ann Fausto-Sterling, *Sexing the Body: Gender Politics and the Construction of Sexuality* (New York: Basic, 2000).

24. I am indebted to Arendt's idiosyncratic account of the Kantian distinction between reason (*Vernunft*) and intellect (*Verstand*). Whereas the faculty of reason is concerned with matters of meaning, which animate an unending process of thinking, that of intellect turns on matters of truth, which demand testable criteria. For Arendt, this distinction (between reason and intellect, thinking and knowing, meaning and truth) is at the core of her critique of the philosophical tradition. "The basic fallacy, taking precedence over all specific metaphysical fallacies, is to interpret meaning on the model of truth" (Hannah Arendt, *The Life of the Mind*, 1-vol. edition [New York: Harcourt Brace & Co., 1978], vol. 1, *Thinking*, 15. Hereafter cited in the text and notes as *LMT* with page references). Failure to register this distinction between questions of meaning and questions of truth is one of the many reasons that someone like Luce Irigaray is read as an "essentialist" (her advocacy of sexual difference, i.e., fails to question cognition of "sex difference"); why Monique Wittig is read as a "social constructionist" (her opposition to sexual difference does question the aforementioned cognition); and why it is practically impossible to establish a dialogue between them. The tendency to treat sexual difference as if it were only a matter of truth and practices of knowing characterizes not only science but feminism in the age of science.

25. As Cornelius Castoriadis explains, the phantasm is the basis of the imagination's capacity to generate images rather than merely reproduce objects absent to intuition. The discovery of the phantasm and thus the imagination is in book 3 of Aristotle's *De Anima*, where we are told that "for the thinking soul the phantasms are like sensations. . . . That is why the soul never thinks without phantasm" (3.7–8). Quoted in Castoriadis, "The Discovery of the Imagination," 217. Grassi makes a similar argument about the phantasm in *Die Macht der Phantasie*, 184–86.

26. Castoriadis, "The Discovery of the Imagination," 242. "If the soul never thinks without phantasm [as Aristotle affirms], the idea that most of the products of the imagination are false becomes insignificant. The true-or-false is uninteresting when it is a question of those functions of the first imagination that are the presentation of the object, separation and composition, and, finally and above all, the Schematism" (ibid., 241–42).

27. Ludwig Wittgenstein, *On Certainty*, trans. Denis Paul and G. E. M. Anscombe (New York: Harper, 1972), §205, §94. "The proposition is either true or false only means that it must be possible to decide for or against it. But this does not say what the ground for such a decision is like" (ibid., §200).

28. Wittig, "The Category of Sex," 8. In light of Wittig's account of an omniscient heterosexuality, it is easy to see why she might be read as trying to jump over her own shadow and construct a lesbian subjectivity which would be fully outside heterosexual norms. As Judith Butler critically interprets Wittig's project, "Lesbianism that defines itself in radical exclusion from heterosexuality deprives itself of the capacity to resignify the very heterosexual constructs by which it is partially and inevitably constituted." For Butler, the problem is attenuated in Wittig's literary texts, which use the strategy of "redeployment and transvaluation" (Butler, *Gender Trouble*, 128, 124). Wittig does not try to get outside heterosexuality— there is no outside, as she recognizes—but to disrupt it from within (what I call her "Trojan Horse strategy"). This disruption cannot be understood properly in terms of the strategy of resignification as Butler understands it. Wittig's project is to create new imaginary significations which, operating at an archaic or metaphorical level, would create the minimal conditions of visibility for that which is at best a "ghost" in heterosexual frames of reference. This approach, we shall see, also entails a continual destruction of concepts (*renversement*), including those created by the revolutionary subject of the text, because even these modified concepts tend to repeat the figures/phantasms that belong to the heterosexual social contract.

29. Bergson writes, "For the possible is only the real with the addition of an act of mind which throws its image back into the past, once it has been enacted. But that is exactly what our intellectual habits prevent us from seeing" (*The Creative Mind*, 100). Although Arendt seems to be saying that the past presents itself to us in a certain way (e.g., as necessity), her view is different from empiricist accounts that put meaning in the object. Whether we see an object under multiple aspects depends not on something in the object but on the space in which the object is seen. Totalitarian societies and mass societies, for example, are those in which objects present themselves under only one aspect.

30. This possibility, says Arendt, is suggested by the medieval philosopher Duns Scotus, who, in contradistinction to the entire philosophical tradition before him, affirms "the contingent character of processes": "the theory that all change occurs because a plurality of causes happens to coincide, and the coincidence engenders the texture of reality." This coincidence of causes, as Arendt explains, saves both freedom and necessity. To say something "is caused contingently," as Scotus does, is to affirm that "it is precisely the causative element in human affairs that condemns them to contingency and unpredictability" (*LMW*, 138, 137, 138).

31. The point here is not that so-called biological sex corresponds to gender, which is factually untrue, but that any combination of the two, as well as every effort to identify differently sexed bodies, remains within a two-sex system of reference. This system cannot be doubted (in the radical sense skeptics assume), denied, or jumped over. It can only be reimagined. And this imaginative language is not the production of a solitary subject but of praxis, human beings talking with one another.

32. Wittig, "The Category of Sex," 5.

33. Monique Wittig, "The Straight Mind," in *The Straight Mind and Other Essays*, 21–32; quotation is from p. 27.

34. Wittig, "The Straight Mind," 28. "The consequence of this tendency toward universality is that the straight mind cannot conceive of a culture, a society where heterosexuality would not order not only all human relationships but also its very production of concepts and all the processes which escape consciousness, as well"

(ibid.). On Wittig's references to the ancient conception of Being, see Monique Wittig, "Homo Sum," in *The Straight Mind and Other Essays*, 46–58. I have discussed in greater detail the relation of form to universality in Linda M. G. Zerilli, "This Universalism Which Is Not One," *Diacritics* 28, no. 2 (Summer 1998): 3–20.

35. Miguel Vatter, *Between Form and Event: Machiavelli's Theory of Political Freedom* (Dordrecht: Kluver Academic Publishers, 2000), 9.

36. Wittig, "On the Social Contract," 41.

37. Ibid., 38.

38. David Hume, "Of the Original Contract," in *Political Writings*, ed. Stuart D. Warner and Donald Livingston (Indianapolis: Hackett, 1994), 164–81.

39. Wittig, "On the Social Contract," 38.

40. Stanley Cavell, *The Claim of Reason: Wittgenstein, Skepticism, Morality, and Tragedy* (Oxford: Oxford University Press, 1979), 25.

41. Wittig, "On the Social Contract," 34, 40.

42. Monique Wittig, "The Trojan Horse," in *The Straight Mind and Other Essays*, 68–75; quotation is from p. 68.

43. Ibid., 69.

44. Monique Wittig, "The Point of View: Universal or Particular?," in *The Straight Mind and Other Essays*, pp. 59–67; quotations are from pp. 62–63.

45. Language is not only meaning, argues Wittig, but also "letter." Wittig seems to have in mind the figurative power of language, or what Ernesto Grassi calls its "rhetorical aspect." The original presence of letter is lost in meaning, much as that of rhetorical speech is lost in rational speech: "[M]eaning hides language [i.e., letter] from sight." Wittig substitutes "letter and meaning" (which "describe the sign solely in relation to language") for the traditional semiotic distinction between signifier and signified in order "to avoid the interference of the referent prematurely in the vocabulary of the sign" (Wittig, "The Point of View," 65). "Meaning is not visible, and as such appears to be outside of language [i.e., given in the nature of things]" (ibid., 67). When language takes form, she writes, "it is lost in the literal meaning. It can only reappear abstractly as language while redoubling itself, while forming a figurative meaning, a figure of speech. This, then, is writers' work—to concern themselves with the letter, the concrete, the visibility of language, that is, its material form" (ibid.). Wittig's literary practice turns in large part on the employment of tropes and figures to combat certain political formations and their entombment in the concept (e.g., "sex").

46. Ibid., 72.

47. Ibid., 63.

48. Ibid., 64, 65.

49. Describing the return to beginnings in Machiavelli, Vatter observes: "In these [revolutionary] events . . . the necessity of a given legal and political order is revoked ('reduced to its beginnings,' as Machiavelli says) to the contingency of its emergence, and therefore lets itself be overthrown; while, conversely, the contingency of new orders are given the appearance of necessity. Without this possibility of 'repeating' the necessary as the contingent, and the contingent as the necessary, there would be no radical political change" (*Between Form and Event*, 10).

50. Erika Ostrovsky, *A Constant Journey: The Fiction of Monique Wittig* (Carbondale: Southern Illinois University Press, 1991), 3–9, 35; Laurence M. Porter, "Feminist Fantasy and Open Structure in Monique Wittig's *Les guérillères*," in *The Celebration of the Fantastic: Selected Papers from the Tenth Anniversary*

International Conference on the Fantastic in the Arts, ed. Donald E. Morse, Marshall B. Tymn, and Csilla Bertha (Westport, CT: Greenwood Press, 1992), 261–69.

51. Porter, "Feminist Fantasy and Open Structure," 261. Porter correctly notes, "[E]ven fine feminist critics like Toril Moi and Nina Auerbach have read *Les guérillères* as a closed structure, in which women win the war and institute a new equilibrium of women ruling men" (ibid.). See also Zerilli, "The Trojan Horse of Universalism."

52. Recall Arendt's claim: "Men *are* free . . . as long as they act, neither before nor after; for to *be* free and to act are the same." Arendt, "What Is Freedom?," 153.

53. Porter, "Feminist Fantasy and Open Structure," 267. I've addressed similar issues in Zerilli, "Rememoration or War?" Porter's essay is virtually alone in its attempt to thematize freedom as an open structure in Wittig's work rather than as something that follows from the overthrow of patriarchy and that is founded in the creation of a new political form.

54. Wittig, *Les guérillères* (Paris: Les Éditions de Minuit, 1969), 49, 68. See pp. 14, 17 of the English translation by David Le Vay (Boston: Beacon Press, 1985). Hereafter cited in the text as G. The first number refers to the English translation and the second to the French original. Due to problems with the translation I have amended the translation of some passages. The most serious problem, discussed in detail below, is the translation of "*elles*" as "the women." A typical locution in Wittig's text is "*elles disent*," which the translator renders as "the women say" and which I translate as "they say." In order to capture the repetitive character of this locution, whose grammatical brilliance is destroyed by its translation as "the women" and barely captured by the neuter "they," I have inserted the original French in brackets in each relevant passage.

Erika Ostrovsky argues that the feminaries "represent traditional notions of a particular kind that must be annihilated and reformulated," and that "their authors, judging from the contents, are obviously male" (*A Constant Journey*, 56). I agree that the feminaries are texts that must be contested and eventually annihilated, but it is not clear to me that they were written by men. They contain stories that amount to rewritings of the central myths of Western culture and a wealth of sexual symbolism that could very well be associated with a *female*-centered culture, and which must therefore be rejected. The feminaries seem somewhat like the books found in the New Age section of feminist bookstores.

55. Porter, "Feminist Fantasy and Open Structure," 261.

56. This mode of interaction is akin to what James Tully describes as governance. In its less restrictive sense, governance involves "relations of intersubjective recognition, power, modes of conduct and strategies of freedom." This older meaning has been lost to an equation of government with formal institutions of political power. The recovery and reimagining of this older notion of governance, he argues, animates the work of Foucault and Arendt. The distinction is crucial for those feminists who refuse to reduce the sphere of the political to the official public sphere or democratic practices to the institutions of representative democracy. James Tully, "The Agonic Freedom of Citizens," *Economy and Society* 28, no. 2 (May 1999): 161–82; quotation is from p. 177.

57. Bergson, *The Creative Mind*, 101.

58. Ostrovsky, *A Constant Journey*, 61.

59. Monique Wittig, "The Mark of Gender," in *The Straight Mind and Other Essays*, 76–89; quotation is from pp. 85–86.

60. Ostrovsky, *A Constant Journey*, 43.

61. Hannah Arendt, "The Concept of History," in *Between Past and Future*, 41–90; quotation is from pp. 64–65.

62. In his reading of the return to beginnings in Machiavelli, Miguel Vatter (drawing on the work of Derrida, Lacoue-Labarthe, and Deleuze) asks, "But how can something like repetition or return coincide with something like innovation or beginning?" The problem is that "if history amounts strictly to repetition of the same events, then there exists no innovation, and as a consequence it is possible to remain, forever, at the beginning (of history)." Arguing that Machiavelli's account of the return to beginnings "rejects the belief that repetition is itself 'secondary', dependent on the 'firstness' or 'priority' of the form (archetype)," Vatter shows that "there is no beginning to return to because what begins is this very return" (*Between Form and Event*, 238, 239).

63. Arendt writes, "We have the Biblical story of the exodus of Israeli tribes from Egypt, which preceded the Mosaic legislation constituting the Hebrew people, and Virgil's story of the wandering of Aeneas, which led to the foundation of Rome." These two foundation legends, says Arendt, were invoked by "men of action of later generations"—the Roman and the American founders—"desperate to find paradigms that would explain and legitimate their actions" (*LMW*, 204). Arendt neglects to mention another Roman foundation legend, namely the story of Romulus, which was important to Machiavelli.

64. Ostrovsky, *A Constant Journey*, 34, 33.

65. Cornelius Castoriadis, "The Imaginary: Creation in the Social-Historical Domain," in *World in Fragments*, 14; emphasis in the original.

66. Wittig, "The Mark of Gender," 84–85.

67. Ibid., 86.

68. Ibid., 87. This translation works, however, only if one changes the last section of the book, in which the men share the pronoun *they*. "In a new version [English translation] the masculine gender must be more systematically particularized than it is in the actual form of the book. The masculine must not appear under *they* but only under *man, he, his* in analogy with what has been done for so long to the feminine gender (*woman, she, her*)." (Ibid.)

69. Similar literary strategies characterize two of Wittig's other novels, *The Opoponax* and *The Lesbian Body*. In *The Opoponax*, she works with the pronoun *on* (one), which is neuter and which can represent a certain number of people all at once while remaining singular. With this pronoun, she builds a universal perspective around the central character of the text, a little girl. In *The Lesbian Body*, Wittig works creatively with the pronoun *j/e*, which she describes in "The Mark of Gender" (87) as "a sign of excess." See Zerilli, "The Trojan Horse of Universalism."

70. Auerbach, *Communities of Women*, 191.

71. Toril Moi, *Sexual/Textual Politics* (New York: Metheun Press, 1985), 80. Moi contends that Auerbach longs for an end to the war and for a time when, in Auerbach's words, "it would be possible to return to the individuality of Meg, Jo, and Amy," characters in another text, *Little Women*, that Auerbach examines (ibid.).

72. This description, found on the back cover of the English translation, is from the *New York Times*. It is followed by a wise comment from Edna O'Brien: "Ms. Wittig is a dazzling writer. Her words are lucid and gleaming like moonlight."

73. Grassi, "Rhetoric as the Ground of Society," 95.

74. Ibid., 99.

75. Ibid., 100.

76. Rosi Braidotti with Judith Butler, "Feminism by Any Other Name," *differences: A Journal of Feminist Cultural Studies* 6, nos. 2–3 (Summer–Fall 1994): 27–61; quotation is from p. 51.

CHAPTER THREE

1. According to Teresa de Lauretis, co-translator of *Sexual Difference*, "Italian feminism is not well known in North America. With very few, very recent exceptions, its critical texts are not translated, discussed, or cited by American and other anglophone feminists." "The Practice of Sexual Difference and Feminist Thought in Italy: An Introductory Essay," in The Milan Women's Bookstore Collective, *Sexual Difference*, trans. Patricia Cigogna and Teresa de Lauretis (Bloomington: Indiana University Press, 1990 [*Non credere di avere dei diritti: la generazione della libertà femminile nell'idea e nelle vicende di un gruppo di donne* (Turin: Rosenberg & Sellier, 1987)]), 1–21; quotation is from p. 1. Hereafter cited as *SD* in the text and notes with page references. This fact was not altered by the English translation of *Sexual Difference*. In the 1980s and 1990s, the situation looked rather different in Europe, where Italian feminism was not, as it is in the United States, equated with—or, as Rosi Braidotti complains, reduced to—that of "the women's bookshop in Milan and the Diotima collective in Verona," but hotly debated. Rosi Braidotti, *Nomadic Subjects: Embodiment and Sexual Difference in Contemporary Feminist Theory* (New York: Columbia University Press, 1994), 209. In Germany, for example, a wide array of responses to the Italian concept of sexual difference appeared. For a good review of the debates see Heike Kahlert, *Weibliche Subjektivität: Geschlechterdifferenz und Demokratie in der Diskussion* (Frankfurt am Main: Campus Verlag, 1996); Britta Kroker, *Sexuelle Differenz: Einführung in ein feministisches Theorem* (Pfaffenweiler, Germany: Centaurus-Verlagsgesellschaft, 1994).

2. de Lauretis, "Sexual Difference and Feminist Thought in Italy," 12. As de Lauretis explains, this claim

> is bound to appear reductive, idealist, essentialist, even reactionary unless one keeps in mind, first, the paradox on which it is founded and which has been the first task of feminist thought to disentangle—the paradox of woman, a being that is at once captive and absent in discourse, constantly spoken of but of itself inaudible or inexpressible, displayed as spectacle and yet unrepresented; a being whose existence and specificity are simultaneously asserted and denied, negated and controlled. And hence the task of feminist philosophy: "thinking sexual difference through the categories of a thought that is supported by the non-thinking of difference itself."

This paradox, she continues, has an explicitly political dimension: it "is not solely discursive, but is grounded in a real contradiction for women in a world designed and governed by men," and only feminism has sought fit to address this contradiction (ibid., 12). It is the Milan Collective's concern to bring together the symbolic and political aspects of the paradox as it bears on the question of freedom that makes the absence of their text in American feminist discussions both curious and disturbing.

3. For a powerful critique of the Western conception of freedom, see Hannah Arendt, "What Is Freedom?," in *Between Past and Future: Eight Exercises in Political Thought* (New York: Penguin, 1993), 143–72.

4. In the introduction I argued that feminism has been caught in two different but related frames for thinking about freedom: the "social question" and the "subject question." Within the frame of the social question, feminist claims to freedom get articulated in terms of expediency and social utility (e.g., women as free citizens will make society better). Within the frame of the subject question, these claims get articulated in terms of problems associated with subject formation (e.g., the project of freedom is to transform femininity as a compulsory social identity). Both frames, I argue, take for granted a means-ends conception of politics that excludes the possibility of freedom as action.

5. The Milan Collective is deeply indebted to Luce Irigaray's attempt to inscribe sexual difference into culture, society, and law. Irigaray's more recent work on changes in the Italian civil code has not dispelled the concern that she continues to rank the difference between the sexes as somehow of a different order than other forms of difference. In *Democracy Begins between Two* she writes, "Sexual difference is perhaps the hardest way, but it is also the key, to achieving civil coexistence between other forms of difference. An apprenticeship in respect for the other at the most instinctive, emotional level, leads to peaceful coexistence with all forms of otherness." Such claims are rooted in Irigaray's belief that the fantasy of sovereignty that, in her view, continues to pose the greatest threat to humanity and to nature is sustained primarily by the denial of sexual difference, by the exclusion of the feminine as the condition of the masculine subject. That is why sexual difference is "the most radical limit opposed to the totalizing will of the subject." Luce Irigaray, *Democracy Begins between Two*, trans. Kirsteen Anderson (New York: Routledge, 2001), 12, 6. A similar worry arises in her more recent writing on the relationship of cultures in *Entre Orient et Occident: De la singularité à la communauté* (Paris: Bernard Grasset, 1999). For a critique of the quasi-transcendental idea of sexual difference in Lacanian-informed theory, see Judith Butler, *Antigone's Claim: Kinship between Life and Death* (New York: Columbia University Press, 2000); "Competing Universalities," in Judith Butler, Ernesto Laclau, and Slavoj Žižek, *Contingency, Hegemony, Universality: Contemporary Dialogues on the Left* (New York: Verso, 2000), 136–81, esp. 143–48. Butler argues that, "as a transcendental claim, sexual difference should be rigorously opposed by anyone who wants to guard against a theory that would prescribe in advance what kinds of sexual arrangements will and will not be permitted in intelligible culture" (ibid., 148). I agree. The question is, can we imagine another claim to sexual difference that would not be transcendental, but rather political and therefore contingent and contestable?

6. See the issue on "The Essential Difference: Another Look at Essentialism," *differences: A Journal of Feminist Cultural Studies* 1 (Summer 1989). Monique Wittig, "One Is Not Born a Woman," in *The Straight Mind and Other Essays* (Boston: Beacon, 1992), 9–20; quotation is from p. 13.

7. For a good overview of what is at stake in this debate, see Rosi Braidotti with Judith Butler, interview, "Feminism by Any Other Name," *differences* 6, nos. 2 and 3 (Summer–Fall 1994): 27–61.

8. For a good example of these two ways of framing sexual difference, see the

essays by Slavoj Žižek and Judith Butler in Judith Butler, Ernesto Laclau, and Slavoj Žižek, *Contingency, Hegemony, Universality*.

9. *Sexual Difference* does not pretend to offer a master theory of feminist world-building that could be applied in rule-like fashion to other contexts or cultures. "[P]utting a political practice into words," recounting the emergence of a "genealogy of women ... who were legitimized by referring to their female origin," the text relates an experience that is "only one of the many historical vicissitudes of the fragile concept of woman" (*SD*, 25).

10. Carole Pateman, *The Sexual Contract* (Stanford, CA: Stanford University Press, 1988). According to Pateman, the classic tale of the social contract cannot accommodate the demands of feminists, for there is no way to add women to a pact that was made (albeit metaphorically) in their absence and is premised (historically) on their exclusion: "to begin to create a free society in which women are autonomous citizens, the story must be cast aside" (ibid., 220).

11. Luce Irigaray, "Equal or Different," in *The Irigaray Reader*, ed. Margaret Whitford (Oxford: Blackwell, 1991), 30–33; quotation is from p. 32.

12. For an account of the occlusion of sexual difference in political thought, see Iris Marion Young, *Justice and the Politics of Difference* (Princeton, NJ: Princeton University Press, 1990); Seyla Benhabib, *Situating the Self: Gender, Community and Postmodernism in Contemporary Ethics* (New York: Routledge, 1992). For an account of its occlusion in law, see Drucilla Cornell, *The Imaginary Domain: Abortion, Pornography, and Sexual Harrassment* (New York: Routledge, 1995).

13. As I argue elsewhere,

> The difference versus sameness debate tends to assume that equality claims confront and are at odds with claims about difference. We are thus faced with an either/or proposition: to claim equality is to eliminate difference, and vice versa. . . . [Ute] Gerhard argues that equality claims do not (simply) eliminate difference but (also) articulate it, that is, they shape what will count as socially and politically significant difference. Equality claims, in other words, do not confront and oppose a static field of already existing differences; they transform socially recognized differences of sex and gender into politically meaningful ones that are contestable and thus subject to change, and, further, they bring into existence new social differences which, in turn, may be transformed into political ones.

Linda M. G. Zerilli, foreword to Ute Gerhard, *Debating Women's Equality: Toward a Feminist Theory of Law from a Feminist Perspective* (New Brunswick, NJ: Rutgers University Press, 2001), ix–xiv; extract is from p. xi.

14. The locus classicus of the feminist argument for equality and against difference is Catherine MacKinnon, *Feminism Unmodified: Discourses on Life and Law* (Cambridge: Harvard University Press, 1987).

15. Refusing this choice, Joan Scott holds that feminism is characterized by a paradox—the need both to accept and to refuse "sexual difference"—that cannot be solved, but only accepted as "the constitutive condition of feminism as a political movement throughout its long history." Joan Scott, *Only Paradoxes to Offer: French Feminists and the Rights of Man* (Cambridge: Harvard University Press, 1996), 3–4. Likewise, Nancy Cott argues that "feminism asks for sexual equality

that includes sexual difference." Nancy Cott, *The Grounding of Modern Feminism* (New Haven, CT: Yale University Press, 1987), 5.

16. Arendt, "What Is Freedom?," 165.

17. Although it has roots in separatism, this social contract demands a political space which calls into question "the space of a presumed female authenticity, which has *no social consequences*" (*SD*, 79). Separatism is "a political form invented by feminism, . . . [which] functions as protection and shelter for an otherwise insignificant difference, and in the group one thinks in terms of an inside and an outside" (*SD*, 116). Separatism reproduces the sameness among women that feminism set out to combat.

18. Ti-Grace Atkinson, *Amazon Odyssey* (New York: Links Books, 1974), 49.

19. Friedrich Nietzsche, *Also sprach Zarathustra*, bk. 2, "Von der Erlösung," in *Sämtliche Werke*, Kritische Studienausgabe, ed. Giorgio Colli and Mazzino Montinari, 15 vols. (Berlin: de Gruyter, 1999), 4:179.

20. Wittig, "One Is Not Born a Woman," 13; Wendy Brown, *States of Injury: Power and Freedom in Late Modernity* (Princeton, NJ: Princeton University Press, 1995), xii.

21. Brown, *States of Injury*, 7. "Ideals of freedom ordinarily emerge to vanquish their imagined immediate enemies, but in this move they frequently recycle and reinstate rather than transform the terms of domination that generated them" (ibid., 16).

22. Ibid., 73–74.

23. Think of feminism's figure of the "Third World Woman" as the embodiment of female wretchedness. For a vivid critique of this figure in Western feminist texts, see Chandra Mohanty, "Under Western Eyes: Feminist Scholarship and Colonial Discourses," in *Third World Women and the Politics of Feminism*, ed. Chandra Mohanty, Ann Russo, and Lourdes Torres (Bloomington: Indiana University Press, 1991), 51–80.

24. Cynthia Eller rightly argues that the myth of a matriarchal past has been used in feminism to give women a sense of their own value in a society that despises femininity. But the myth of an ancient matriarchy works "to flatten out the differences among women; to exaggerate differences between women and men; and to hand women an identity that is symbolic, timeless, and archetypal, instead of giving them the freedom to craft new identities that suit their individual temperaments, skills, preferences, and moral and political commitments." Cynthia Eller, *The Myth of a Matriarchal Prehistory: Why an Invented Past Won't Give Women a Future* (Boston: Beacon, 2000), 8.

25. "[W]omen are afraid of exposing their own desire," writes the collective, "and this induces them to think that others prevent them from desiring; thus they cultivate and manifest desire as that which is prohibited to them by an external authority. Female desire feels authorized to signify itself only in this negative form. Just think of the politics of equal rights, carried out by women who never put forward a will of their own but always and only claim what men have for themselves and is denied to women" (*SD*, 54).

26. In some respects, the direct work on the self, what the collective calls the practice of the unconscious, had taken up this task. "However, since it was confined to the female sex and aimed at the transformation of each individual woman, it provided political knowledge useful in developing relations between women, but not

between women as members of the social body." Although it was assumed "that relations would consequently change in that direction," it turned out that the changes in female experience, brought about in feminist practices, still had "no social inscription." An altered female desire still had no place in the social world, and had either to conform itself to traditional female roles or to become neuter and evade them (*SD*, 106–7).

27. Defined in terms of the subject question, it is difficult to imagine freedom as anything but paradoxical, unless one alters the nature of modern subjectivity. Accordingly, Brown's proffered solution, "the replacement—even the admixture—of the language of 'being' with 'wanting,'" takes the form of work on the self: "a recovery of the more expansive moments in the genealogy of identity formation, a recovery of the moment prior to its own foreclosure against its want, prior to the point at which its sovereign subjectivity is established through such foreclosure and through eternal repetition of its pain" (Brown, *States of Injury*, 76).

28. Although it had a more limited number of participants than *autocoscienza*, this practice was focused on female desire, and women's reluctance to express it in anything but negative form, i.e., reparation. Apart from "keeping feminism from turning into an ideology which served as a front for a politics of equality," the practice of the unconscious was deeply limited: it "tended to end up in interpretation and commentary instead of direct social change" (*SD*, 58).

29. These included not only women's bookstores in a variety of other Italian cities (Turin, Bologna, Florence, Pisa, and Cagliari), but also the founding of publishing houses, in Rome (Edizioni delle donne) and Milan (La Tartaruga), devoted exclusively to women's literature; women artist collectives (e.g., Via Beato Angelico); the Women's Library in Parma; and the "Virginia Woolf Cultural Center was established in Rome, offering regular courses and its own publications" (*SD*, 93).

30. Hannah Arendt, *The Human Condition* (Chicago: University of Chicago Press, 1989), 182.

31. Ibid., 182–83.

32. Ibid., 183.

33. "In *autocoscienza*, its solution consisted in the possibility of reciprocal modification: juxtaposing women's differences is significant in itself, even without judgment, insofar as it induces each woman thus confronted to change. The practice of doing . . . balanced, on the one hand, the natural tolerance of things—I do this, you do that—with, on the other hand, the words that tell the meaning of things and that, in order to tell it, cannot avoid judging" (*SD*, 94).

34. Hannah Arendt, *Lectures on Kant's Political Philosophy*, ed. Ronald Beiner (Chicago: University of Chicago Press, 1982), 13.

35. "Disparity in social relations appears in intricately confused forms. Our need for others is confused with exploitation by those who have more power; unjust forms of disparity are valorized, or at least resist elimination by piggybacking on those differences which we feel are unavoidable and even beneficial in certain cases. . . . Among the productive forms of disparity, the one between adult and child is the only one which can be cited as an example in our culture, but others exist or could exist. There are forms of disparity, in beauty or health, which often cannot be eliminated; it is senseless to call them unjust even if they unfortunately provide the occasion for some of the worst injustices—think of the condition of the sick or of the old who do not have the power of money" (*SD*, 132).

36. Arendt, *The Human Condition*, 215.

37. Ute Gerhard, *Debating Women's Equality*, 8. I make these points in the foreword, ix–xiv.

38. Ibid., 165.

39. Ibid.

40. In *Tribute to Freud*, H. D. relates what she told Freud in 1930 about her 1920 trip to Corfu with a young acquaintance, whom she calls "Bryher." At the center of the analysis, writes H. D., was a "series of shadow—or of light pictures I saw projected on the wall of a hotel bedroom in the Ionian island of Corfu, . . . [which] belong in the sense of quality and intensity of clarity and authenticity, to the same psychic category as the dream of the Princess, the Pharaoh's daughter, coming down the stairs." Continuing the story, H. D. writes,

> But it was no easy matter to sustain this mood [which became more and more intense], this "symptom" or [poetic] inspiration. And there I sat, and there is my friend Bryher . . . I say to Bryher, "There have been pictures here—I thought they were shadows at first, but they are light, not shadow. They are quite simple objects—but of course it's very strange. I can break away from them now, if I want—it's just a matter of concentrating—what do you think? Shall I stop? Shall I go on?" Bryher says without hesitation, "Go on." (*SD*, 33)

Tribute to Freud: Writing on the Wall—Advent (Boston: David R. Goodine, 1974; reprint, New York: New Directions, 1984).

41. The women who first put forward the idea of entrustment were criticized for supporting hierarchy among women. The collective remarks that the charge—which is deemed "laughable" for the reasons just outlined in my text—"originated from the difficulty of attributing authority, in acknowledging superiority without associating it with domination, with the sanction of power, with the form of hierarchy" (*SD*, 133).

42. Stanley Cavell, "Knowing and Acknowledging," in *Must We Mean What We Say?* (Cambridge: Cambridge University Press, 1969), 238–66; quotation is from p. 257.

43. Arendt, *The Human Condition*, 244.

44. Ibid., 233.

45. Ibid., 245.

46. See Luce Irigaray, "Towards a Citizenship of the European Union," in *Democracy Begins between Two*; "Comment devenir des femmes civiles?" and "Droits et devoirs civils pour les deux sexes," in *Le Temps de la différence: Pour une révolution pacifique* (Librairie Générale Française, 1989); "Why Define Sexed Rights," in *je, tu, nous: Toward a Culture of Difference*, trans. Alison Martin (New York: Routledge, 1993).

47. For a lucid account of this point in relation to the recent work of Jürgen Habermas, see Bonnie Honig, "Dead Rights, Live Futures: A Reply to Habermas's 'Constitutional Democracy,'" *Political Theory* 29, no. 6 (December 2001): 792–805.

48. Irigaray, "The Representation of Women," in *Democracy Begins between Two*, 174.

49. Ibid., 175.

50. Gerhard, *Debating Women's Equality*, 176.

51. Refiguring rights, as Kirstie McClure argues, entails "a politics of direct address": "a politics that begins not with the object of constructing similarities to

address rights claims to the state, but opens rather with the object of addressing such claims to each other, and to each 'other,' whoever and wherever they may be." Kirstie McClure, "On the Subject of Rights: Pluralism, Plurality, and Political Identity," in *Dimensions of Radical Democracy: Pluralism, Citizenship, Community*, ed. Chantal Mouffe (New York: Verso, 1993), 108–27; quotation is from p. 123.

52. This demand for something more may be part of what animates the charge that gay and lesbian people seek "special rights" when they claim equal rights. Whatever the homophobic sentiment behind that charge, it is also the case that this most recent and divisive struggle for equal rights confronts us with a demand for something that equality as such can never satisfy—namely, freedom.

53. The Milan Collective emphasizes this point time and again. Aware of the unprecedented character of their actions, they were also aware of the lack of a guarantee. "The action of those women who met only with other women, and consequently changed the methods and contents of their politics, is an example of liberating transgression. Their example legitimized others, but nothing and no one guaranteed that what they were doing was right. The value of female difference is not inscribed in the system of social relations, nor does anything which has to be done so that it will exist appear with a guarantee that it is the right thing to do. We, in flesh and blood, have to take the place of the missing guarantee" (*SD*, 126).

54. Gerhard, *Debating Women's Equality*, 10.

CHAPTER FOUR

1. "Human action, projected into a web of relationships where many and opposing ends are pursued, almost never fulfills its original intention," writes Arendt. "Whoever begins to act must know that he has started something whose end he can never foretell, if only because his own deed has already changed everything and made it even more unpredictable." Hannah Arendt, "The Concept of History," in *Between Past and Future: Eight Exercises in Political Thought* (New York: Penguin, 1993), 41–90; quotation is from p. 84.

2. Cited in ibid., 85.

3. "To our modern way of thinking nothing is meaningful in and by itself. . . . What the concept of process implies is that the concrete and the general, the single thing or event and the universal meaning, have parted company. The process . . . alone makes meaningful whatever it happens to carry along" (ibid., 63–64).

4. Immanuel Kant, *Critique of Pure Reason*, trans. Paul Guyer and Alan Wood (Cambridge: Cambridge University Press, 1977), B171.

5. The basis for all cognition, recognition requires that the faculties of reason, imagination, and understanding form a "common sense," i.e., that they collaborate with each other to produce "a form of the Same," in Gilles Deleuze's apt formulation. Gilles Deleuze, *Difference and Repetition*, trans. Paul Patton (New York: Columbia University Press, 1994), 137. Common sense is a harmony of the faculties that makes the object I now see the one I now touch or smell, securing this object as recognizable under a concept, i.e., something already known.

6. Hannah Arendt, "Understanding and Politics," in *Essays in Understanding, 1930–1954*, ed. Jerome Kohn (New York: Harcourt Brace & Co., 1994), 307–27; quotation is from p. 325, n. 8. For Arendt, totalitarianism was the paradigmatic example of a new event that demands our judgment, for "the death factories erected

in the heart of Europe" confront us with an unprecedented sense of meaningless-ness. How are we to judge an event that has brought to light the ruin of "our cate-gories of thought and standards of judgment"? she asks (Arendt, "Understanding and Politics," 313). Nonetheless, we are reluctant to relinquish inherited rules. This reluctance suggests that what we have gotten used to is not so much the substance of any particular rule for subsuming particulars but the sheer fact of having rules under which to subsume. Rules are like a mental crutch to which we cling for fear of not being able to understand or judge at all. The real threat of nihilism is not the loss of standards, in Arendt's view, but the refusal to accept the consequences of that loss. Hannah Arendt, "Thinking and Moral Considerations," *Social Research: Fiftieth Anniversary Issue* 38, no. 3 (Autumn 1971): 416–46; see especially p. 436.

7. On the relationship of judgments (*Urteile*) to prejudices (*Vorurteile*) see Hannah Arendt, *Was Ist Politik?*, ed. Ursula Ludz (Munich: Piper Verlag, 1993), 17–23. Hereafter cited in the text and notes as *WIP* with page references. All trans-lations are my own.

8. "Maybe it is preposterous even to think that anything can ever happen which our categories are not equipped to understand," quips Arendt. "Maybe we should resign ourselves to the preliminary understanding, which at once ranges the new among the old, and with the scientific approach, which follows it and deduces methodically the unprecedented from precedents, even though such a description of the new phenomena may be demonstrably at variance with the reality" (Arendt, "Understanding and Politics," 313). Arendt is not willing to concede this point, for that would deny human freedom. She does not dispute here the idea that there is no place outside our preliminary understanding from which we could judge. The pre-cognitive basis of our capacity for judgment belongs to the world-disclosing func-tion of language associated with the linguistic turn carried out by thinkers like Heidegger. In his challenge to the philosophy of consciousness and its idea that lan-guage is a mere tool for expressing prelinguistic thoughts, Heidegger held that the meanings already given in a language are constitutive of what we can think or of anything we could encounter as an object. We do not *first* encounter an entity given independently of language and *then* take it—in a cognitive judgment—as something (e.g., first as a bare object, then as a door). Rather, we encounter every entity from the start as an object of such-and-such a kind; our prepredicative seeing already exhibits an "as-structure."

9. Arendt, *WIP*, 21.

10. Deleuze, *Difference and Repetition*, 136.

11. As Sonia Kruks summarizes this problem,

[I]dentity politics tends toward what I call an epistemology of provenance. By this, I mean it tends toward an epistemological and ethical relativism. . . . [T]his ten-dency is grounded in claims about group specificity of experiences and the exclu-sive capacity of particular identity groups to evaluate those experiences. Although important in enabling previously marginalized and silenced groups to speak, an epistemology of provenance can also be problematic. For it threatens to undercut notions of shared (or even communicable) experience to such an extent that pos-sibilities for a broadly based emancipatory politics are de facto subverted.

Sonia Kruks, *Retrieving Experience: Subjectivity and Recognition in Feminist Politics* (Ithaca, NY: Cornell University Press, 2001), 85.

12. Kirstie McClure, "The Issue of Foundations: Scientized Politics, Politicized

Science, and Feminist Critical Practice," in *Feminists Theorize the Political*, ed. Judith Butler and Joan Scott (New York: Routledge, 1992), 341–68; quotation is from p. 345. According to McClure, second-wave feminism became entangled in strategies of authorization that rejected "extreme positivist versions of 'objectivity'" (352) but sustained the belief in "systematic causal explanation" (359) and "the desire for comprehensive causal theory as a reflection of the 'truth' of the social world" (364–65). Although the quest for such a theory is no longer credible, the problems of authorization and validity remain.

13. Richard Bernstein provides a useful description of objectivism:

> By "objectivism" I mean the basic conviction that there is or must be some permanent, ahistorical matrix or framework to which we can ultimately appeal in determining the nature of rationality, knowledge, truth, reality, goodness, or rightness. An objectivist claims that there is (or must be) such a matrix and that the primary task of the philosopher is to discover what it is and to support his or her claims to have discovered such a matrix with the strongest possible reasons. Objectivism is closely related to foundationalism and the search for the Archimedean point. The objectivist maintains that unless we can ground philosophy, knowledge, or language in a rigorous manner we cannot avoid radical skepticism.

Richard J. Bernstein, *Beyond Objectivism and Relativism: Science, Hermeneutics, and Praxis* (Philadelphia: University of Pennsylvania Press, 1983), 8.

14. Immanuel Kant, *Critique of Judgment*, trans. Werner S. Pluhar (Indianapolis: Hackett, 1987), Introduction, 4, p. 18. Hereafter cited in the text and notes as *CJ* with section and page references.

15. As Béatrice Longuenesse explains, "the peculiar feature of aesthetic and teleological judgments is not that they are reflective judgments (*for every judgment on empirical objects as such is reflective*); it is rather that they are *merely* reflective judgments, judgments in which reflection can never arrive at conceptual *determination*." *Kant and the Capacity to Judge: Sensibility and Discursivity in the Transcendental Analytic of the "Critique of Pure Reason"*, trans. Charles T. Wolfe (Princeton, NJ: Princeton University Press, 1998), 164; emphasis in the original.

16. Hannah Arendt, *Lectures on Kant's Political Philosophy*, ed. Ronald Beiner (Chicago: University of Chicago Press, 1982), 13. Hereafter cited in the text and notes as *LKPP* with page references.

17. The same point applies in reverse: "For example, I may look at a rose and make a judgment of taste declaring it to be beautiful. But if I compare many singular roses and so arrive at the judgment, Roses in general are beautiful, then my judgment is no longer merely aesthetic but is a logical judgment based on an aesthetic one" (*CJ*, §8, p. 59).

18. Kant is emphatic on this point:

> [A]n aesthetic judgment is unique in kind and provides absolutely no cognition (not even a confused one) of the object; only a logical judgment does that. An aesthetic judgment instead refers the presentation, by which an object is given, solely to the subject; it brings to our notice no characteristic of the object, but only the purposive form in the [way] the presentational powers are determined in their engagement with the object. (*CJ*, §15, p. 75)

19. The pleasure obtained in the act of judging is subjective. It entails the agree-

ment or harmony of the faculties (understanding and imagination in the case of beauty; imagination and reason in the case of the sublime) in the absence of a concept, for reflective judgment fails to produce any conceptual determination. That is why Kant speaks of aesthetic and teleological judgments as "merely reflective judgments" [*nur reflektierende, bloß reflektierende*]. See *CJ*, First Introduction, 5, p. 399. On this point, see Rodolphe Gasché, *The Idea of Form: Rethinking Kant's Aesthetics* (Stanford, CA: Stanford University Press, 2003), chap. 3.

20. Since aesthetic judgments cannot be justified on the basis of proofs, writes Kant, "there is no science of the beautiful, but only critique" (*CJ*, §44, p. 172).

21. If there were no common sense, as the skeptic assumes, we would be unable to identify the object in other people's descriptions. But we are able to communicate, which in turn implies that we must possess the feelings and use of faculties in common, says Kant.

> If judgments of taste had (as cognitive judgments do) a determinate objective principle, then anyone making them in accordance with that principle would claim that his judgment is unconditionally necessary. . . . So they [judgments of taste] must have a subjective principle, which determines only by feeling rather than by concepts, though nonetheless with universal validity, what is liked or disliked. Such a principle, however, could only be regarded as a *common sense*. This common sense is essentially distinct from the common understanding that is also sometimes called common sense (*sensus communis*); for the latter judges not by feeling but always by concepts, even though these concepts are usually only principles conceived obscurely. (*CJ*, §20, p. 87)

Kant is talking not about the empirical opinions of a given community but about an "attunement" of the faculties in a judgment that must be universally communicable. Thus the validity of a judgment of taste is "not to be established by gathering votes and asking other people what kind of sensation they are having" (*CJ*, §31, p. 144). Although this attunement is also "the subjective condition of [the process of] cognition" (*CJ*, §21, p. 88), in a judgment of taste it is determined solely by feeling, not concepts.

22. For critiques of Arendt's reliance on Kant, see Ronald Beiner, "Hannah Arendt on Judging," in Hannah Arendt, *Lectures on Kant's Political Philosophy*, 89–156; Jürgen Habermas, "Hannah Arendt's Communications Concept of Power," in *Hannah Arendt, Critical Essays*, ed. Lewis Hinchman and Sandra Hinchman (Albany: State University of New York Press, 1994), 211–30; Seyla Benhabib, "Judgment and the Moral Foundations of Politics in Hannah Arendt's Thought," in *Judgment, Imagination, and Politics: Themes from Kant to Arendt*, ed. Ronald Beiner and Jennifer Nedelsky (New York: Rowman & Littlefield, 2001), 183–204; Hans-Georg Gadamer, *Truth and Method* (New York: Continuum, 1994); Albrecht Wellmer, "Hannah Arendt on Judgment: The Unwritten Doctrine of Reason," in *Hannah Arendt: Twenty Years Later*, ed. Larry May and Jerome Kohn (Cambridge: MIT Press, 1996), 33–52; Ronald Beiner, "Rereading Hannah Arendt's Kant Lectures," in *Judgment, Imagination, and Politics*, 91–102.

23. Beiner, "Hannah Arendt on Judging," 133–34.

24. Ibid., 136.

25. Habermas claims, "An antiquated concept of theoretical knowledge that is based on ultimate insights and certainties keeps Arendt from comprehending the process of reaching agreement about practical questions as rational discourse"

(Habermas, "Hannah Arendt's Communications Concept of Power," 225). Agreeing with Habermas, Albrecht Wellmer adds that Arendt's failure to question Kant's "distinction between judgments that are open to argument or dispute . . . and judgments that are only open to 'contention'" (i.e., *disputieren* versus *streiten*) leads to "a *mythology* of judgment—a mythology of judgment because the faculty of judgment now begins to emerge as the somewhat mysterious faculty to hit upon the truth when there is no context of possible arguments by which truth claims could be redeemed." Wellmer, "Hannah Arendt on Judgment," 38.

26. Arendt, *WIP*, 20.

27. As Beiner writes, "*[A]ll* human judgments, including aesthetic (and certainly political) judgments, incorporate a necessary cognitive dimension." (You will be a better judge of art if you know something about the art you are judging.) "Hannah Arendt on Judging," 137. Such comments fail to recognize what is involved in an aesthetic or political judgment. It is not that all knowledge is by definition excluded—as if we forgot everything we knew—but that the judgment is of beauty—and beauty is not an object but a feeling, a subjective response. Such a judgment has no purpose, no place in the nexus of causal relations that ground our knowledge of nature. "If we judge objects merely in terms of concepts, then we lose all presentation of beauty" (*CJ*, §8, p. 59), writes Kant. The judgment refers to what the subject *feels*, not what he *knows* (i.e., concepts of the object). A botanist *knows* that a flower is "the reproductive organ of a plant," as Kant observes, yet he "pays no attention to this natural purpose when he judges the flower by taste" (*CJ*, §16, p. 76). Arendt's argument regarding political judgments is similar: it is not that we don't know things about the objects of the common world (e.g., totalitarianism). But when we judge these objects politically, we are making something other than a knowledge claim.

28. See Beiner, "Hannah Arendt on Judging," 136–37.

29. Hannah Arendt, *The Life of the Mind*, 1-vol. edition (New York: Harcourt Brace & Co., 1978), vol. 1, *Thinking*, 69. Hereafter cited as *LMT*.

30. "If the understanding in general is explained as the faculty of rules, then the power of judgment is the faculty of subsuming under rules, i.e., of determining whether something stands under a given rule (*casus datae legis*) or not. . . . *Now if we wanted to show generally how one ought to subsume under these rules, i.e., distinguish whether something stands under them or not, this could not happen except once again through a rule. But just because this is a rule, it would demand another instruction for the power of judgment, and so it becomes clear that although the understanding is certainly capable of being instructed and equipped through rules, the power of judgment is a special talent that cannot be taught but only practiced.* Thus this is also what is specific to so-called mother wit, the lack of which cannot be made good by any school; for, although such a school can provide a limited understanding with plenty of rules borrowed from the insights of others and as it were graft these onto it, nevertheless the faculty for making use of them correctly must belong to the student himself, and in the absence of such a natural gift no rule that one might prescribe to him for this aim is safe from misuse" (Kant, *CPR*, A133/B172; my emphasis).

31. Arendt, *LMT*, 69. Deleuze writes, "A first mistake would be to believe that only reflective judgment involves inventiveness. . . . Every time Kant speaks of judgment as if it were a faculty it is to emphasize the originality of its act." Gilles

Deleuze, *Kant's Critical Philosophy: The Doctrine of the Faculties*, trans. Hugh Tomlinson and Barbara Habberjam (Minneapolis: University of Minnesota Press, 1984), 58–59.

32. Without a rule to guide us, we experience what Kant describes as pressure toward articulation, a noncognitive awareness of an order, which leads us to search for a concept or meaning. This pressure, however, is different from the pressure we feel when confronted with a (cognitive and logical) claim to truth, which is better described as a sense of compulsion to agree on the basis of shared criteria or concepts. The noncognitive awareness of an order in a reflective judgment, in contrast, generates not the sense of compulsion to judge like *this* (i.e., based on shared criteria), but the need to judge itself. The point here is to recognize both the autonomy of reflective judgment (i.e., that it does not stand under the laws of another faculty) and that even determinant judgments involve skill, because there is no rule for the application of rules.

33. For readings of Arendt contra Habermas, see Dana Villa, *Arendt and Heidegger: The Fate of the Political* (Princeton, NJ: Princeton University Press, 1996), 72; Lisa Jane Disch, *Hannah Arendt and the Limits of Philosophy* (Ithaca, NY: Cornell University Press, 1994), 87–91.

34. Ludwig Wittgenstein, *Philosophical Investigations*, trans. G. E. M. Anscombe (Oxford: Blackwell Press, 2000), §437, p. 129. As Salim Kemal explains,

> Proofs usually begin with generally accepted premises, asserting that certain relations hold between concepts and, from these, on the basis of inferential rules, draw relevant conclusions. If we accept the premises and the validity of the argument, then, unless there is a mistake, we must accept the conclusion. In some sense our agreement is compelled, for a dissenting individual's claim will be dismissed as false—because it does not tally with some part of the premises; or as irrational—because it cannot tally with any proof of procedure. Disagreement is still possible, because premises are questionable and proofs may be inadequate. But such arguments and conclusions are objective and universally valid on the basis of given procedures. Agreement between subjects does not determine the truth of cognitive claims; rather the truth of judgments depends on the nature of objects and their relations in the world.

Salim Kemal, *Kant's Aesthetic Theory* (New York: St. Martin's Press, 1997), 76.

35. Susan Hekman, "Truth and Method: Feminist Standpoint Revisited," in *Signs: Journal of Women in Culture and Society* 22, no. 2 (Winter 1997): 341–64; quotation is from p. 342.

36. Ibid., 359.

37. In their responses to Hekman, Nancy Hartsock, Patricia Hill Collins, and Sandra Harding (three giants of feminist standpoint theory) agree that Hekman's account of standpoint theory is flawed, as Hill Collins puts it, "because standpoint theory never was designed to be argued as a theory of truth or method." Rather, it was designed to be an account of "knowledge/power." Patricia Hill Collins, "Comment on Hekman's 'Truth and Method: Feminist Standpoint Theory Revisited': Where's the Power?," in *Signs: Journal of Women in Culture and Society* 22, no. 2 (Winter 1997): 375–81; quotation is from p. 375. Hekman's "misreading" is invited by the primary texts themselves. Standpoint theory has always had a fraught relationship to the very epistemological frameworks it puts into question

(e.g., rationalist, empiricist, and positivist). Although it has argued for a situated conception of truth, standpoint theory (even in its most sophisticated versions) has never doubted the basic if unstated premise, shared with the epistemologies it criticizes, that our fundamental relation to the world and to each other is rational and cognitive, one of knowing. Standpoint theorists have never relinquished the claim that some subject positions and discursive accounts are epistemically privileged.

38. Hekman, "Truth and Method," 362.

39. Arendt, *WIP*, 96. This ability, argues Arendt, is based on a refusal to view the Trojan War through the prism of "victory and defeat, which moderns have felt expresses the 'objective' judgment of history itself" (Arendt, "The Concept of History," 51), a judgment that is based on a means-end conception of politics.

40. Arendt, "The Concept of History," 51. See also *WIP*, 94–96. The modern conception of objectivity, in contrast, is premised on the idea that standpoints, intrinsically deceptive, should be eliminated, based as they are on subjective sense experience. "[T]he 'extinction of the self'. . . [becomes] the condition of 'pure vision,'" in Ranke's phrase. Objectivity is a clean relation to the facts; it requires abstention from judgment (cited in Arendt, "The Concept of History," 49).

41. Ibid., 51.

42. Ibid.

43. "The limits of a decisionistic treatment of practical questions are overcome as soon as argumentation is expected to test the generalizability of interests, instead of being resigned to an impenetrable pluralism of apparently ultimate value orientations," writes Habermas. "It is not the fact of this pluralism that is here disputed, but the assertion that it is impossible to separate by argumentation generalizable interests from those that remain particular." Jürgen Habermas, *Legitimation Crisis*, trans. Thomas McCarthy (Boston: Beacon Press, 1975), 108. Citing this passage, Richard Bernstein equates it with Arendt's claim that "judgment must liberate itself from 'subjective private conditions' and the idiosyncrasies that determine the outlook of each individual in his or her privacy" (Bernstein, *Between Objectivism and Relativism*, 220–21). This equation fails to account for her very different understanding of objectivity and argument in the political realm.

44. Hannah Arendt, *The Human Condition* (Chicago: University of Chicago Press, 1989), 57–58. See also Arendt, *WIP*, 96.

45. For a vivid account of realness as unthinkable apart from plurality, see Kimberly Curtis, *Our Sense of the Real: Aesthetic Experience and Arendtian Politics* (Ithaca, NY: Cornell University Press, 1999), esp. chap. 2.

46. Stanley Cavell, *The Claim of Reason: Wittgenstein, Skepticism, Morality, and Tragedy* (Oxford: Oxford University Press, 1979), 45.

47. Ludwig Wittgenstein, *On Certainty*, ed. G. E. M. Anscombe and G. H. von Wright (New York: Harper & Row, 1972), §612.

48. Stephen Mulhall, *Stanley Cavell: Philosophy's Recounting of the Ordinary* (Oxford: Clarendon Press, 1994), 25.

49. Ibid., 26; emphasis in the original.

50. See *CJ*, §32, pp. 145–46.

51. Hannah Arendt, "The Crisis in Culture," in *Between Past and Future*, 197–226; quotation is from p. 220.

52. Standpoint theory never developed this political understanding of plurality because, focused on a concept-governed notion of validity, it had no way of thinking about differences that was not haunted by the specter of subjectivism. It there-

fore had no way to think about such differences as elements susceptible to political articulation. For an excellent account of articulation in this political sense, see Ernesto Laclau, *Emancipation(s)* (London: Verso, 1996); Ernesto Laclau and Chantal Mouffe, *Hegemony and Socialist Strategy: Towards a Radical Democratic Politics* (London: Verso, 1985).

53. Jacques Rancière, *Dis-agreement: Politics and Philosophy*, trans. Julie Rose (Minneapolis: University of Minnesota Press, 1999), 56.

54. Jürgen Habermas, *The Philosophical Discourse of Modernity: Twelve Lectures*, trans. Frederick Lawrence (Cambridge: MIT Press, 1987), 204. Habermas accuses Derrida, among other "postmodern" thinkers, of foregrounding the rhetorical, world-creating capacity of language over its communicative, problem-solving capacity.

55. Discourse ethics is based not on a substantive conception of what is right and good, but rather on an empty rule of argumentation. It is a proceduralism that holds that what is rational is universalizable, hence speakers must be able to justify their views and reach agreement. This supposedly empty rule of argumentation offers a way of adjudicating a putatively "impenetrable pluralism," but is already an attempt to come to "a right answer" in moral and political affairs. The requirement of justification itself only makes sense if the practice of justification itself is governed by the idea of reaching such an agreement. As Christina Lafont observes, "this premise [of a single right answer] implies excluding certain kinds of pluralism and disagreement that are perfectly rational alternatives to rational argument on practical questions." Christina Lafont, *The Linguistic Turn in Hermeneutic Philosophy*, trans. José Medina (Cambridge: MIT Press, 1999), 348. For a good account of this problem, see Thomas McCarthy, "Legitimacy and Diversity: Dialectical Reflections on Analytical Distinctions," *Cardozo Law Review* 17, nos. 4–5:1083–1127. Arendt, in contrast, does not think that attempts at justification are pointless if we do not reach agreement (i.e., that arguments must lead to an agreement in conclusions to be valuable) for their purpose is not—not simply or primarily—to generate agreement but rather to open the world to us in new ways.

56. Rancière, *Dis-agreement*, 58.

57. Hannah Arendt, "What Is Authority?," in *Between Past and Future*, 91–142; quotation is from p. 93.

58. Rancière, *Dis-agreement*, 50.

59. The task of aesthetic and teleological judgment, as Kant explains, is to judge without a concept and thus the notion of a "purpose" (end [*Zweck*]). But judgment is only possible if we assume that nature has an order that we can discern and could potentially cognize, hence a purposiveness (finality [*Zweckmässigkeit*]). Thus aesthetic judgments have "finality without an end" or "purposiveness without a purpose" [*Zweckmässigkeit ohne Zweck*] (*CJ*, Introduction, 8, pp. 32–35).

60. Arendt, "The Crisis in Culture," 215, 216.

61. This criticism applies to the two types of social interaction that Habermas calls "strategic" and "communicative." Whereas in strategic interaction actors "are interested solely in the *success*, that is, the *consequences* or *outcomes* of their action," in communicative interaction actors "are prepared to harmonize their plans of action through internal means, committing themselves to pursuing goals only on the condition of an agreement . . . about definitions of the situation and prospective outcomes." Jürgen Habermas, *Moral Consciousness and Communicative Action*, trans. Christian Lenhardt and Shierry Weber Nicholsen

(Cambridge: MIT Press, 1990), 133–34; emphasis in the original. In both cases we are dealing with a form of interest, but the normative procedures and assumptions are changed.

62. Hannah Arendt, "Truth and Politics," in *Between Past and Future*, 227–64; quotation is from p. 241.

63. Arendt, "The Crisis in Culture," 220. Kant calls this process the "enlargement of the mind," in which "we compare our judgment not so much with the actual as rather with the merely possible judgments of others, and [thus] put ourselves in the position of everyone else" (*CJ*, §40, p. 160). Citing this passage, Arendt, like Kant, in no way *excludes* the role that the actual judgments of other people might play in our own. But neither does she dispute his claim that enlarged thought is not a practice of re-presenting to oneself opinions one has heard any more than it is a matter of transposing oneself into the actual place of another person. Arendt, *LKPP*, 43.

64. Arendt, "Understanding and Politics," 323.

65. Iris Marion Young, "Asymmetrical Reciprocity: On Moral Respect, Wonder, and Enlarged Thought," in *Judgment, Imagination, and Politics*, ed. Ronald Beiner and Jennifer Nedelsky (New York: Rowman & Littlefield, 2001), 205–28; quotations are from pp. 225, 223.

66. Disch, *Hannah Arendt and the Limits of Philosophy*, 168.

67. Beiner, "Rereading Hannah Arendt's Kant Lectures," 97. Beiner, Young, and Disch share the view that Arendt was mistaken to turn to Kant, for she is really interested in empirical sociability as the basis for judgment and he is not. But Kant's argument for an a priori *sensus communis* begins with the actual social practices of judgment, not to dismiss these as totally irrelevant to the validity of aesthetic judgment, but to discern what he calls the existence of the mutual human attunement that is the basis for validity.

68. This limited view of imagination as empirical and reproductive is tied to certain suppositions about the status of normative political claims and the kind of rationality that is proper to politics, both of which are central to Habermas's discourse ethics: (1) that political claims are cognitive and can be treated like claims to truth; (2) that the justification of claims requires that a *real* discourse be carried out, i.e., that speakers engage in an actual practice of argumentative justification. Even defenders of Arendt's account of political judgment against Habermas's charge of incoherence (e.g., Lisa Disch) take for granted (2), largely because they never really find a way to counter (1), caught as they are in the validity problematic that structures our understanding of politics.

69. Sarah Gibbons, *Kant's Theory of Imagination: Bridging Gaps in Judgment and Experience* (Oxford: Clarendon Press, 1994), 32.

70. Hannah Arendt, "What Remains? The Language Remains," in *Essays in Understanding*, ed. Jerome Kohn, 1–23; quotation is from p. 20.

71. For Habermas, the perspective of the third person never arises except in the form of a problematic departure from the first- and second-person engagement that he mistakenly equates with what Arendt calls representative thinking. Habermas, advocating the "interpersonal relationship" of first- and second-person perspectives as the irreducible condition of achieving mutual understanding and the general interest, rejects the third-person perspective as intrinsically objectifying. Habermas, *The Philosophical Discourse of Modernity*, 297.

72. David Carroll, "Rephrasing the Political with Kant and Lyotard: From

Aesthetic to Political Judgments," *Diacritics* 14, no. 3 (Autumn 1984): 73–88; quotation is from p. 82.

73. Arendt's discussion of imagination focuses on the schematism, which (quoting Kant from the *Critique of Pure Reason*, B180) "'provid[es] an image for a concept'" (Arendt, *LKPP*, 81), and on the function of imagination in the logic of recognition. See ibid., 79–85.

74. Deleuze, *Difference and Repetition*, 139.

75. Hannah Arendt, *The Life of the Mind*, 1-vol. edition, vol. 2, *Willing* (New York: Harcourt Brace & Co., 1978), 20. This power, she writes, is "distinguished from the faculty of choice between two or more given objects (the *liberum arbitrium*, strictly speaking)." Whereas the *liberum arbitrium* merely decides between things already given, the idea of a free will entails "a power to begin something really new" (ibid., 20, 29). I discussed this point in chapter 2.

76. On imagination as the faculty of presentation, see Rudolph A. Makkreel, *Imagination and Interpretation in Kant: The Hermeneutical Import of the "Critique of Judgment"* (Chicago: University of Chicago Press, 1990), 55. Sarah Gibbons similarly argues that

Kant tends to use the verb "to exhibit" (*darstellen*) when he wishes to emphasize the productive and presentational character of the imagination, whether in schematizing, mathematical construction, or art. Imagination performs a presentational function involving its capacity to present a whole as a "synthetic universal," and this activity involves more than is suggested by thinking of imagination as "running through and holding together" parts of the intuited manifold.

Gibbons, *Kant's Theory of Imagination*, 139.

77. Arendt discusses the Kantian sublime in her lectures in connection with Kant's account of war in the third *Critique*. She refers to this section only to say that the position of the spectator is impartial, and that it does not carry maxims for action. Rather, were one to act in accordance with how one judges, one would be immoral, so says Kant. See Arendt, *LKPP*, 52–53.

78. Makkreel, *Imagination and Interpretation in Kant*, 67–68.

79. For a similar reading, see Gibbons, *Kant's Theory of Imagination*, 128–29. As Kant explains, reason demands that the imagination grasp and present a large magnitude (e.g., "a progressively increasing numerical series") in a single intuition (*CJ*, §26, p. 111). To do so, "the imagination must perform two acts: apprehension (*apprehensio*), and comprehension (*comprehensio aesthetica*)" (*CJ*, §26, p. 108). Apprehension has no problem continuing a series, in which each part is added successively, even to infinity. But when it proceeds by generating more and more comprehensive units of measure (e.g., comprehending 100 or 100 as a single unit), it encounters difficulty and, at a certain point, a limit. The first presentations of sensible intuitions (e.g., the series 1–100) are "extinguished in the imagination, as it proceeds to apprehend further ones" (ibid.). This is the moment of the sublime. As Tamar Japaridze usefully glosses this point: "Imagination at the limit of what it can present does violence to itself in order to present that it can no longer present. Reason, for its part, seeks, unreasonably, to violate the interdict it imposes on itself and which is strictly critical, the interdict that prohibits it from finding objects corresponding to concepts in sensible intuitions. In these two aspects thinking defies its

own finitude, as if fascinated by its own excessiveness." Tamar Japaridze, *The Kantian Subject: "Sensus Communis," Mimesis, Work of Mourning* (New York: State University of New York Press, 2000), 148n17.

80. Makkreel, *Imagination and Interpretation in Kant*, 72. Kant elaborates this regress of imagination in a passage on the "absolutely great" as an idea of reason:

> Measuring (as [a way of] apprehending a space) is at the same time describing it, and hence it is an objective movement in the imagination and a progression. On the other hand, comprehending a multiplicity in a unity (of intuition rather than of thought), and hence comprehending in one instant [*Augenblick*] what is apprehended successively, is a regression that in turn cancels [annihilates, *aufhebt*] the condition of time in the imagination's progression and makes *simultaneity* [coexistence] intuitable. Hence, (since temporal succession is a condition of the inner sense and of an intuition) it is a subjective movement of the imagination by which it does violence to the inner sense. (*CJ*, §27, p. 116)

81. Makkreel, *Imagination and Interpretation in Kant*, 73. See also Jean-François Lyotard, *Lessons on the Analytic of the Sublime (Kant's 'Critique of Judgment,' §§23–29)*, trans. Elizabeth Rottenberg (Stanford, CA: Stanford University Press, 1994), 144.

82. "[I]nstead of the linearly ordered time required for the progressive apprehension and mathematical determination of nature, we have an instant or moment in time which allows for aesthetic comprehension or reflection" (Makkreel, *Imagination and Interpretation in Kant*, 74). For Makkreel, the idea of the supersensible that attends the imaginative regress in the sublime "may be used in a transcendental philosophy of mind to ground a theory of the subject as a whole" (ibid., 80). For Lyotard, by contrast, insofar as it destroys the inner sense necessary to the "I think," "the 'regression' of the imagination in sublime feeling strikes a blow at the very foundation of the 'subject.'" *Lessons on the Analytic of the Sublime*, 144. For a good discussion of this difference, see Peter Fenves, "Taking Stock of the Kantian Sublime," *Eighteenth-Century Studies* 28, no. 1 (Autumn 1994): 65–82; see especially pp. 72–76.

83. Lyotard, *Lessons on the Analytic of the Sublime*, 123. "This conflict [between reason and imagination, between the power to conceive and the power to present] is not an ordinary dispute, which a third instance could grasp and put an end to, but a differend, a *Wiederstreit*" (ibid., 124).

84. Ibid., 140, 141.

85. Ibid., 18.

86. Jean-François Lyotard, *Peregrinations: Law, Form, Event* (New York: Columbia University Press, 1988), 38. Citing Lyotard, David Carroll conflates Arendt's thought with the communicative theory of Habermas and accuses her of lacking a critical understanding of community. David Carroll, "Community After Devastation: Culture, Politics, and the 'Public Space,'" in *Politics, Theory, and Contemporary Culture*, ed. Mark Poster (New York: Columbia University Press, 1993), 159–96, esp. 170. A similar idea of community as being at odds with any empirical form is given by Jean-Luc Nancy, *The Inoperative Community*, trans. Peter Connor, Lisa Garbus, Michael Holland, and Simona Sawhney and ed. Peter Connor (Minneapolis: University of Minnesota Press, 1991).

87. Ewa Plonowska Ziarek, *The Rhetoric of Failure: Deconstruction of*

Skepticism, Reinvention of Modernism (Albany: State University of New York Press, 1996). I discussed this idea of failure in signification in chapter 1.

88. Judith Butler, "Competing Universalities," in Judith Butler, Ernesto Laclau, and Slavoj Žižek, *Contingency, Hegemony, Universality: Contemporary Dialogues on the Left* (New York: Verso, 2000), 136–81; Michael Warner, *The Trouble with Normal: Sex, Politics, and the Ethics of Queer Life* (New York: Free Press, 1999), esp. chap. 3.

89. Arendt, "The Crisis in Culture," 223.

90. On this point, see Mulhall, *Stanley Cavell*, 28–29.

91. Kemal, *Kant's Aesthetic Theory*, 44.

CONCLUSION

1. Claude Lefort, "The Question of Democracy," in *Democracy and Political Theory*, trans. David Macey (Minneapolis: University of Minnesota Press, 1989), 9–20; quotation is from p. 19; emphasis in the original.

2. Claude Lefort, "The Image of the Body in Totalitarianism," in *Political Forms of Modern Society: Bureaucracy, Democracy, Totalitarianism*, ed. John B. Thompson (Cambridge: Cambridge University Press, 1986), 303–4.

3. Judith Butler, "Contingent Foundations," in *Feminists Theorize the Political*, ed. Judith Butler and Joan Scott (New York: Routledge, 1992), 3–21; quotation is from p. 16.

4. Ibid.

5. Alan Keenan, *Democracy in Question: Democratic Openness in a Time of Political Closure* (Stanford, CA: Stanford University Press, 2003), 7.

6. Ibid.

7. Ibid., 8.

8. Jean-Jacques Rousseau, *On the Social Contract*, published together with *Geneva Manuscript and Political Economy*, ed. Roger D. Masters, trans. Judith R. Masters (New York: St. Martin's Press, 1978), bk. 2, chap. 7, p. 69.

9. Bonnie Honig, *Democracy and the Foreigner* (Princeton, NJ: Princeton University Press, 2001), 20.

10. Ibid.

11. Keenan, *Democracy in Question*, 49.

12. Ibid., 52.

13. Rousseau, *On the Social Contract*, 69.

14. Keenan, *Democracy in Question*, 52; emphasis in the original.

15. On this point see Stanley Cavell, *The Claim of Reason: Wittgenstein, Skepticism, Morality, and Tragedy* (Oxford: Oxford University Press, [1979] 1982), 25.

16. Ibid., 27.

17. Ernesto Laclau, *Emancipation(s)* (London: Verso, 1996). I discuss Laclau's argument in Linda M. G. Zerilli, "This Universalism Which Is Not One," *Diacritics* 28, no. 2 (Summer 1998): 3–20.

18. Charlotte Bunch and Samantha Frost, "Women's Human Rights: An Introduction," electronic publication by the Women's Center for Global Leadership, Rutgers University (http://www.cwgl.rutgers.edu/Global_Center_Pages/whr.html). Also published in *Routledge International Encyclopedia of Women: Global Women's Issues and Knowledge* (New York: Routledge, 2000).

19. Claude Lefort, "Human Rights and the Welfare State," in *Democracy and Political Theory*, 37.

20. Ibid., 37–38.

21. Hannah Arendt, *The Origins of Totalitarianism* (New York: Harcourt Brace Jovanovich, 1975), 298.

22. Ibid., 300.

23. Hannah Arendt, *On Revolution* (New York: Viking Press, 1965), 102.

24. Lefort, "Human Rights and the Welfare State," 37.

25. Ibid., 36.

26. Ibid., 37.

27. Joan Scott, *Only Paradoxes to Offer: French Feminists and the Rights of Man* (Cambridge: Harvard University Press, 1996). Scott does not suggest that logic is the proper way to understand feminist demands, but points us to the seeming irreconcilability of its political history with the requirements of logic.

28. For a good discussion of this point in relation the democratic theory, see Keenan, *Democracy in Question*, chap. 1.

29. Joan Copjec, "Sex and the Euthanasia of Reason," in *Read My Desire: Lacan against the Historicists* (Cambridge: MIT Press, 1994), 201–36; quotation is from p. 225. Although Copjec is right to criticize the historicist tendency in feminist theory, the problem is different from what she suggests. The problem with a historicist account of women as an unstable category is not that it functions as a judgment (e.g., about the impossibility of collecting women into a whole), but that it functions as a substitute for judgment. Historicism claims to attend to the particular, but just the opposite is the case: by submerging all actions in an overarching notion of process and precedents, historicism obliterates the particular and, with it, the new, that which calls for our judgment. It is, however, in no way clear that such a notion of historicism can plausibly be attached to the name Judith Butler. What makes Butler a historicist for Copjec, finally, is her emphasis on the empirical, i.e., on the actual or concrete instantiations of concepts in society and history.

30. Ibid.

31. Ibid.

32. Immanuel Kant, *Critique of Judgment*, trans. Werner S. Pluhar (Indianapolis: Hackett, 1987), §2, p. 45.

33. Hannah Arendt, *The Life of the Mind*, 1-vol. edition, vol. 1, *Thinking* (New York: Harcourt Brace & Co., 1978), 71.

34. Judith Butler, *Antigone's Claim: Kinship between Life and Death* (New York: Columbia University Press, 2000), 20–21.

35. Ibid., 21.

36. Arendt, *The Origins of Totalitarianism*, 302.

37. Margaret Canovan, "Politics as Culture: Hannah Arendt and the Public Realm," *History of Political Thought* 6, no. 3 (1985): 617–42; quotation is from p. 634.

38. Arendt, *On Revolution*, 210.

39. Ibid., 214.

40. Hannah Arendt, *The Life of the Mind*, 1-vol. edition, vol. 2, *Willing* (New York: Harcourt Brace & Co., 1978), 204.

Milan Women's Bookstore Collective
(*continued*)
discovery of, 110; disparity,
political value of, 107; disparity,
practice of, 110, 112; and
entrustment, 114; and equality,
110; equality, break with, 107;
and female desire, 215n25,
215–16n26; and female freedom,
97, 114, 122; female freedom,
and gratitude, 116; female plus,
notion of, 113; as feminist space,
104; freer, as feeling, 108;
freedom, as political association,
98; and freedom, as world-
building, 93–94; inequality
among, 108; and injury identity,
100, 101; and interlocutors, 118;
judgments, taboos against, 106,
107; judgments, of other women,
106; and masculine social
contract, 96; and new social
contract, 114; past, redeeming
of, 99; as political space, 104;
and politics of doing, 107;
practice of doing, 104, 105, 106,
109; and prototypes, 113;
reparation, 100, 114, 216n28;
sexual difference, political
symbolization of, 104; sexual
difference, politics of, 94, 99,
104; sexual difference, and
problem of new, 98; as shared
interest, 104–5; social contract,
tearing up of, 96, 97; and
sovereignty, 94, 97; and symbolic
mother, 114; turning point of,
107; utility, logic of, 94;
voluntary associations,
development of, 97–98; women,
free relations among, 104, 105,
112, 125; women, as victims,
100; and women's literature,
107, 108; on women's
movement, 101; and world-
building, 95; and worldly in-
between, 29; and Yellow
Catalogue, 107

Mill, John Stuart, 4, 75, 187n28;
feminism of, as ambivalent,
185–86n20
modernity, 15
Moi, Toril, 89, 210n51, 211n71
Montesquieu, 192n58
Moore, G. E., 42
Morante, Elsa, 113
Mouffe, Chantal, x, 2
Mulhall, Stephen, 142

National American Woman Suffrage
Association (NAWSA), 183n2,
185n11
National Organization for Women
(NOW), 183–84n3
nature: necessity of, 76
necessity, 74; and contingency, 76, 91,
126; description of, 76; and free
act, 85; and freedom, 137
new: problem of, 81–82
Newton, Isaac, 203n84
New York City: feminist movement
in, 183–84n3
New York Radical Feminists,
183–84n3
New York Radical Women (NYRW),
183–84n3
Nietzsche, Friedrich, 13, 191n52; and
gender identity, 189–90n44; and
self-loathing, 99
nihilism, 218–19n6
noble lie, 68
nonsovereignty: and democratic
politics, 19; and freedom, 20
normative heterosexuality, 71
Nussbaum, Martha, 137, 138, 157

objective truth, 132
objectivism, 131, 132;
foundationalism, related to,
220n13; and plurality, 140; and
validity, 138
objectivity, 132, 133, 151, 224n40;
and political realm, 147
O'Brien, Edna, 211n72
October 17th Movement, 183–84n3
Okin, Susan, 137, 138, 157; women,

"women," as subject, 14, 28, 33; destruction of, 1; and domesticity, 6; loss of, in feminism, 36; as new concept, 65; particularity of, 95; political freedom of, ix; and public life, 5; and sameness, 95; as sociological group, 6–7; as virtuous sex, 4; Western concept of, 174

women's freedom: and social problems, 9

women's human rights, 7, 173, 174; difference, demand for, 176; equality, demand for, 176; nature, appeal to, 175

women's liberation, 8, 122

Women's Library (Parma), 105–6, 107, 216n29

women's movement: of nineteenth century, 183n2; and Mary Wollstonecraft, 185n11

women's rights, 94; ballot, as means to end, 7; and gender differences, 186n22; and sameness-difference debate, 5; society, betterment of, 7; and voting, 5, 7, 185n11

women's suffrage, 8

Woolf, Virginia, 113; Vita Sackville-West, friendship between, 114

workers' rights, 7

world-building: and feminism, 25, 38, 180; feminism, as practice of, 177, 181; and freedom, 16, 20, 27, 29; and freedom-centered feminism, 65; and Milan Women's Bookstore Collective, 95; and political freedom, 125; and politics, 22; and sexual difference, 119; and standpoint theory, 138

World Conference on Human Rights, 173

Young, Iris Marion, 149, 156, 226n67

Ziarek, Ewa: rhetoric of failure, 157